Sexy Recipes for Lovers

Linda De Villers, PhD

**FREE DVD and 50% off streaming offer at
www.lovingsex.com/food** *see last page for details*

Copyright 2016 Linda De Villers, PhD
First published as *Simple Sexy Food*, Aphrodite Media, 2012

Published by
1 to 1 Publishers, Inc.
12439 Magnolia Blvd.
Suite 100
Valley Village, CA 91607 USA
www.1to1publishers.com
+1-818-508-1296

Table of Contents

Author's Preface

I created this book to help you enjoy the remarkable relationship between food and sex. These two themes run brightly through my own life both personally and professionally, and are inseparable from my sense of who I am. Having counseled and taught thousands of people on the loving arts, and having fed nearly as many in my kitchens over the years, I find myself in a state of barely contained excitement over the opportunity to share what I know with you. I am the only author in this field to be credentialed in both sexual health and food, having worked and presented internationally and conducted research on the joint topic over the course of my career.

With the 1997 publication of my first book, *Love Skills*, now in its sixth edition, I was able to reach a broad audience of couples hungry for a fun, upbeat guide to more enjoyable lovemaking. My sense was, and is, that many of us bring a fairly narrow framework of understanding of four key skills - love talk, touch, body knowledge and playfulness - to our intimate relationships. I set about with that book to gently and positively awaken a deeper, joyful, satisfying experience for all who wished for more.

That approach continues with *Sexy Recipes for Couples*, along with my sense that many of us are ready and willing to enrich our mutual love of our partners and of food by the use of everyday aphrodisiacs. I'm not talking about pills, powders, and potions, here.

For our simple, sexy purposes, we'll use and enjoy food ingredients whose chemical makeup, flavor, aroma, texture, or appearance can both please and arouse. I won't be slipping any crushed beetle between your filo pastry sheets, I promise, but I will make suggestions for adding pleasure, playfulness, and variety to your eating and loving. Many of you will be astonished at the range of ordinary foods possessing aphrodisiac qualities.

It turns out, of course, that there are now many books on the market highlighting the aphrodisiac qualities of food and drink. Several are quite good from the perspective of the recipes, but I've found most of them lacking in terms of explanations about aphrodisiacs and in terms of valid sexual advice for couples. Most lack a thorough listing of aphrodisiac foods and their effects, for example. In the sex department, they're either too flippant, too focused on singles and one-night-stands, or too unstudied about what people actually need and want to enhance their sex lives. One or two of the most prominent of these books belongs on the coffee table, but not in the kitchen or the bedroom!

With *Sexy Recipes for Couples*, I've overcome those issues by creating what I believe is a one-of-a-kind book. The basic premise, beginning with the title, takes into account how hectic and busy everyone is these days. While singles looking for seduction enhancers will find plenty of ideas to amuse themselves, my primary focus is on couples in committed relationships.

The organization of the book is based on the time of day and the scenario you want to create, from breakfast in bed to a sit-down dinner to a midnight snack, and everything in between. To my knowledge this is the only book that includes actual survey data about what foods people think are sexy. You'll find a more extensive listing and explanations of the wonderful variety of aphrodisiac foods than I've seen anywhere. Throughout these pages I share tips and suggestions not only for food preparation, but for "love skills," setting the scene, serving, and even what (or what not) to wear!

In other words, you're getting a lot of bang for your buck. The truth is that millions of ordinary folks want help in spicing up their sex lives. Eating and loving are everyday actions that sometimes become too every day. It's my hope that with *Sexy Recipes for Couples*, you're able see the world through a more sensual lens. I want you to discover—or re-discover—a joyful, playful relationship with your partner, one in which sharing great food together helps you connect emotionally as well as physically, and is both fuel and inspiration for loving each other more.

Linda De Villers, PhD
Los Angeles, California

Introduction

In a world where instant gratification, medical intervention, and ridiculous demands on our time and attention have mechanized and "routinized" our eating and lovemaking, *Sexy Recipes for Lovers* offers a new perspective. You can think of it as the art and science of food hooking up with the art and science of sex, an intoxicating mixture of fact and fantasy, of ultra-modern and ancient, of physical and emotional. It's all of these things and more.

At very least it will help you perk up your sex life and your eating habits! The beauty of it is that, at their essences, both food and sex are deliciously simple pleasures. A bit of heat, some stirring, a light touch, some gentle words, and Presto! Yes, they can get complicated, but they don't need to be. So first and foremost is the concept of simplicity. You've got enough going on in your life without having to stress out over whether you're sexy enough, or attractive enough, or a good enough cook. You are, right now. No questions asked.

If food and sex are valued parts of your life, or if you'd like to make them more so, what you might need is a bit of inspiration, along with good information. This cookbook is designed to help stimulate and satisfy your creative appetites and get your home fires burning.

Simple Sexy Background

Beyond the fact that food and sex have deep human biological and psychological value, for many people both are at the core of their enjoyment of life. At their best, both enhance life nearly beyond description. At their worst they fall without control into pathology.

Most of us live somewhere in between, and are in search of ways to enjoy both food and sex to the fullest. Enjoying them in combination is an immeasurable bonus, and will contribute to both the quality and quantity of your experiences. Of course, this applies foremost to those in committed relationships, but it must also be said that nothing builds early relationship bonds better than sharing a great meal. Typically, though, new couples aren't as dissatisfied with their sex lives as those who've been together for years, or even decades. The newness is exciting, and in some ways the idea of re-creating a new and fresh context for lovemaking is what this book is all about.

What's been missing in the discussion over why we're increasingly discontent in our sex lives is that arousal, attraction, even good old-fashioned horniness, are influenced by many factors, including but not limited to whether you believe something is sexy, i.e. it contributes to, enhances, or initiates the sexual experience. In other words, it's a partly a mental thing. Viagra doesn't cause men and women to become aroused. In theory it helps the body to function properly in the presence of sexual stimulation, opportunity, and belief. You need all three. The "medicalization" of sexuality and the application of principles that work for men to women have actually pushed us away farther away from that fact.

Typically we still need and/or want the scent, the sight, the feel, the flavor of (at least the thought of) something or someone to spark arousal. Sometimes we want them all! Food is often the answer, for whether or not it directly turns us on, it draws us together in a shared, sensual experience with nearly limitless erotic potential. It gives us energy, relaxes us, and keeps us healthy. It's pleasing both superficially and deep-down, a quality good food shares with good sex.

There's a rich and well-documented history of the relationship between the food and sex, as well as misconceptions galore, starting with aphrodisiacs.

Some misconceptions result from the fact that very few natural aphrodisiacs cause immediate or even obvious contributions to the sex drive or act. Modern science has shown us that the chemical compounds in, say, oysters, stimulate or are needed by sex-related physical functions, though their effect may not be immediate. In short, oysters are loaded with zinc, a must-have mineral for testosterone production, which in turn is a must-have hormone in the pas-de-deux of sexual arousal.

But what about the appearance, texture, manner of preparing and eating, even the odor of oysters? They, too, might contribute to arousal.

And what about chocolate, that universal treat of sweethearts and lovers-to-be? Of all the aphrodisiac foods available to modern society, a simple sweet made from cocoa beans, milk and sugar remains the most cherished for its effect on our libidos. It is the ultimate simple, sexy food, available everywhere in myriad forms, delicious and decadent, easy to prepare and consume. As science has shown us, chocolate is loaded with "feel good" neurotransmitters that release endorphins and boost serotonin, is high in caffeine-like theobromine, and contains the cannabinoid anandamide, a chemical that connects to the same brain receptors as marijuana smoke. No wonder the Aztec ruler Montezuma was said to have consumed up to 50 cups of honey-sweetened chocolate before diving into his harem of 600 women! He didn't know about the science, but apparently he enjoyed the results.

A quick glance at the comprehensive list of aphrodisiac foods reveals both well-known and lesser known items, those with which you may have experimented and those you'd never have considered until now. All these ingredients have interesting and often humorous historical identities, further confirmation not only of their reputed love-enhancing effects, but also of the fact that we humans have been consuming food to boost sexual pleasure since the dawn of civilization.

As with most long-standing myths and legends, the specific origin of a given aphrodisiac is often shrouded in mystery, a by-product of time, the era or cultural context in which it came into use, and the reason for its use in the first place. By the same token, as with most myths and legends, even though their veracity may not be provable, a kernel of truth usually lies somewhere beneath the obfuscating layers of time and re-telling.

To bring some modern sensibility to the history of aphrodisiacs, I have conducted surveys of over 3000 adults to determine their sexy food preferences, usage, and suggestions. The survey data are not exhaustive, yet give insight into what regular folks do with food to enhance their sexuality.

The surveys revealed that chocolate is the aphrodisiac of choice for modern Americans, and that a romantic dinner prepared by someone else is the sexiest setting, but the data also reveal something of a lack of knowledge about the variety and potential of aphrodisiac foods, something this cookbook addresses to the extreme.

Healthy, Simple and Sexy

Of all the reasons to enjoy great food and great sex, perhaps the most underrated are their roles in maintaining physical and mental health. As we've seen, both have value beyond biological necessity, and both are linked in obvious and not-so-obvious ways to healthy living. For most people, the obvious contributions to our health are physical. Good nutrition is the cornerstone of good health, along with exercise, a category in which we can certainly place good sex.

But it's in the area of mental health that food and sex have more to contribute to, or detract from, our well-being than you might have thought.

For women, there are numerous and complex subtleties at work in our minds and bodies when it comes to food and sex. Poor body image, a puritanical upbringing, or hormonal changes brought on by childbirth or simply by age can create unhealthy patterns of thought and behavior. Add to that complexity a growing awareness of our mental and physical health needs and almost inhuman demands on our time, and many women find themselves in a state of stress and worry that goes beyond whether or not they'll have sex tonight.

And men are certainly not immune. Unhealthy eating habits, lack of exercise, and aging all contribute to many a man's impotence, or at least a reduction of performance and interest in sex. Combine these factors with long work hours and other demands on one's time, and guys are equally challenged in both quantity and quality of sex.

If conventional approaches to taking care of your body have eluded you because they felt too dutiful (should-focused), too mechanical, or just too impractical, I may have an answer. When it comes to turning around your relationship with food and sex, this book offers an indulgent, pleasure-focused approach to making your body happy and healthy. I want to help you pop out of the rut you're in and get back on a delightful new road paved with confidence and joy. In so doing, you'll discover a better body image, one that comes with a big upside: Feeling great about yourself is key to a fuller expression of sexuality. Few things are as sexy as a person who's completely at ease with her body.

The fact is, you are beautiful, inside and out, and the sooner you believe that about yourself, the sooner you'll be able to relish the give-and-take of a more sensual relationship.

That said, this is not by any stretch a diet cookbook. You'll find butter and sugar, fats and carbohydrates. Wherever possible, I've included "healthier" alternatives, but the reality is that better dietary health is achieved through portion control, moderation, proper hydration and exercise, not religiously avoiding everything that tastes good. In keeping with modern practice, however, I have also included nutrition facts, a handy feature for anyone trying to eat healthier.

Making Time for Simple, Sexy

Beyond healthier eating, however, is the concept of "slow food." That's not to say that great food must take forever to prepare and consume, but rather that in slowing down our relationship with food we improve our food choices, our bodies' digestion and often our appreciation of food. And it's also there we may begin to find time to appreciate the curve of a lover's hips, the beauty of his smile, the fragrance of her skin.

In my experience, one of the greatest obstacles to a more sensual, romantic relationship can be loosely described as our ridiculously fast-paced, hectic lives. From soccer moms to stay-at-home dads, from single parents to two-career couples, we're constantly on the go. For couples with kids, the demands multiply exponentially. Parents of younger kids, especially, are often hard-pressed to find the time or the energy for much more than a bite of fast food and a perfunctory roll in the hay from time to time. While that may be better than nothing, it can also take its toll on a relationship (not to mention your digestion!).

Regardless of your schedule, I implore you to find time to slow down and appreciate good food, and in the process, your partner. I do share some tips throughout the book for finding ways to spend "alone" time together at home. For some it may be as simple as tapping grandparents for a weekend with the kids or trading kid sleepovers with another couple. For others it may mean a Friday midnight snack and sleeping in together Saturday morning, maybe followed by breakfast in bed. My point is, just do it. Make it happen. Put your relationship on the front burner from time to time and you just might find you like the heat coming from the kitchen!

How to Use *Sexy Recipes for Lovers*

Speaking of busy schedules, the overall organization of *Sexy Recipes for Couples* is by time of day. I did so for two reasons. One, it saves you precious time! If you are in a hurry and need a quick idea for, say, an edible "nooner," you can go right to Part II and find what you need. The other reason is that, other than midnight snacks, our days are often scheduled around mealtimes, and it's a familiar and comfortable new way to look for food ideas.

The basic sections are as follows:

Part I - Tease Me Anytime
     (appetizers, soups, salads, quickies)
Part II - Daytime is the Right Time
     (breakfast, brunch, lunch, afternoon delight)
Part III - Love-Feasts
     (sit-down dinners, complete meals)
Part IV - Late Night Rendezvous
     (desserts, drinks, and more)

You've probably noticed that all these sections contain items that are not limited by time of day. In fact, with the possible exception of some of the dinner items, all the recipes in *Sexy Recipes for Couples* can be enjoyed pretty much anytime. You might want dessert in the afternoon, for example, or an appetizer or two in place of a full meal. The organization of recipes is intended to be a handy starting point. What you do with them in your own home is utterly and joyously up to you!

The complete list of aphrodisiac foods follows this introduction. All listings are cross-referenced with where they appear in the recipes and elsewhere in the book. This list alone is fun reading. I learned a great deal in researching this list, finding both humor and numerous "aha" moments when I came across an item I had heard about but whose details I hadn't known.

Another unique feature of *Sexy Recipes for Couples* is the "factoid" blurbs I've sprinkled throughout. The blurbs are color-coded in boxes to keep things simple and include:

Survey Secrets
I've polled over 3000 people on their food/sex preferences, habits, and more. Look for some of the results sprinkled throughout the recipes! (quotes and data)

Love Skills
Wherever appropriate I'll share sensual/sexual suggestions for spicing up your love life, including physical details like scene setting, dressing up (or down), and co-preparation of meals. Many come from my book of the same name.

Simple, Sexy Kitchen Tips
Keep an eye out for tips related to obtaining ingredients, food preparation, recipe variations and more!

Aphrodite Says
Throughout the book I'll share tidbits about the love-inducing qualities and historical reputations of various ingredients. To check the descriptions of particular aphrodisiacs, see the summary following this introduction.

Bon Appétit, et Bon Amour!

Aphrodisiac Food History, Lore and Facts

Simple, Sexy Disclaimer: While most people acknowledge the interplay of food's chemical properties and a physical or psychological impact, the purported aphrodisiac qualities of the following foods have not been acknowledged by the USFDA, which in general doesn't recognize any food ingredient as having aphrodisiac qualities. **This listing is designed for educational purposes only and the author is not engaged in rendering medical advice or professional services. If you feel that you have a general or sexual health problem, you should seek the advice of your physician or other appropriate health care professional.**

What does the term *aphrodisiac* mean?
As you might guess, the origin of the noun *aphrodisiac* is Greek, derived in the early 18th century from *aphrodisia*, meaning heterosexual pleasures, and from *aphrodisios*, or "of Aphrodite."

The myth of Aphrodite, the Greek Goddess of Love who rose from sea foam, or in some versions, from the sea, dates back to the 9th century BCE. She was revered for her fertile, feminine energy, and turned to for support with reproductive power, from abundant crops to gardens to human reproduction.

The modern definitions include 1. an agent (as a food or drug) that arouses or is held to arouse sexual desire, and 2. something that excites (www.Merriam-Webster.com). Given that my research focuses on food and drink, we will use the term to mean any food or drink that contributes to sexual intimacy either through increasing arousal, excitement, playfulness, or enjoyment.

Why the interest in aphrodisiacs?
There's no question there's been a recent uptick in interest in aphrodisiacs in North America and around the world. A recent check of internet searches for the term revealed 90,500 per month in the U.S., and 246,000 worldwide for the same month. Several aphrodisiac books have been published in recent years, adding greatly to what had been a somewhat limited list. Before we look at what may be driving this current phenomenon, let's take a brief look at history.

In pre-Judeo-Christian times, sexuality and sexual expression were highly valued both for procreation and recreation. For example, the ancient Greeks and Romans held orgies that were celebrations of all the senses. They featured food, drink and sex—their version of "Eat, drink, and be merry." Both sexes, but particularly men, were interested in anything that could enhance their sexual vigor. For women, foods and elixirs that would enhance both fertility and pleasure held the greatest value.

The advent of Christianity put the brakes on sexual appreciation and experimentation in the West, or at least pushed in underground, but obviously didn't stop it altogether. Some cultures and societies have retained their historical knowledge and use of aphrodisiacs to enhance sexuality—perhaps due to never having experienced the stultifying effects of medieval Christendom or the Victorian era—and continue to use them today in various forms. Certain Asian societies are somewhat infamous for their use of endangered animal parts in potency formulas, for example. But individuals and couples in otherwise Christian, or Catholic, cultures also valued aphrodisiacs even as they upheld, or pretended to uphold, strict moral guidelines.

One reason for this ongoing use of aphrodisiacs must be the need for fertility. Procreation has held value for societies and families since the dawn of time. More children meant more help in securing livelihood, the survivability of a lineage, and of a culture in general. It's not as if the Victorians, for example, quit having sex. It could be argued, however, that they took a lot of the fun out of it, especially for women.

I deal elsewhere in this book with the debilitating effects of prudish Victorian-style morality on women's sexuality in particular, so I won't extend that dialogue here. Still, it's instructive to consider the possible root causes of our current fascination with enhancing our sexuality. We're certainly bombarded with sexual messages everywhere we turn. And while it's true that women no longer suffer en masse from claustrophobic sex roles, the high value placed on youthful sexuality, at least in symbolic form, has never been greater.

Body image and sex role issues contribute to many a woman's struggles, but that's not the whole story. We're wildly overstressed, too, and have ridiculous demands on our minds and bodies.

These modern-day stressors result in a variety of sexual side effects, first and foremost among them the oldest mood-killer in the book: fatigue. Being tired keeps many couples from having sex, but that's the tip of the iceberg. Stress constricts blood flow, decreases serotonin and other "happy" hormones, increases irritability, and distracts us from simpler, more pleasurable pursuits. Add to that a catch-as-catch-can diet and precious little down time, and you have the perfect recipe for infrequent, lackluster sex.

No wonder, then, that a society seemingly preoccupied with sex has so much trouble in the bedroom. Still, people still want to have sex, and seek quick fixes for a variety of lust-related problems. If the frequency and volume of Viagra™ and Cialis™ commercials is any indication, it appears that men, at least, are searching for a "cure." And it also stands to reason that many of us would prefer a more "natural" solution to what ails us, and that, I believe, is a driving force in our current interest in aphrodisiacs.

Fortunately, the relationship between food and sex is largely a relaxed, expansive affair. Eating disorders and obesity aside, I believe we can find our way back to better sexual, mental, and physical health by paying closer attention to this relationship. Few things bring us closer together as humans than sharing food and sharing our bodies. Doing so slows us down, boosts our communication, and makes us feel better. Not bad for a couple basic necessities of life!

Aphrodisiacs Lore and History
If the entire history of aphrodisiac lore were documented, it would surely fill many volumes and cover every cultures and geographic area of the world. While that would make for fun and interesting reading, our goal here is to capture the essence of aphrodisiac foods by first taking a look at a few historical references to their use, and then looking at individual aphrodisiac foods, (many, most?) of which can be sampled in the recipe sections.

Certain themes run through the history of aphrodisiacs. Their use often begins among the ruling classes, nobility, and the wealthy, but with the exception of caviar, eventually finds their way down to the masses, who then indulge without prejudice whenever and wherever they can!

Another curious theme is timing. It's interesting to note that formulas for love potions have often stipulated that ingredients must be gathered or prepared on a Friday. The French word *Vendredi*—*Siernes* in Spanish, *venerdi* in Italian— all come from the Latin *veneris dies*, meaning "Venus' Day." And in English, the word "Friday" derives from "Frija's Day." Frija was the Norse goddess of love. No wonder we all look forward with such unbridled joy to the weekend. Friday's a great day for passion!

And aphrodisiacs are no stranger to literature and the arts. The 2nd century CE Hindu sex book, *The Kama Sutra*, and the 15th century CE Arabic love text, *The Perfumed Garden*, both mention various foods and concoctions to aid and enhance sexuality.

More recently, Nobel Prize winner Octavio Paz asserted that eroticism and gastrosophy (sex and eating) are the two most fundamental pleasures of human life. Eroticism is the most intense and gastrosophy is the most extended. Desire in both of these initiates a movement among substances, the bodies, and the sensations.

And in Laura Esquivel's exquisite novel, *Like Water for Chocolate*, the main characters' love for one another is consummated through the sensual and erotic act of eating and drinking, even though they are forbidden to have sex.

So eating is deeply entwined in our experience of sex, both literally and metaphorically, as both reflect, in the words of Angel Montoya in *Theology of Food*, "our strongest feelings of hunger, desire, greed, delectation, and satiety." But where does the idea that certain foods actually improve sexual function come from, and how has that idea evolved over time?

Mythical vs. "Proven" Powers

Just about any food that resembles the reproductive organs—penis and testicles in men, and breasts, labia, vagina and ovaries in women—has been cited for aphrodisiac powers. Further, animals and plants with perceived reproductive power (masculine or feminine) are thought by many to aid human sexuality.

The formal reference for this concept is called the Doctrine of Resemblances, aka the Doctrine of Signatures. It dates back to Galen, but was at its peak during the European Renaissance, as it was promulgated by a Swiss professor of medicine during the first half of the 16th century.

The idea was that the shape of a food was thought to be an indication of its virtues. Thus asparagus and carrots were aphrodisiacs. The logic actually used in the Renaissance was that asparagus was hot and incisive and the carrot caused flatulence. The Doctrine of Resemblances that was applied universally to all aphrodisiacs reached its zenith in the work of a 20th century Belgian sociologist/professor, Leo Moulin. He suggested that carrots, asparagus, and leeks were phallic; truffles resembled testicles; parsley, cress, and tarragon looked like pubic hair; and the fig was shaped like a womb. Such connections were not made in the Renaissance, however, and his entire list can be reduced to that era's concepts of nourishing foods (figs), hot, stimulating foods (herbs), and windy foods (leeks, carrots, and truffles).

It's here we run into the conflict between science and belief, and the difference between the physiological and psychological effects of aphrodisiacs. If you eat something that looks like a penis, or an actual animal penis, will your penis reap any benefits? Probably not. Yet who can deny the stimulating potential of seductively enjoying a banana in the company of your lover? Or biting into a juicy peach? Or hand-feeding your partner a freshly-shucked oyster?

But with oysters, for example, as with many simple, sexy foods, we enter a crossover area. Certain foods not only possess perceived aphrodisiac power due to their appearance or reproductive ability, but also contain chemicals or ingredients known by science to improve, enhance or otherwise impact sexual performance or pleasure. When it comes down to it, as long as the food is relatively healthy for your body and mind, does it really matter why it trips your trigger? If it enhances your sexual experience, it's an aphrodisiac.

The following is a brief summary of aphrodisiac foods, along with their reputed and scientifically-known qualities. It's by no means an exhaustive list, but you may be surprised by many of the foods that appear here.

Apples

Lore and Fun Facts
No fruit has been more frequently used as a symbol of love or sexual temptation as the apple, despite the fact that few scholars today believe it was the "forbidden fruit" that led Adam and Eve to fall from grace in the Garden of Eden. Much debate continues over the precise identity of the tree that bore that "forbidden fruit," Suggestions range from pomegranates, a belief held by a number of Jewish scholars, to figs, apricots, or quinces.

Ever since, historical accuracy aside, the lure of the apple, including its use in several love charms, has continued through to the present day.

One 9th century Arabic poem turns the apple into a sexy simile for love:

The apple,
which I received from the hand
Of the most charming,
gazelle-like maiden
Which she had plucked herself
from a branch
That was as supple as her own body.
And sweet it was
to place my hand upon it
As though it was the breast
of the one who gave it.
Pure was the fragrance of the apple,
Like the breath of the giver.
One could see
the color of her check on it,
And I thought I was tasting her lips
When I began to eat the apple.

The thirteenth century handbook of the *Ancren Riwle*, or "nun's rules," warns young women about to become religious recluses as follows: "This apple, dear Sisters, is a token of everything that arouses lust and sensual delights." A modern reviewer of this text adds: "Fortunately, most everyone but nuns ignored his advice and an apple a day still helps keep sexual lassitude away."

And then there's Paulus Silentiarius, a 6th century Greek poet, who begged, "If, my pet, you gave me these two apples as tokens of your breasts, I bless you for your great kindness. But if your gift does not go beyond the apples, you wrong me by refusing to quench the fierce fire you lit." Is it getting warm in here?

Rabelais, the 15th century Renaissance writer and humanist, called the breasts *pommes d'amour*, or apples of love, and the testicles *pommes de cas pendre*, which means, rather literally, hanging, encased apples!

By the 17th century, perception of the apple as aphrodisiac was universal, and particularly strong in Latin countries. Priests of the era, like Juan Ludovico de la Cerda, stated that "the apple (is) under the jurisdiction of Venus."

Similarly, in the same era, Milton in *Paradise Lost* says the first act of Adam and Eve after tasting the apple was to make love in a bed of flowers. "So the first man and woman lost one paradise only to find another. Through their lustful behavior the apple became the symbol of earthly desires and an aphrodisiac of the highest quality."

Now, what would you say about the apple of *your* eye?

Sexy Nutrients
Apples are an excellent source of fiber, which helps get rid of bad LDL cholesterol and regulates blood sugar; it's also high in vitamin A and is a top source of several phytochemicals, including the antioxidant flavinoid, quercetin, associated with reduced risk for prostate cancer, lung cancer, and cardiovascular disease. Keep that beautiful red (or yellow) skin on the apple to maximize its sexy benefits.

Apricots

Lore and Fun Facts
Apricots trace back 5000 years to the Far East, initially spreading Middle East and parts of Egypt. They then traveled to the Greeks and Romans via the conquests of Alexander the Great.

Like the pomegranate, some contemporary botanists and biblical scholars make a compelling case for the apricot, not the apple, as the sexy fruit of temptation in that very erotically focused *Song of Solomon* (this is the psalm in the Old Testament that Queen Victoria banished from English Bibles printed during her reign).

Why vote for the apricot over the apple? The psalm makes metaphoric allusion to "sweet fruit" and the female lover imagines her male lover as a tree under which she tasted its voluptuous fruit. Apricot trees grew in abundance in the region and were then, as now fragrant, velvety, fleshy and golden. By contrast, apple trees were not native to the region and only a few grew in the wild. They bore fruit that was acidic, hard and small. What we know as apple trees were introduced to the region much later in history.

On a slightly more contemporary note, in Shakespeare's *A Midsummer's Night Dream*, Titania, queen of the fairies, commands her fairy servants to feed apricots, along with dewberries, to the mortal object of her desire (Bottom) to give him the "royal treatment" as part of her seduction ploy. I'm not suggesting you dress up in a fairy servant costume and hand feed your lover apricots, but . . . well, perhaps I am suggesting that!

Sexy Nutrients
Apricots are a well-known source of Vitamin A, and are also a very good source of Vitamins C and E. They also offer significant amounts of B-complex vitamins. Additionally, apricots pack a powerful surprise: lycopene, that miracle phyotochemical that helps protect against prostate cancer, as well as stomach and lung cancers. That's a happy, sexy prospect!

Artichokes

Lore and Fun Facts
Artichokes are native to Sicily or possibly northern Africa, but likely earned their sexy reputation elsewhere.

This highly distinctive veggie was among the more fashionable foods of late Medieval and early Renaissance European courts.

In 16th century Europe, only men were allowed to consume artichokes because of their reported libido-enhancing qualities. The French Court considered Catherine De Medici scandalous for eating such a large quantity of artichokes, but her husband wasn't complaining. Henry the VIII was extremely fond of artichokes as well. The fleshy leaves were reputed to induce euphoria and restore natural powers. Catherine was quoted as saying, "If one of us had eaten artichokes, we would have been pointed out on the street. Today young women are more forward than pages at the court."

In centuries past, French street vendors cried out: "Artichokes! Artichokes!

Heats the body! Heats the spirit! Heats the genitals!"

Meanwhile, a 16th century English schoolmaster, Thomas Cogan, essentially concurred, stating that "(artichokes) procure a more ernest desire both of man or woman to the venereal acte," further specifying that "the hearts are better than the leaves for this purpose."

In the Tudor era (15-17th centuries) "Artichokes were aphrodisiac, preserved in sugar syrup…".

And this funny tidbit, From the Book of Nature, by Dr. Bartolomeo Boldo in 1576: "It has the virtue of . . . provoking Venus for both men and women; for women making them more desirable, and helping the men who are in these matters rather tardy."

On a more contemporary note, can you name the woman crowned "Miss California Artichoke Queen" in 1947 at the Artichoke Festival in Castroville, California? It was one Norma Jean Baker, whose crown provided a decided boost to her budding career as the sex goddess icon, Marilyn Monroe. The burning question: Did Marilyn and Catherine De Medici both grow their amorous reputations on the back of the noble artichoke, or just on their backs?

Speaking of Italians (work with me here: Catherine De Medici, Marilyn, Joe DiMaggio!), when they came to the US in the early 1900s, they so missed artichokes that they started growing them in California. Problem was, all the New York Italians wanted them, too, but since they were hard to grow and preserve in that climate, the mafia got involved in distribution!

And last but not least, the famous chef Mario Batali calls artichokes one of his "fave vegetables" because of their "very sexy flavor."

Sexy Nutrients
One large artichoke packs 170 milligrams of potassium, and the US Department of Agriculture now ranks the artichoke as the number one vegetable in antioxidant count, especially the phytonutrients cynarine and silymarin. Cynarine stimulates the taste buds and enhances the sweetness of any food eaten right after artichokes—that's why any wine accompaniment must be carefully selected. Cynarine also helps trigger the production of bile needed for the digestion of fats. Silymarin is another powerful antioxidant that may aid the liver in regenerative tissue growth, which may explain why artichokes have also been reputed to cure hangovers! Artichokes are also a good source of vitamin C, folate, magnesium and dietary fiber.

Asparagus

Lore and Fun Facts
Small wonder that this blatantly phallic shaped vegetable, a stellar example of the Doctrine of Resemblances, has been valued for its aphrodisiac qualities for millennia!

Coming to us from the Greek word *asparagos*, this member of the lily family is native to both the eastern Mediterranean and Asia Minor, and it was cultivated by the Romans as early as 200 BCE.

According to one source, Roman emperors were foodies who cultivated asparagus for its diuretic and blood cleansing properties. Apparently their obsessive appreciation of it required that they build special boats in order to transport it for storage.

There's even an old Roman saying, "As quick as cooking asparagus," meaning something accomplished rapidly. Hey honey, how about we cook up some asparagus over our lunch hour?

During the Renaissance, its aphrodisiac reputation was so intense that it was banned in most convents. In French, the word *asperge* is slang for penis. 19th century French bridegrooms were mandated to eat several courses of asparagus on their wedding eve to assure the groom of sexual stamina (and in the Renaissance, it was recommended for "timid" newlyweds). The asparagus' graceful spears have also been a sign of elegance, and in the past were a delicacy only the wealthy could afford.

Few foods are regaled as explicitly in ancient sexual or obscene love poetry as asparagus. Greek, Roman, and Chinese literature sings its praises, as does the Indian *Kama Sutra*, which tells us that asparagus "is provocative of sexual vigor."

In England the plant is mentioned from earliest times and cited again and again in medicinal recipes, as it was throughout Europe, which led Rabelais to have Panurge declare, "My better end is my uniterminal, intercrural asparagus stalk. I hereby vow and promise to keep it succulent, with good measure pressed down and running over," a promise I'm sure was pleasing to his female partners!

Asparagus was a common food in the Renaissance in both France and Italy, an elegant food associated with southern Europe.

The Arabs also loved it, perhaps enamored by its prolific growth, sometimes ten inches in one day and the need to harvest twice a day. Modern men might see this as a new way of bragging about their size and stamina!

In *Culpeper's Complete Herbal* (1652), Nicholas Culpeper suggests, "A decoction of asparagus roots boiled in wine and being taken fasting several mornings together, stirreth up bodily lust in man or woman, whatever some have written to the contrary."

The famous Arabic erotic love manual, *The Perfumed Garden*, recommends a daily dish of asparagus for "great erotic effect" or, as a "stimulant for his amorous desires."

And then there's the sexy way asparagus is eaten: with your fingers. Warm and tender, slightly messy, there's no better way to enjoy this erotic delicacy!

Oops! There is one, tiny downside to the sexy appeal of asparagus. Anyone who's eaten much of it has likely detected its aroma when they urinate. As you might guess, the rumor is true: it adversely affects taste of semen, so oral sex and asparagus don't mix too well! Condom, anyone?

Sexy Nutrients
All varieties of asparagus (green, white, and violet) contain asparagine, the amino acid likely responsible for diuretic properties that support kidney function and reduce high blood pressure. Asparagus is also the leading vegetable that supplies folic acid, needed for the prevention of liver disease and for blood cell formation. Folic acid is said to boost histamine production necessary for the ability to reach orgasm in both sexes. It's also good source of potassium and fiber, a significant source of thiamin and vitamin B6, and one of the richest sources of rutin, a compound that strengthens capillary walls. It also contains glutathione (GSH), an antioxidant that reduces free radicals.

Avocados

Lore and Fun Facts
The very name for this extraordinary fruit is R-rated! It's derived from the Aztec word for testicle, *ahuacat*. Avocados are not merely shaped like testicles; the richer, better tasting Hass (California) varieties are "warty" like the scrotum. They even hang from trees in pairs! Meanwhile, some find the voluptuous egg-like shape and texture of the fruit itself evoke feminine imagery, so take your pick! The Aztecs concocted a sexy spread called *ahuaca-mull*, a mix of mashed avocados, chiles, onions, and tomatoes, an

ancient version of guacamole.

Early explorers to the Americas were enamored by the fruit and took it back to Europe, where France's Sun King, Louis XIV, swore by their capacity to restore his libido, dubbing them *la bonne poire*, or "the good pear." They frequently appeared on the banquet tables of the licentious 17th century court. Their reputation is so strong that Spanish Catholic priests once considered it a forbidden fruit and admonished their parishioners to avoid them.

Much more recently, the famous stripper Mae West continued the long-standing reputation of avocados by reputedly eating at least one every day and giving them credit for her healthy sexual appetite and well-preserved good looks.

Similarly, across the border, in contemporary Mexico, the avocado is valued for its lust-provoking powers.

Sexy Nutrients
Avocados contain 20 essential nutrients, including soluble fiber, potassium, vitamin E, B-vitamins and folic acid. Avocados predominantly contain the monounsaturated fat oleic acid, which maintains levels of the beneficial high-density lipoproteins (HDL) and reduces the harmful low-density lipoprotein (LDL) cholesterol that contributes to atherosclerotic heart disease. They also act as a "nutrient booster" by enabling the body to absorb more fat-soluble nutrients, such as alpha and beta-carotene and lutein, in foods that are eaten with the fruit. Very recent research confirms these nutrients help prevent Age-Related Macular Degeneration. All the better to visually appreciate the lines and curves of your lover!

Bananas

Lore and Fun Facts
If the Doctrine of Resemblances needed a poster child, it would surely be the banana. Long, thick and slightly curved, you have to "undress" it to eat it. Whew! It almost makes me blush to write about it!

Ancient 6th century BCE Buddhist texts written in the region of Malaysia first mention bananas. From there, they moved west to India, where Alexander the Great in 327 BCE savored them during his conquests. He's even given credit for introducing them to the Western world. Although Alexander's special attraction to bananas is up for speculation, many languages, from French to Arabic, use this fruit's name as a common slang term for the male sex organ. Perhaps the late of arrival of bananas to the United States in 1876 explains why we don't have the same slang tradition. On the other hand, up until the 1930s, a common expression for sexual intercourse among the English was "I had a banana with Lady Diana."

This versatile fruit conjures up eroticism. In addition to its erotic shape, the banana is associated with erotic energy in classic Tantric tradition. It's also widely believed, in both Moslem and Roman traditions, that the serpent that tempted Eve camouflaged itself in a bunch of bananas, not behind a fig leaf. A fascinating fact: If you're allergic to bananas, you probably steer clear of latex condoms as well, since an allergy to both, known as the "latex-fruit syndrome," is a common condition!

Sexy Nutrients
Bananas are renowned for their manly supply of potassium, lowering blood pressure and reducing cardiovascular disease, their fiber content, and their defense against a precipitous drop in blood sugar, making them a diabetic's favorite fruit. Consuming twice as much potassium as sodium helps prevent bloating, hardly a sexy sensation/feeling. In the long run, eating bananas and other high potassium foods helps reduce blood pressure and might halve your risk of dying from cardiovascular disease. Bananas also offer a healthy supply of B vitamins, believed to help manufacture sex hormones, and vitamin B6, an energy booster. Makes you want to peel and eat one right now, doesn't it?

Beans

Lore and Fun Facts
Contrary to their reputation in the US for producing unsexy sounds and smells, for thousands of years beans of all types have been held in high esteem by many cultures. They've been praised both as a satisfying food and for their potential to stir passion or enhance fertility.

It is believed that the ancient Mesopotamians cultivated chickpeas (garbanzo beans) in part because they thought they encouraged ovulation. Galen, the personal physician of Marcus Aurelius, believed that garbanzos offered excellent nourishment. He wrote that they stimulated a desire for sex and enhanced sperm production. The reputation of chickpeas continued into the Renaissance, when Benedict, a court professor who later became a Milanese physician, included them in his list of "hot" foods that promoted male erectile functioning. Who needs Viagra when you've got garbanzo beans!?

As for black beans, the famous Roman Pliny wrote in his *Natural History* that they were eaten for their aphrodisiac qualities by the peasants, presumably because of their reputed ability to "stir up action in the lower abdominal organs." In an ironic twist of fate, and an explosion of a different natural gas, he died when he got too close to an erupting volcano!

In the 4th century, St. Jerome, a Croatian ascetic and scholar, forbade nuns to eat beans because he thought they would invoke sexual cravings (his words: "excite genital titillation"). You simply can't have titillated nuns!

By the Renaissance era, beans were counted among the "windy" foods that coursed through the bloodstream and "inflated" both the extremities and the genitals, making them an obvious aphrodisiac. Care for a little extremity inflation?

Sexy Nutrients

Beans are rock stars in the world of sexy food! They're a great source of soluble fiber and low-fat protein, especially when combined with rice. They help lower bad cholesterol levels and have a very low glycemic index, making them great for controlling blood sugar levels. They're also packed with antioxidants, especially the darker varieties. The folate in beans reduces homocysteine, and independent risk factor for heart attack, and they are also rich in anthocyanin, the same antioxidant compounds found in grapes and cranberries, fruits long appreciated for their healthy qualities.

As for the really sexy part, cultures in which beans are regularly eaten report lower risks of dying from breast, prostate or colon cancer. That's likely because beans are rich in compounds such as saponin, inositol, resistant starch and oligosaccharides, which several studies have linked to cancer prevention. The more beans you eat, the longer you live. The longer you live, the more sex you have. Pass the beans!

Beets (Beetroot)

Lore and Fun Facts

In the ancient world, beets were white and bore a greater resemblance to testicles, which may be why the aforementioned Pliny the Elder, Roman naturalist and scholar, considered them an aphrodisiac. According to him, they were "… guaranteed to inflame the passions" and often used in recipes designed to stir the libido.

The modern beet, with its rich red color, came into existence in the 16th century. Russian women in centuries past reputedly used red beets to color their cheeks to draw suitors to them. Many today are drawn to the voluptuous texture and evocative, passionate color of beets. They have a sweet, earthy flavor and are easy to store and preserve.

Given their high sugar content, it's likely that beets convert well to energy, which is a good thing when it comes to love in all its forms!

Sexy Nutrients

Although various colors of beets are currently in vogue, it's the beautiful rich red ones that are packed with the highest nutrient levels. Beets provide impressive amounts of folate, manganese, potassium and fiber, along with being a good source of tryptophan, iron, vitamin C and magnesium. Potassium is associated with good cardiovascular health.

Getting enough folate is particularly important for pregnant women, as it helps prevent birth defects. Both red and other pigmented beets contain betalains, which act as free-radical scavengers that may offer protection against cancers, especially colon (not a sexy prospect!) and stress-related conditions. Beets' anti-inflammatory power also reduces the odds of contracting type-2 diabetes.

After eating red beets, prepare yourself for the possible intrigue of producing red-tinted urine or even stools! "Beeturia" occurs in about 10-14% of the population and its cause is likely related to iron absorption, although there's some debate about it. Typically, it's perfectly harmless, and with a positive perspective, certainly adds "color" to everyday potty breaks.

Capers

Lore and Fun Facts

Capers are the piquant flowering buds of the caper shrub native to the Mediterranean. In the 15th century, Bartolomeo Sacchi, known as Platina, wrote the first printed cookbook, *De Honesta Voluptate et Valitudine (On Right Pleasure and Good Health)*. Platina proclaims that capers "expel humors and melancholy pressures as well as excite the passions."

Similarly, a contemporary, Benedictus de Nursia, a professor at Perugia (until the pope expelled him), became a Milanese physician and included capers on his list of "heating" foods recommended for enhancing male sexual performance (literally—"extending" the penis). Clearly the Doctrine of Resemblances was ignored by these two highly regarded gentlemen of the middle ages! Who knew such tiny round buds could be inspire such phallic blossoming?

Sexy Nutrients

Packed into those tiny flower buds is a remarkable host of sexy nutrients. Impressively, they are loaded with quercetin and rutin, powerful antioxidant flavinoid compounds. Rutin helps to strengthen capillaries and is sometimes included in treatments for varicose veins, hemorrhoids and hemophilia. Quercetin is highly regarded for its ability to fight free radicals and its anti-inflammatory, anti-bacterial, analgesic, and anti-carino-genic properties. Interestingly, the quercetin levels in capers exceed the levels in apples, onions or blueberries! What's more, they also provide a variety of vitamins and minerals, including vitamins A, K, niacin, and riboflavin as well as calcium, iron and copper. Yes, they've got sodium in them, but surely adding capers to meals is a much sexier form of adding kick to a dish than reaching for the salt shaker! Unless your salt shaker conforms to the Doctrine of Resemblances ... but I digress!

Carrots

Lore and Fun Facts
In ancient Greece, carrots were called "philon" or "philtron," based on the Greek word "philo," or "loving." Only later did their current name derive from Latin and French words. The ancient Greeks used them to "cure sexual problems and also to make men more ardent and women more yielding."

Caligula, the famously licentious Roman emperor, once convened the senate and then fed the assembly a spread of carrot dishes in the hope that they'd all get down to business in the form of an orgy.

Some say the phallic shaped carrot, a classic example of the "Doctrine of Resemblances," makes up in firmness what it lacks in girth. Of course, I've seen carrots that would make the average guy jealous, but that's another story. The Arabs in the era of Scheherazade and Aladdin especially valued slender carrots as a potent aphrodisiac. They spiced the carrots and cooked them in milk in this belief this would double the erotic effects.

In the Middle Ages and Renaissance era, carrots were among the "windy" foods considered aphrodisiac because they produced flatulence. "In the Renaissance era, carrots were among the "venerous roots" made into sweet composts and served at banquet feasts as a "a great furtherer of Venus her pleasure." (sic)

Sexy Nutrients
Carrots are hot! In addition to being packet with beta carotene, the better to see your lover and protect his prostate, they're packed with lots of other nutrients that are good for your sex life. They provide fiber, B-complex vitamins and potassium. Danish research has found they also contain a compound, falcarinol, that is linked to a reduction in cancer risk.

Caviar

Lore and Fun Facts

Its very name is evokes sexy elegance, elitism and indulgence—the platinum of aphrodisiacs. As fabulous fish roe (eggs), they literally evoke images of the sea, Aphrodite herself and fertility. "Real" caviar—like "real" champagne—has a specific designation: it must be roe from one of three species of sturgeon (beluga, osetra, and sevruga).

After Alexander the Great brought Beluga caviar to the west, the Romans so lusted for it that they had their servants bring live sturgeon from the Caspian sea, while the Greeks began their "cocktail" parties (aka orgies) with a plate of hors d'oeuvres that included caviar, oysters and roasted grasshoppers.

In the boudoir, Dostoevski's wife reputedly treated her husband to caviar—and more—after the completion of each chapter of Crime and Punishment. Pab lo Picasso, known for his amorous intentions, insisted on Beluga, the largest fish roe, produced by the largest species of sturgeon. It's delicate and gray in color. A specific kind of Beluga, Alma, is white and comes from fish that are more than 100 years old; its rarity and quality (older fish generally make the best caviar) make it the most expensive of all. The osetra sturgeon produces a smaller "golden" caviar, the favorite choice of British author Ian Fleming, whose pen created the debonair and always randy James Bond. The third type of "real" caviar comes from the sevruga sturgeon, which is the smallest and most common type of sturgeon found in the Caspian Sea. That makes its eggs the least expensive, and happily, they're the favorite of many chefs because of their excellent flavor and texture. Top quality sturgeon caviar of all types is labeled "Mallosol," which means "little salt."

Jackie Kennedy indulged in it frequently (because she could—at about $140/ounce)! Her favorite meal at the Four Seasons in New York was a baked potato heaped with caviar and a glass of champagne.

In ultra-modern times, there's even a reality TV show star from the VH1 series, *For the Love of Ray J*, who has not only dubbed herself, "Caviar," but has also become a porn star! Whether or not she actually consumes fish eggs is less clear, but her choice of *nom de guerre* makes it clear that the reputation of caviar is alive and well.

Although the various sturgeon species produce the crowning glory of fish roe, other fish including cod, herring, sea urchin (*uni* at sushi bars), and even salmon also produce very delectable roe that are far more affordable. Or you can get sturgeon fish roe from the world's leader in sustainable sturgeon farming,

Tsar Nicoulai, an aqua farm in Northern California. As with many aphrodisiacs, a little goes a long way, too!

Sexy Nutrients
Caviar is an excellent source of vitamin B12. Recent Finnish research suggests this vitamin may reduce the risk of Alzheimers disease by lowering homocysteine levels (it's good to remember your lover's name in the heat of passion!). Caviar also provides significant amounts of magnesium, iron, and vitamin A and protein.

In just one tablespoon and 40 calories, is also provides 15% DV (Daily Value) of selenium, which may help keep a man's prostate gland healthy. But its immediate effects may be even sexier! All types of caviar are loaded with L-arginine, which boosts the vasodilator Nitric Oxide (NO), as does Viagra. Caviar, however, surely offers a much more sensual and satisfying approach to "building wood!" (One fairly un-sexy caveat: If you get herpes outbreaks often, L-arginine is not your friend, as it can help trigger an outbreak).

Celery

Lore and Fun Facts
Many cultures, from Haitians to Chinese, have been struck by suggestive power and zesty crunch that celery offers. Early Romans believed celery to be an aphrodisiac and used it liberally through many of their recipes in order to stimulate sexual arousal. and given its long shape and rigid texture, it's a candidate for the Doctrine of Resemblances.

During the Renaissance, celery was known as a "hot" aphrodisiac that "provoked" coitus. For that reason, sadly, it was a food that wet nurses were to avoid, since it would presumably harm both the quality and quantity of milk production by drying it up!

By the 18th century, the mistress of Louis XV, Madame de Pompadour, so believed in the powers of celery soup that she ate it each morning to overcome her "frigidity." Unfortunately, she remained "frigid," and this and other aphrodisiac "remedies" did not help. She ultimately became the king's chief procurer and managed the king's royal whorehouse.

Sexy Nutrients
Celery's perfect ratio of potassium to sodium makes it an excellent diuretic, the better to banish unsexy bloating! In Asia, its use as a folk remedy to lower blood pressure is believed to trace back to BCE. University of Chicago research has confirmed that a chemical in celery called 3-n-butyl-phthalide

accounts for its aroma and is especially effective in reducing stress-induced hypertension by relaxing the smooth-muscle lining of blood vessels.

Popular references assert that celery contains a male hormone called androsteron, which when released as a pheromone in a man's sweat man attracts women; actually, celery contains androstenone, a different, unpleasantly smelly substance. We should be grateful that humans can't typically smell it!

But a word of warning before you grab that sexy stalk: In a few individuals, an allergy to celery can induce anaphylactic shock, which is highly unsexy in every way!

Cherries

Lore and Fun Facts

Cherries hold lots of sexy allure; they're juicy, tasty, and bright red to deep crimson. Easily popped into the mouth, they're a natural to serve a lover in diverse settings, from a picnic to the boudoir. These reasons and more explain why they ranked in the top 10 of personal aphrodisiac favorites in my 21st Century Aphrodisiac Foods Survey.

Cherries were once considered a particularly luxurious and erotic fruit and luscious lips were frequently compared to them, as this 17th century poem by Robert Herrick shows. The "cry" here is by someone selling them in the market.

CHERRY-RIPE, ripe, ripe, I cry,
Full and fair ones, come and buy.
If so be you ask me where
They do grow? I answer There,
Where my Julia's lips do smile
There's the land or cherry isle,
Whose plantations fully show
All the year, where cherries grow.

Then there's the erotic slang use of "cherry," which can be "popped" or "picked" depending on the user. I'll leave it to you to decide how that term came into being.

Sexy Nutrients

Cherries are loaded with extremely high levels of antioxidants that can keep your sex life thriving by reducing the risks of developing heart disease and diabetes. Cherry-enriched diets have been found to lower bad cholesterol and triglycerides (another bad fat), and they're a natural source of vitamin A, vitamin C, potassium, magnesium, iron, fiber and folate. Tart cherries are one of the few foods rich in melatonin, which helps regulate the body's natural sleep patterns and aids with jet lag (you'll be ready for action sooner after a long-distance trip!).

Cherries are great for your body image, too! A recent University of Michigan study found a cherry-enriched diet lowered total weight and body fat—especially the notorious "belly" fat—to keep you smiling and confident when you look at your gorgeous self in the mirror.

Chilies

Lore and Fun Facts

Throughout history, from China to the Yucatan peninsula, chilies have enjoyed a worldwide reputation for putting fire on your palate and in your loins! In 1132 the monks of Cluny, under the pious leadership of Peter the Venerable, were forbidden to eat "pimento" because of its lust-provoking qualities.

Similarly, a 16th century Jesuit priest, Jose de Acosta, warned Spanish colonists in Mexico and Peru to avoid chilies because of their aphrodisiac nature. As recently as the 1970s, the Peruvian government banned them from prison food because they considered their reputed aphrodisiac properties inappropriate for men living in a "limited lifestyle." Maybe the Doors' 1967 hit song, "Light My Fire" reminded those government officials of the lusty dangers of chilies!

Sexy Nutrients

Think pleasure in pain! The active ingredient of chilies, capsaicin, triggers the release of endorphins, the brain's "feel-good," morphine-like polypeptide compound, the same one that triggers "runner's high" in long-distance runners and, surprise, surprise, gushes forth during orgasm. Capsaicin also helps to clear the lungs, improve circulation and acts a pain killer for various types of chronic pain, including arthritis. Research comparing the effectiveness of an aspirin a day versus the ingestion of chilies suggests they're equally effective in keeping your blood vessels free and clear, lowering bad cholesterol, and even in reducing the odds of developing diabetes! Cool news for a hot food! Both sweet and hot chilies are packed with vitamins A, C, and E, especially the sweet red ones.

Chocolate

Lore and Fun Facts

We can't forget chocolate! Every Valentine's Day, we are reminded of the huge aphrodisiac reputation of chocolate. Especially for 21st century sensibilities (and my survey data), chocolate is the winner!

If there were a single food that meant "sexy," it would have to be chocolate. No review of aphrodisiacs seems complete without an extensive detailing of chocolate's mythical properties, tangled history, and incredible variety of forms. While we can't devote the time or space to a detailed accounting of its influence, a brief summary, a little sip of its goodness, will be, like the food itself, just enough to leave us wanting more.

Certain facts about chocolate are unquestioned, but questions remain. It's believed that the wild cocoa plant originated in what is now South America, likely in the Amazon or Orinoco basins. Archeological evidence suggests that the Maya brought it to the Yucatan when they migrated there in the 7th century CE. Chocolate's name is certainly Mayan in origin, from *chocolatl*, the name given to a cold, bitter drink they enjoyed, but the actual meaning of *chocolatl* is unclear.

Aztec emperor Montezuma may have drunk 50 glasses of honey-sweetened chocolate a day to sustain his virility while pouncing on his harem of 600 women, but I don't recommend either that much chocolate or that many partners! Enjoy in moderation!

The Spanish explorer Cortez almost certainly brought chocolate back to Europe, where from Spain it spread to Italy, Austria, and then France. In Europe it was at first something of a secret indulgence, and as its popularity grew, so did rules and restrictions on its consumption. And this may very well be explained by chocolate's effect on both mood and libido, brought about by the release of endorphins, opiate-like neurotransmitters thought to mimic that falling-in-love feeling.

Chocolate's early reputation was as a "food for the Gods," first for Mayan nobility, then Aztec nobility, then European nobility. It was also used as currency as late as 1850 in the Yucatan, and given that it had to be imported for European enjoyment, only the wealthy could afford it at first.

In 17th century England, an immoderate use of chocolate was thought to be aphrodisiac: In that era, chocolate was prepared with vanilla, another aphrodisiac.

Thankfully, chocolate now enjoys a more widespread following, due in part to how versatile it is. It's not coincidental that the one holiday devoted to love, Valentine's Day, cannot be properly celebrated or appreciated without indulging in chocolate. It mixes well with a wide variety of foods, is consumed hot, warm or cold, in solid, powdered or liquid form. If we had to survive with just one aphrodisiac food, surely it would be chocolate!

Sexy Nutrients
Historically, chocolate has been valued as a tonic, as a medicine, and as a powerful aphrodisiac. It's loaded with what are called the "feel good" neurotransmitters, releasing endorphins and boosting serotonin (mood stabilizers).

Chocolate is a stimulant that's high in theobromine (0.5 to 2.7 percent), which is similar to but milder than caffeine, and caffeine itself (0.25 to 1.7 percent), which may be why it perks you up but without the jitters!

And then there's anandamide, discovered in chocolate by San Diego researchers, which is similar to THC but not highly discussed because some chocolate manufacturers were concerned that chocolate would be labeled a drug! Anandamide is a cannabinoid, a chemical that hooks up to the same brain receptors that catch similar ingredients in marijuana smoke. Your brain produces some anandamide naturally, but you also get very small amounts of the chemical from chocolate.

In addition, chocolate contains two chemicals similar to anandamide, which slow the breakdown of the anandamide produced in your brain, intensifying its effects. Maybe that's why eating chocolate makes you feel very mildly mellow. Not enough to get you hauled off to the hoosegow or bring in the Feds to confiscate your candy, just enough to wipe away the tears of lost love. (Don't worry: You'd need to eat at least 25 pounds of chocolate at one time to achieve any marijuana-like effect.)

PEA, or phenylethylamine, is also in chocolate, and although this has been popularized as raising dopamine and also contributing to the "chocolate high," it's really only present in traces. PEA in excess dilates the blood vessels and can trigger headaches. It's also rapidly broken down, and much higher levels are found in salami, pickled herring and cheddar cheese.

The fat of chocolate—cocoa butter—is heart healthy because it is converted into a monosaturated fat by other fatty substances in chocolate. Chocolate also contains trace amounts of iron, magnesium and copper. Milk chocolate has calcium, but also has more simple sugars and doesn't have the antioxidant phenolics found in dark chocolate.

Cilantro

Lore and Fun Facts

Cilantro, the Spanish name for the leaves and stems of the coriander plant, is also known as coriander, or Chinese parsley, and grows wild in south East Europe. Coriander is believed to be named after koris, the Greek word for the "bedbug" which was said to emit a similar odor! Today most people refer to the seeds of the plant as coriander, and to the stems and leaves as cilantro or Chinese parsley.

The Egyptians, Indians and Chinese have all cultivated this member of the carrot family for thousands of years. Its culinary and medicinal uses are mentioned in the *Ebers Papyrus* from about 1550 BCE. The herb was among those offered by the king to the temple, and coriander seeds were found in King Tut's tomb. The ancient Egyptians included it in unguents to treat various ailments, including herpes, which was around even then! It is mentioned in Sanskrit text and in the Bible Spanish conquistadors introduced to Mexico and Peru, where it now commonly paired with chilies in local cuisine.

The book of the *Arabian Nights,* which in various versions is at least 1000 years old, tells a tale of a merchant who had been childless for 40 years, only to be cured by a concoction that included coriander. Cilantro was also known to be used as an "appetite" stimulant.

Coriander seeds have often been included in love potions, including a Chinese version believed to induce immortality, which of course would be highly beneficial from a sexual point of view! At wedding banquets during the Tudor era, a spiced wine known as "hippocras" included coriander and was served to induce "feelings of well-being."

It was one of the first herbs brought by the colonists to North America, reaching the shores of Massachusetts before 1670. Cilantro has since become very popular in the Southwest and Western part of the United States and is a staple of Mexican and Tex-Mex cuisine. It's easily found fresh at farmers markets and supermarkets alike across the United States.

You say you just don't like cilantro? If so, you're likely of European descent and quite possibly genetically predisposed to dislike it, according to research conducted at the Monell Chemical Senses Center in Philadelphia, and it has not gained in popularity in Europe as it has in many other parts of the world. On the other hand, given its millions of devoted followers across the Americas, North Africa, India and Asia, you might want to consider acquiring a taste for it!

Sexy Nutrients

For most of us, cilantro's health benefits extend way beyond our enjoyment of its flavor. It gets major kudos for helping to manage blood sugar levels and controlling diabetes. Animal research has found that it reduces LDL even when the animals were fed a high fat diet. It's also an excellent herbal source of vitamin K, which helps to keep your bones strong and hence more capable of engaging in intriguing sexual positions!

Cilantro is loaded with both phytonutrient and flavinoid antioxidants and possesses anti-inflammatory benefits as well as dietary fiber. It's a very good source of vitamins A and C, thiamine, riboflavin, folate, calcium, iron, magnesium, and potassium, as well as a good source of niacin, vitamin B6, phosporus, zinc and selenium.

Various studies have also confirmed its anti-microbial alcohols and aldehydes help ward off various infections, from the common cold to bacteria associated with food poisoning, such as salmonella and listeria. Perhaps the Egyptians were on to something when using it to treat herpes infections!

Clams

Lore and Fun Facts

The reputation of the lowly clam is nearly as long-standing as the oyster, and although it's sometimes referred to as the "poor-man's oyster," it carries a solid reputation for both its nutritional and aphrodisiac benefits. Its value extends even to the clam shell's ancient use as currency, leading perhaps to the modern vernacular use of "clams" as "money."

Today, we "clam up," feel "clammy," get into spots as "tight as a clam" and, somewhat counterintuitively, can go through life "happy as a clam." In an interesting nod to the Doctrine of Resemblances, "clam" has also a nickname for female genitalia, and there's some evidence to show that many have thought the bulbous meat of the clam resembles the male testicles, as well!

Then, of course, there's Boticelli's famed "Birth of Venus," or "Venus on the Half Shell," depicting a nude Venus standing on a large shell looks a lot more like a clam than an oyster. The popular American hardshell clam, *Venus mercenaria*, was probably so named because clams have frequently been associated with both Venus and with currency.

But the primary historical reference to clams as aphrodisiacs appears in Japanese folklore, which suggests long baking to dry them and then ingesting the powder mixed with water every night for a week 2 hours before bedtime to restore sexual function for both men and women.

Sexy Nutrients
Like oysters, clams pack an immediate biochemical punch. A team of researchers recently found that clams deliver two types of amino acids that spark a rush of sex hormones in even greater quantities than oysters. They're also loaded with protein, vitamin C, vitamin B12, iron, phosphorus, copper, manganese, and selenium. All of these vitamins and minerals keep your immune system going and contribute to cardiovascular health. Iron keeps you energized and is especially important for pregnant women. Selenium helps to protect against certain cancers. If that weren't enough, they're also a good source of riboflavin, niacin, potassium, and zinc.

Clams have lots of omega-3s, which are great for many reasons (see seafood), and are also low fat. Some worry about their cholesterol content, which is actually moderate. It also turns out that the cholesterol found in low-fat seafood is metabolized differently than the cholesterol in meat that is also high in saturated fatty acids.

Coconuts

Lore and Fun Facts
The great Moroccan 14th century geographer/traveler, Ibn Battuta, who traveled over 75,000 miles just 60 years after Marco Polo, sang the praises of coconuts, bananas, and mollusks after finding them in abundance in Dhofar, Oman. Referring to the coconut, he wrote: "As for its aphrodisiac quality, its action in this respect is wonderful."

Coconut is an integral part of many tropical cuisines, including in Thailand, the Philippines, Sri Lanka, and India. It has been revered for thousands of years both as a food and as a folk medicine to treat a variety of ailments, from irregular or painful menstruation to sexually transmitted infections.

Coconut oil is part of a traditional aromatic mixture used to anoint a bride on the eve of her wedding in some Afro-Caribbean and modern Muslim cultures.

Sexy Nutrients
Contemporary Western medicine is divided on the health benefits of coconut and its oil. It is one of the few sources of lauric acid, a key component of human breast milk and formulas used to nourish hospital patients. Research on Pacific Island and Asian populations whose diets include lots of coconuts have very low rates of heart disease, On the other hand, their diet is mostly plant-based, and they're a lot more active than the typical American, so a direct

comparison isn't necessarily reliable.

The medical community in the US regularly advises us to steer clear of products that include coconut oil, because it is a highly saturated fat. Other recent research suggests it's more likely to raise HDL, the good cholesterol, but pure coconut milk should not be confused with processed, partially hydrogenated coconut oil used in packaged goods.

In an effort to keep it simple and sexy, coconut milk and unsweetened coconut flakes are a delicious addition to many classic Asian recipes and deserve to be enjoyed from time to time. If it feels a bit naughty to indulge, so much the better for revving up the erotic engines!

Dates

Lore and Fun Facts
The domestication of dates can be traced back to about 5000 BCE, when date trees grew along the Nile. In ancient Egypt, the goddess Nephtyz resided in the date palm and offered dates and the water of life to the dead. Palace reliefs from the period depict the high priest holding the cone of a male date palm and worshipping the tree. Scholars today believe this represents a fertilization ceremony. The 2nd century physician Galen included date piths in the love potion he recommended to "excite the desire of women."

A single male date palm typically produces enough pollen to fertilize 25-50 female date palms. Sometimes, female palms lean distinctly toward a neighboring male palm. Even so, the ancients in date-growing regions throughout the Middle East assisted in fertilizing the female trees by gently brushing them with male flower bundles. It's no secret that many women today find it erotic to be gently brushed by her man's flower bundle!

Today, dates are a staple in Mediterranean cuisines, and date shakes are popular and well known in southern California, where date palms are grown. The Shields Date Farm near Palm Springs, CA keeps alive the centuries-old "date-mating" process, and even promotes it in the form of a vegetative super-soft porn film seen by thousands: "The Romance and Sex life of a Date."

Sexy nutrients
Dates are fat-free, sodium-free, cholesterol-free and packed with both soluble and insoluble fiber, which helps to keep both your cardiovascular system and colon humming along nicely. They're an excellent source of potassium, which helps to keep your blood pressure down.

Dates are also loaded with a remarkable variety of minerals and vitamins, including iron, copper, B-complex vitamins, vitamin A and antioxidant flavonoids such as beta-carotene, lutein, and zeaxanthin. These antioxidants offer protection against a variety of cancers, including prostate, breast, and colon. Dates offer a sumptuous alternative to candy, and a little of their delicious sweetness goes a long way. A marvelous size and shape for finger food, they are a sexy alternative to raisins.

Egg

Lore and Fun Facts
As a metaphor for sexuality throughout the millennia, few foods are as powerfully associated with passion, fertility and regeneration as the egg. An Australian Aboriginal tale holds that the universe emanated from an egg. A clear majority of cultures feature the egg in their creationist versions of how the world came into being.

The Greeks believed Eros was born from an egg, and Ovid praised their aphrodisiac qualities. The Romans believed that if a woman even offered to make eggs for a man, her sexual intent was clear, and the object of her desire would be helpless to resist. Perhaps now you won't respond so casually to your lover's offer of making you eggs for breakfast!

Sheikh Nefzawi provides several love potions featuring eggs in the 15th century *Perfumed Garden*. One suggests he make a daily practice of eating egg yolks to provide "an energetic stimulant towards coitus." Another, directed at being able to enjoy repeated acts of pleasure throughout the night, suggests frying a "great number" of eggs and then immersing them in honey.

The Venetian Casanova, arguably the historical figure most known for his sexual escapades, made egg the primary ingredient in his secret, egg salad "love recipe" to assure his "stamina" throughout the night. Humpty Dumpty might not have been so lucky, but Casanova knew to crack a few eggs to hold up his part of the sexual bargain!

Sexy Nutrients
Whole eggs are loaded with many sexy nutrients, from iodine for making thyroid hormone to vitamins A, D, lutein and zeaxanthin (for healthy eyes) to amino acids, omega 3s, and minerals. Eggs are also the richest food source for choline, a nutrient needed for good brain function and health and in which many Americans are deficient. It's especially important for pregnant women and nursing women to assure healthy brain development of the fetus and infant. What's more, one large egg contains 6.25 grams of protein, which is

roughly 8-10% of an adult's recommended daily allowance.

This just in on the sexy news front! Recent studies and major literature reviews conducted both in the United States (Physician's Health Study) and England (University of Surrey) conclude that the health benefits and risks of eggs have been given a very bum rap! Saturated fatty acids (SFA) found in processed foods, including meats, are much more responsible for elevating LDL "bad" cholesterol levels than are cholesterol-rich foods, such as egg yolks. Only those whose diets are high in SFAs, or who have diabetes (the cholesterol is metabolized differently) need to exercise caution in egg consumption. Otherwise, the research concludes eggs actually help to reduce coronary risk factors, including obesity—they're low in calories and leave you feeling full. That's a sexy prospect! If you have any concerns that eggs aren't all that the recent research says they're cracked up to be, talk to your health care professional.

Eggplant

Lore and Fun Facts
Eggplant, often referred to as aubergine (France and England) made its way into kitchens some 5000 years ago, traveling westward from India to Persia and North Africa. When it showed up in southern Europe during the 15th century, some physicians contended it was dangerous and might contribute to the production of black bile and cause melancholia (it's a member of the nightshade family). Despite that temporary bad press, its aphrodisiac history is long-standing and prevails. The *Kama Sutra* (2nd century, BCE) offers a remedy to "weakened sexual power" that includes rubbing an eggplant along the length of the lingam (penis) to produce a "swelling" said to last up to a month! Apparently, they were oblivious to the risks of priapism! In the 17th century, Cardinal de Richelieu, known for his debauched leanings, introduced eggplant to France. Other sexy legends abound, from the Middle East to England, and even the West Indies, where eggplants were also reputed to evoke genital excitement. What else would you expect from a vegetable with such a "meaty" texture!

Sexy Nutrients
Eggplant offers lots of dietary fiber with very few calories. It's also a very good source of potassium, copper, manganese and vitamin B1. The US Department of Agriculture also reports that it contains high levels of phenolic acid, which offers protection from oxidative stress and bacterial and fungal infections—the better to keep you happy, healthy and hot! If that's not enough, the skin of eggplant contains an anthocyanin, nasunin, which helps protect brain cell membranes from free xradical damage, the better to keep your neurons—and their sexy thoughts—firing!

Fennel

Lore and Fun Facts
With its distinctive, delicate fragrance of mild licorice, its bulbous base and feathery, green tendrils, fennel is an aromatic herb in the same family of plants as celery, coriander/cilantro, anise and dill, to name just a few. The stalks are typically used as a vegetable. Still, its shape, flavor, nutrients and history place is squarely in the category of sexy foods.

It was worn as a crown during orgies in ancient Greece to celebrate Dionysius, the God of wine and fertility. It is also featured in recipes in both *The Perfumed Garden* and *The Kama Sutra* to boost sexual vigor. For centuries, it's been used to promote milk flow in nursing mothers, and 19th century eclectic physicians recommended it to promote menstruation.

Research on rats has supported its libidinal effects, though it remains a challenge to get the critters to talk about it! A Mediterranean fennel soup is popular today for its aphrodisiac potential. Due to its versatility, fennel enhances recipes calling for meats, poultry, seafood, soups, and vegan dishes. It adds an exotic, aromatic twist to a traditional vichyssoise.

Sexy Nutrients
Fennel's phytoestrogens help regulate hormone levels in women, and some herbalists suggest it has been used to augment breast size (don't some women—and their lovers— wish that were true!). An important nutritional value of fennel is that it contains large amounts of vitamin C, one cup containing nearly 20% of your daily vitamin C requirement.

It's a very good source of folate, fiber and potassium, all of which contribute to cardiovascular health. Its abundance of potassium helps to lower blood pressure by diminishing the adverse effects of regular table salt. High blood pressure is generally bad for lovemaking, so maybe it's time to start including fennel in more of your simple, sexy cooking!

Figs

Lore and Fun Facts
The ancient and widely revered fig has a long and sexy history. Like the androgynous avocado, figs should get a nod from the Doctrine of Resemblances, by resembling both male and female genitals. Their external appearance is suggestive of testicles, while the interior has a curvy shape and feminine rosy color. Even the sexy fig leaf, used historically in the biblical Garden of Eden and in Western art to cover genitals, now graces a woman in the playful

Desperate Housewives television logo!

Figs are thought to have been first cultivated in Egypt. They spread to ancient Crete and then, around the 9th century BCE, to ancient Greece, where they became a staple foodstuff in the traditional diet. Figs were held in such esteem by the Greeks that they created laws forbidding the export of the best quality figs.

Figs were also revered in ancient Rome where they were thought of as a sacred fruit. According to Roman myth, the twin founders of Rome, Romulus and Remus, were suckled by a she-wolf beneath a fig tree.

Both the ancient Greeks and Romans valued figs for their impact on sexual potency. Plutarch wrote that figs were featured during the lively and lusty festival of Dionysia, which was and is renowned for its carnal excesses.

And then there's this sexy little ditty from the Athenian playwright Aristophanes' The Peace, from around 421 BCE:

Now live splendidly together
Free from adversity
Pick [your] figs
May his be large and hard,
May hers be sweet!

Figs are so sexy they're even mentioned in a lover's context in the Bible, from the Song of Solomon: "The fig tree putteth forth her green figs, and the vines with the tender grape a good smell. Arise, my love, my fair one, and come away." Come away, indeed!

Among the Hindus, the fig is a symbol of the lingam and yoni, referring to male and female creative energy. The French expression *faire la figue,* or "make the fig," refers to an obscene gesture similar in context to "flipping the bird," while Greeks and Italians used the word as slang for the female genitalia, finding similarities between that lovely region and the appearance of a newly split fig.

And who could blame anyone for being enamored of figs? From their mild but deeply sweet flavor to the complex textures of smooth skin, chewy flesh, and crunchy seeds, they are also notoriously delicate. For this reason, they're often dried to keep them around longer, but fresh figs are available in the US from June through early autumn.

Sexy Nutrients
The complexity of figs extends to their health benefits. Included in their over 80 nutrients is a high concentration of magnesium, needed to produce

sex hormones. They are a good source of calcium, and their high potassium content counteracts the loss of calcium through urination, providing a synergistic boost for your bones.

One fig serving offers about 30% of your daily fiber, which helps with in weight management and in keeping your energy levels up. In one study, women who relied on fiber supplements in place of fiber-rich foods like figs showed a significant decrease in their levels of energy. That's not a sexy prospect! So figs can help keep you trim, boost your energy and aid in boning ... sorry, bone strength. What a great little pick-me-up!

Garlic

Lore and Fun Facts
This "stinking rose" member of the onion family has been a staple food, medicine, and aphrodisiac in many cultures since ancient times. Garlic appears in the Bible and the Talmud. Hippocrates, Galen, Pliny the Elder, and Dioscorides all mention the use of garlic for many conditions, including parasites, respiratory problems, poor digestion, and low energy. Its use in China was first mentioned in 510 CE.

On the sexy side of things, Pliny specifically mentioned its aphrodisiac powers. The love manuals, *The Kama Sutra* and *The Perfumed Garden*, sing its praises. In one era, Palestinian grooms wore a garlic close in their buttonhole to ensure a good wedding night. The ancient Egyptians filled King Tutankanum's tomb with massive amounts of garlic, perhaps in the hope of sending their leader to the next world with a big smile on his face. You could say this gives a whole new meaning to rising from the dead!

Korean gods were said to have given certain mortal women an immortal's black garlic before mating with them to give them supernatural powers.

And in the Renaissance, garlic was one of the "hot" foods that could stand in for more expensive cloves to heat things up and promote circulation and sperm count.

Sexy Nutrients
Raw garlic generates antibacterial, antifungal and antiviral activity, the sexual ramifications of which can be guessed at quite easily! In addition to being a fairly good source of vitamins B1, B6 and C, University research has confirmed that garlic compounds in combination with red blood cells trigger the release of polysulfides, which in turn relax the blood vessels. That's not only a good thing for your blood pressure, but also increases blood flow to the genital

regions of both sexes (note: increased blood flow to the genitals is a very good thing sexually!). While correlation studies are as yet inconclusive, cultures in which large amounts of garlic are consumed are known to have lower incidents of several cancers. Its largely positive, blood thinning, cardiovascular properties are so significant that some surgeons tell patients to avoid garlic for several weeks before surgery to avoid excessive bleeding during the procedure.

Ghee (clarified butter)

Lore and Fun Facts
This mainstay of South Asian and African cooking, ghee is butter at its indulgent best. Butter is heated at a low temperature for about thirty minutes, so that all the water and milk products are removed; the remaining "ghee" is a silken yellow liquid with an enhanced flavor and a much higher burning point than regular butter.

Ghee is integral to many recipes of *The Kama Sutra*, as part of a blend with other aphrodisiac substances such as honey and jasmine flowers. It features in numerous sacred Hindu rituals including marriage celebrations. Savor it without dietary guilt by sticking to a small portion and using it as an occasional, special dipping sauce for finger foods like asparagus or artichoke. Because of its richer flavor, a little goes a long way.

Sexy Nutrients
Everyone knows butter provides "fat" and calories! Although the fat in ghee is largely saturated, the process of making it creates short chain fatty acids, not the long chain fatty acids associated with cardiovascular damage. It also contains vitamin A, D, E, and K. Butterfat also helps with the absorption of calcium, magnesium, iodine, and selenium. What's more, Harvard researchers recently reported that as butter and other full-fat food (e.g., yogurt) consumption has declined, fertility and other sexual health problems have increased. Ghee offers advantages over regular butter or oils because it aids digestion by stimulating the secretion of stomach acids. One study in rats found that ghee actually reduced levels of bad LDL cholesterol by increasing the secretion of biliary lipids. For those with lactose intolerance, it offers an opportunity to savor the flavor of butter. Various references suggest it's 60% to 100% saturated fat, so its sexy benefits can and should be savored in small quantities.

Ginger

Lore and Fun Facts
History reveals that some six thousand years ago ancient Austronesian voyagers traveling south through the Malay Archipelago carried ginger with them

on their small boats, with otherwise only essentials on board. As it spread throughout Asia, it became indispensable as both a spice, a medicine, and in antidotes against poison.

As a "heating" agent it was felt that ginger, among other qualities, contributed to sexual potency and fertility. Both sperm and the womb were considered "hot and wet," so the best aphrodisiacs possessed these dual features: . "Hot" alone might boost potency but not fertility. Ginger's rare classification as both hot and wet made it the most prized of all the spices. Any man that has heard his lover say that she is "hot and wet" will appreciate the value of this root.

It is lavishly praised in the *Qur'an*, the sacred Islam text, as the pleasurable spice offered to the righteous in the afterlife. They are served "brimming [silver goblet] cups from the Fountain of Ginger" to protect them from the cold. With its "hot in the third degree" highest ranking, ginger was prescribed by Arabic and Persian dieticians as a treatment for male potency difficulties.

By the 14th century in England, ginger was second only to pepper as the most common spice, and by the Tudor era, it was a key ingredient in both hippocras and gingerbreads, said to "provoketh sluggish husbands." Consider that the next time your lover needs a little "ginger" in his get-me-up!

Sexy Nutrients
Ginger's reputation in the ancient and "old" world is hardly surprising, considering its myriad health benefits, especially in its fresh form! Since the era of Confucius, who refused to eat a meal without it, its use as a digestive has been confirmed by modern science. Recent research establishes its effectiveness in reducing diarrhea, nausea and vomiting, including the morning sickness experienced by many women in early pregnancy. Only a small amount is needed, and it has the great advantage of not potentially causing birth defects, as anti-vomiting medications can. Given that gastrointestinal disturbances can get in the way of a good romp in the hay, ginger might be a healthy and tasty alternative to over-the-counter tummy medications.

Gingerols are potent anti-inflammatory compounds contained in ginger that can help alleviate arthritic pain, and also figure prominently in killing ovarian cancer cells. That's a very sexy prospect since ovarian cancer is tough to diagnose in its early stages, making it more often deadly.

Grapes

Lore and Fun Facts
What is it with grapes? Their popularity cannot be overstated, both as a food

item and as the basis for the lovey-dovey liquids known as wine and champagne. Interestingly, it was probably a hitchhiker on the grape skin, yeast, that gave rise to the alcoholic drinks we know today. The domestication of purple grapes (and yeast) originated in what is now southern Turkey, but historical records indicate their cultivation by Egyptians, Greeks, Phoenicians and Romans. As civilization spread, so did the growing of grapes.

And their popularity was not limited to making wine. Grapes themselves have a storied history as sexy food. They are fondly mentioned in the Bible and highly praised by the Greek poet Euripides. In that era, grape clusters were offered to newlyweds to bless the couple with many offspring. And the Romans so valued the voluptuous grape that the 1st century BCE poet Catullus wrote of a young maiden so alluring that she should be "...hid like ripe black grapes."

During the Renaissance, as a part of the Doctrine of Resemblances, many believed color reflected nutritional value. So it's not surprising that Gazius, a practicing physician in Padua, asserted in his 15th century that sweet red grapes are good for sexual intercourse because they make a full, rich blood, whereas white grapes diffuse through the body quickly and hold less nutritional value.

In the case of grapes, 21st century sentiments are not much different from the ancients! Participants in my survey of 3000 respondents ranked grapes in the top 10 when given a free choice to pick personal favorites, and when it came to selecting from a list of classic favorites, they most often picked champagne grapes or red grapes.

In addition to their sweetness and flavor, part of the allure of grapes must be in their size and shape. They are, in many ways, the perfect sexy finger food.

SexyNutrients
A huge body of research in recent years has focused on the numerous nutritional benefits of grapes, all of which promote a healthy sex life! Grapes owe their beautiful, deep vibrant color to the rich mixture of flavinoid compounds found in them: flavans, anthocyanins, quercetin, myricetin, kaempferol, as well as the highly publicized resveratrol. These compounds do great things for your cardiovascular system and cholesterol levels, such as boosting good HDL cholesterol and keeping your sexy blood flowing. Resveratrol in red

grapes and red wine has received lots of press as the "French factor" accounting for the health and longevity of the French despite their lavish ingestion of saturated fat (e.g., in their fabulous cheeses and butter-based sauces) and other rich staples of the French diet.

Red wine receives more attention for its health benefits in part because its production includes grape skins, which contain the anthocyanins research is finding have an impact on certain cancers. And red grape skins and seeds contain recently discovered compounds that have been shown to reduce the size of estrogen-dependent breast cancer tumors. In my world, anything that's good for the ta-tas is good for sexuality!

Honey

Lore and Fun Facts

Honey is one of the all-time superstars of the sexy food world. It possesses myriad qualities that lend themselves to love: sweet, sticky, liquid, delicious, even antibacterial! Interestingly, honey's source ingredient is nectar, a sugar-rich liquid produced by plant flowers, and honey is produced by bees from a wide variety of flower sources, each giving the honey its own special flavor. The sweetness of honey comes from fructose and glucose, both "sugars" which are easily assimilated and used as fuel by human bodies.

Bee-keeping for honey likely began for medicinal uses in Egypt in the third millennium BCE. It was also the universal sweetener in many parts of the ancient world, although some say its use in cooking was reserved for the wealthy.

Writings from Mesopotamia, widely regarded as the birthplace of civilization, include references to the role of honey in enhancing sensual pleasure. These writings express the sexual act, from "tasting the honey-plant," and "doing the sweet thing," to "bringing the sweetness," which likely referred to orgasm.

Both the Greek physician Galen and the Roman poet Ovid recommended honey as an aphrodisiac. In preparation for the ancient Olympics, athletes were reported to have eaten special foods, such as honey and dried figs, to enhance their sports performance.

Honey is used in numerous recipes in both *The Perfumed Garden* and in *The Kama Sutra*, in some cases to ward off premature ejaculation, and in others as a topical application on the penis to help with erectile dysfunction.

And if more evidence is needed for honey's ancient aphrodisiac reputation, consider this reference from the Bible's Song of Solomon: "Thy lips, my spouse, are as dripping honeycomb, honey and milk are under thy tongue..." Apparently Queen Victoria's delicate (or incredibly stuffy) sensibilities were so offended by this erotic passage that she ordered it deleted from the Bibles of her day.

And then there's the evolution of honey into the lexicons of love. Newlyweds in ancient Europe drank honey wine during the first month of marriage to improve their sexual stamina, giving rise to the term "honeymoon." And what sweetheart, tingling with desire for their partner, hasn't whispered, "Honey, do want to fool around?"

Sexy Nutrients
Most of us have mothers or grandmothers who touted the healing powers of honey to soothe an ailing sore throat, though it's doubtful whether they did so to perk up the recipient for lovemaking.

Regardless, honey embodies many positive sexy benefits, according to recent University of California research. When enjoyed regularly, honey, especially dark varieties such as buckwheat and bamboo, boosted antioxidant levels in participants' bloodstreams, and had another sexy, unanticipated benefit: weight control. Honey's nearly 1:1 ratio of fructose to glucose makes it ideal for the liver and also blood sugar levels, helping to prevent diabetes and making it more tolerated than table sugar for those who already have diabetes. It's also been found to benefit cholesterol levels and reduce two other substances associated with cardiovascular disease: C-reactive protein and homocysteine.

Its legendary wound healing ability has also been documented for recovery following a caesarian section or a hysterectomy. Compared to women treated with the standard iodine/alcohol solution on their incision, women who received a topical application of honey healed more cleanly and spent fewer days in the hospital.

Buckwheat and bamboo honey have also been found to show promise in anxiety reduction and memory enhancement, all the better to help you enjoy and remember last night's sexy romp!

On the other hand, if you're looking forward to an Olympic moment in bed, honey may also contribute to your endurance. Recently, one group of researchers has investigated the use of honey as an "ergogenic aid" in athletes. The study involved a group of 39 weight-trained athletes, both male and female. Subjects underwent an intensive weight-lifting workout and then immediately consumed a protein supplement blended with either sugar, maltodextrin or honey as the carbohydrate source. The honey group maintained optimal blood sugar levels throughout the two hours following the workout. In addition, muscle recuperation and glycogen restoration (carbohydrates stored in muscle) was favorable in those individuals consuming the honey-protein combination.

So whether you're looking for increased stamina, healthier blood flow, or a sweet syrup to drizzle over your lover's best features, honey is one of the simplest, sexiest foods you can find!

Ice Cream

Lore and Fun Facts

Ice cream is a relative newcomer to the sexy stage, but has made up for its short history by creating a huge segment of appreciative lovers. In fact, ice cream ranked in the top five personal aphrodisiac favorites in my 21st Century Aphrodisiac Foods Survey, which is not surprising since it offers such varied and delicious satisfaction.

The precursors of ice cream do have ancient roots. The flavoring of snow and ice appears to have begun in ancient Persia, and was continued throughout the Arab world for centuries. Snow was saved in underground caves or retrieved from mountaintops for consumption during warm weather.

The making of true ice cream became possible in the 1660s with the advent of ice-houses for storing winter ice throughout the year, with the first recipes appearing in 18th century England and America. Ice houses made their first appearance in royal palaces, and allowed royalty to serve distinguished guests sumptuous treats such as ice cream, sorbets and ice-cooled beverages at official celebrations and special feasts. A century later, many among the upper classes built ice-houses for their country homes so that they too could enjoy the sensual pleasures of ice cream.

Sexy Nutrients

As a diary product, traditional ice cream is high in calcium, vitamin A and other important nutrients, including, yes, fat! What's more, a large-scale Harvard study reported that married women of child-bearing age who were trying to get pregnant benefited from eating full-fat dairy foods, including ice cream, on a daily basis. The risk of infertility from ovulatory disorders was 25% less than those who ate full-fat dairy foods just once a week. Of course, if you're not trying to get pregnant, because, say, you're a man, this is one food whose sexy benefits are very related to serving size! A little ice cream with lots of berries ups its sexy potential!

Jalapeno chilies—See chilies

Kiwi (Kiwifruit)

Lore and Fun Facts

Kiwi as an aphrodisiac speaks to the great power of belief and suggestion! Though no reference exists, with its fuzzy skin and testicle-like shape, it's a possible candidate for the Doctrine of Resemblances.

Yet it's a fruit whose very name is quite contemporary. Although indigenous to Southeast Asia and known but not favored by the ancients, it was first introduced to the West (England) in the 19th century, at which time it was called Chinese gooseberry. It was not commercially grown until the 20th century, when both the United States and New Zealand started production. The cold war of the 1950s led the enterprising New Zealanders to create its current, more marketable name, and of course their nickname, kiwi.

Its current popularity showed up in the results of The 21st Century Aphrodisiac Foods Survey. Out of more than 35 fruits, kiwi ranked 7th in recognition as a fruit participants had heard possessed aphrodisiac properties, beating out several others with extensive histories. With their sweetness, and the sexy appeal of their beautiful green flesh, why be surprised?

SexyNutrients

Kiwi is an excellent source of vitamin C, and polyphenols, and a good source of vitamin E, magnesium, potassium, and copper, all of which may function individually or in concert to protect the blood vessels and heart. In one study, human volunteers who ate 2 to 3 kiwifruit per day for 28 days reduced their platelet aggregation response (potential for blood clot formation) by 18% compared to controls eating no kiwi. In addition, kiwi eaters' triglycerides (blood fats) dropped by 15% compared to controls. And anything so delicious that also keeps your blood flowing freely to all the important regions is perfect for keeping the sexy, good times rolling!

Like avocados and bananas, kiwifruit contain compounds associated with the latex-fruit allergy syndrome. There is strong evidence of the cross-reaction between latex and these foods. If you have a latex allergy, you may very likely be allergic to these foods as well. So besides not wearing a condom, you're probably not going to ask your lover to spoon feed you kiwis before lovemaking!

Lettuce –Romaine (Cos) and Arugula (rocket)

Lore and Fun Facts

Given our modern, Western sensibilities, lettuce may be hard to picture as an aphrodisiac. But the ancient Egyptians thought lettuce, specifically romaine, was a potent cure for impotence and its milky sap was believed to promote fertility. (Its Latin name, *lactuca sativa* is based on the Latin word for "milk."). It was regularly offered to King Senusert I by Amun-Re, in his guise as the god of rain, sexual prowess and fertility, Min. On the walls of the White Chapel at the temple of Karnak, Min is depicted sporting a splendid erection while standing by a pile of tall Egyptian lettuce.

Similarly, arugula (also appropriately named "rocket") has a long aphrodisiac reputation. Ancient Romans praised it, from the first century Roman poet Horace who wrote of its capacity to "strengthen members" to Pliny, the Roman historian. He called it a "provocative of lust" and provided a recipe of arugula and honey.

In the Renaissance, its use was advocated "tenere instrumentum virge erectum," or "to keep the rod erect." Arugula was considered a "hot herb" associated with sexual stamina, so its production during wartime was discouraged, lest it distract soldiers from battle.

Today, contemporary Egyptian arugula soup is referred to as the "Soup of Delights" to highlight its hot reputation. Romaine lettuce continues to have a very sexy reputation and is always served during the biggest "pharonic" fertility celebration each year.

Sexy Nutrients
Both Romaine and Arugula are dark, leafy greens and excellent sources of numerous vitamins and minerals to keep you sexually healthy and vital. They provide high levels of vitamins K, A, C, B1 and B2 as well as iron, folate, manganese and lutein-zeaxanthin, the only antioxidant carotenoids that head straight for your eyes. They help you avoid cataracts and macular degeneration, the better to gaze on your lover for a long, long time! And lack of folates (folic acid) plays a big role in heart disease, stroke and cancer, not to mention causing huge problems for newly pregnant women and their fetuses. Low in calories and high in nutrients that keep you healthy, it's time to give lettuce its proper due as a simple, sexy food!

Liver

Lore and Fun Facts
Okay, I know many of you are thinking, "Yuck. Liver? An aphrodisiac?" But the ancient Greeks considered the liver the seat of passion, the soul, and the source of all generative capacity. Although it was also highly prized for its association with power and courage, Shakespeare emphasized a libidinous, "overheated" liver as the cause of Tarquin's uncontrollable desire in *The Rape*

of Lucrece:

Neglected all, with swift intent he goes
To quench the coal which in his liver glows.

Liver has been ascribed various powers throughout history. Some of its reputation may stem from the fact that it is the only body organ capable of regeneration.

The purest liver is *foie gras* or liver from the goose, which some experience as a voluptuous delight. But it is currently very out of favor because force-feeding geese is just, well, disgusting and inhumane! Liver from other species are not force-fed and offer a delicious, sensual alternative. To this day, liver from various animals continues to be valued as a potent aphrodisiac in parts of Europe.

Sexy Nutrients

Liver is one of the few natural sources of vitamin D, and offers the highest concentration of vitamin A of any food. It's high in bio-available iron, which makes it recommended for treating pernicious anemia. It's also a good source of all the B vitamins (particularly B12), copper, vitamin C and trace minerals. Recent research suggests that despite being a highly concentrated protein food, four ounces of chicken liver provides just 144 calories. Many of us know, though, that it also high in cholesterol! So it's a sexy delicacy that's best enjoyed occasionally and in small quantities.

Lobster

Lore and Fun Facts

Today as in the past, rare and expensive items are often used to impress both new and long-standing lovers. In the Renaissance era of France and England, lobster was highly prized for its elegant, aphrodisiac qualities. The 17th century English physician Venner asserted that lobster "maketh a great propensitie unto venereall embracements,"—referring to men of course. A 17th century Frenchman, Nicolas Abraman, embraced lobster as an aphrodisiac in his 1608 book on rules for a long and healthy life.

Even the mating ritual of lobsters is erotic. As a foreplay ritual, the male and female engage in a sexy dance that triggers the release of pheromones. Recent research suggests that lobsters' fertility actually increases with age. Some scientists point to "negligible senescence" as evidence that, barring injury or disease, a lobster could live indefinitely!

There's no question that the lobster's reputation is that of a sensuous, luxurious food to indulge in on special, typically romantic occasions. In my 21st Century Aphrodisiac Foods Survey, lobster ranked in the top 10 of the most recognized aphrodisiac foods. It's a personal favorite for men of all ages, and for both sexes among those over 50. So maybe there's something to the better-with-age thing, and maybe eating lobster can help you experience it!

Sexy Nutrients
Lobster packs lots of lean protein, copper, zinc, and selenium, all of which are good for your sex life. It's extremely low in fat: 1 gram of fat per 3 ounces versus 7 grams of fat in an equal amount of hamburger. Lobster is also a good source of B12, niacin, vitamin E, and pantothenic acid. So why the frequent bum rap, along with other shellfish? Lots of misunderstandings. For starters, dietary cholesterol—the stuff you eat—is not the same as serum cholesterol—the stuff in your bloodstream. For about 2/3 of us, the cholesterol you eat has little to no bearing on what clogs up your blood. For all who are healthy, as well as those who are more susceptible, 300 mg a day of dietary cholesterol is the upper limit.

Contrary to popular belief, lobster and other shellfish are not loaded with cholesterol, unless you think 61 mg per 3 ounces is a lot (again, compare that to 76 mg in a equal amount of hamburger). Even a full lobster provides less than half of the upper limit. The real culprit in boosting serum cholesterol and triggering cardiovascular difficulties is saturated fat, not dietary cholesterol. It's the company lobster often keeps, with gobs of saturated fat found in butter, that's unfairly judged lobster. Lobster itself, with just about no saturated fat, is a sexy winner, actually. So enjoy every foreplay morsel of delicious lobster, in moderation, of course, without a hint of guilt!

Mangos

Lore and Fun Facts
The mango is known as the "king of fruit" and "the love fruit," and has a 5000 year-long sexy history.

Mangos originated in East India, Burma and the Andaman Islands bordering the Bay of Bengal. Around the 5th century BCE, Buddhist monks are believed to have introduced the mango to Malaysia and eastern Asia. Legend has it that Buddha found tranquility and repose in a mango grove. Persian traders took the mango into the Middle East and Africa; from there the Portuguese brought it to Brazil and the West Indies.

The mango is mentioned in the Kama Sutra at least 6 times, including a recommendation to drink the tropical juice before sexual play. There's also a rather homoerotic reference to "sucking the mango fruit," but such pleasures need not be limited to men! To this day mangos are very important for Indian couples, and are featured at weddings and other celebrations as a symbol of love and joy of life.

Another sexy reference to the mango comes courtesy of an anonymous Arabic poet, who, though acknowledging the practice of cunnilingus cannot bring himself to describe it in proper mouth-watering detail:

Her breath is like honey spiced with cloves,
Her mouth delicious as a ripened mango.
To press kisses on her skin is to taste the lotus,
The deep cave of her navel hides a store of spices,
What pleasure lies beyond, the tongue knows,
But cannot speak of.

Mango cultivars arrived in Florida in the 1830s and in California in the 1880s, and today the luscious fruit is widely available in the US. Anyone who has sampled the sweet, soft flesh of a properly ripened mango will have no trouble imagining its role in edible foreplay. Peel, slice, and enjoy!

Sexy Nutrients

Besides containing a generous portion of fruit sugar for energy and stamina, mangos are packed with a full 20 different sexy benefits, from vitamins A, B6, C, K, and even E, to the minerals potassium, calcium, phosphorus, magnesium, copper, and iron. They also contain several antioxidant carotenoids—alpha-carotene, beta-carotene and beta-cryptoxanthin—which help you see your lover better and are also the source of their beautiful, sunny color. Mangos are a great source of dietary fiber, offering 3 grams per one cup serving. A recent Swedish study found that women consuming the most fruit fiber had a 34% reduction in breast cancer risk compared to those women consuming the least. So protect your twins: eat a mango!

Mushrooms

Lore and Fun Facts

Mushrooms, those ground hugging spores of mystical reputation, have been gathered from the wild for consumption since prehistoric times. In the ancient Egyptian era, only Pharaohs were allowed to eat mushrooms or truffles, their even more aristocratic cousin. Both have both divine and aphrodisiac reputations.

The shape alone of some mushroom varieties helps to account for their erotic appeal through the Doctrine of Resemblances. In ancient Greece, a poisonous hallucinogenic species, Amnita muscaria, was used in fertility rites because of its phallic shape. The ancient Romans favored mushrooms at wedding feasts because they were reputed to stimulate the libido. Throughout the world, mushrooms have been included in erotic dishes that energize the body with "meaty" strength.

Their sensual, earthy flavor is a great example of what Western scientists now call "umami," a 5th flavor sense first described by a Japanese researcher over 100 years ago. (See umami). Their aroma is sometimes compared to the smell of semen, or "mushroom spurt."

Sexy Nutrients
Unique from fruits and vegetables, several versions of this munchable fungus are a good source of vitamin D and very good source of selenium, which enhances male fertility. Mushrooms are an excellent source of copper, which helps to produce red blood cells. They provide a variety of B-complex vitamins, including niacin, riboflavin and pantothenic acid, all of which help keep your nerves untangled and your love light burning.

Exciting new research has revealed that numerous species of mushrooms contain beta-glucans. This substance contributes to resistance against allergies and other significant immunity-stimulating effects, including cancer. Clinical trials are currently looking into mushrooms' potential to fight both breast and prostate cancers, which is certainly sexy news for both men and women!

Mushrooms are hearty and filling, and many blend deliciously with spices and herbs, yet they have few calories, which helps you watch your weight. Their rich umami flavor, especially in darker mushrooms, reduces the need for salt, which is also a good thing health-wise. That's a lot of sexy value for a fungus!

Mussels

Lore and Fun Facts
Mussels, like other bivalves, crustaceans and fish, are derived like Aphrodite from the sea. Sometimes called, "the new oyster," mussels are gaining in both popularity and sexy reputation. Rather than relying on nature to do all the work, mussels are now farmed quite extensively throughout the world. But word is that mussel farmers are a secretive lot, and enjoy keeping the benefits of the love mussel to themselves and their partners!

Want to get a woman worked up for a bit of frolicking? According to the Roman satirist Juvenal, hard-shell mollusks, including mussels, lead women to wanton and reckless abandon. By the 14th century Chaucerian era, "mussel" was a naughty reference to the vulva, yet another example of the Doctrine of Resemblances.

Slightly less slurpy than oysters and less often eaten raw, mussels lend themselves to culinary experimentation. Perhaps a double-blind, "mussel-bound sex-periment" and taste test should be on your menu tonight!

Sexy Nutrients
As a high protein/low fat food, sexy mussels are also low in calories. Like other shell fish, they are also excellent source of B12, folate, and selenium, as well as a good source of Vitamin C, iron and manganese, which helps produce thyroid and sex hormones. All contribute to sexual health. Mussels contain mucopolysaccharides, which control inflammation and also increase the production of semen.

What's more, the immediate love potion potential of mussels actually exceeds that of oysters. Both are packed with two unusual amino acids, D-aspartic acid (D-Asp) and N-methyl-D-aspartate (NMDA). But a joint American-Italian research team found mussels are packed with even higher levels than oysters. These amino acids trigger a quick release of testosterone, which means lovely mussels are beneficial for the love muscle!

Nuts, including almonds, cashews, hazelnuts (filberts), macadamia nuts, pecans, walnuts (also see "pine nuts," a seed)

Lore and Fun Facts
It's hard to imagine a more appropriate example of the Doctrine of Resemblances than nuts, especially the testicle-like walnut. The Latin origin of walnuts, *juglans*, literally translates "glans of Jupiter."

According to archeological evidence, walnuts trace back 8000 years and aphrodisiac references are numerous and lusty. When the Greek god Dionysus lost his beloved Carya (Greek word for "nut"), he turned her into a walnut tree. Then the nature goddess Artemis, also distraught, had a temple built to commemorate her. Walnut columns for the temple were sculpted into female statues, known as caryatids, which represent the nymphs or maidens of the walnut tree. The completed temple was dedicated to Artemis Caryatis. Because of walnuts' associations with Artemis, they also became symbols of love and fertility.

In today's parlance, *Carya* refers to a plant genus including 17-19 species of deciduous trees with pinnately compound leaves and, forgive me, big nuts.

Both the Dionysian myth and the more blatant Roman reference to sexual prowess help to explain the Roman use of walnuts during fertility rites, including the practice of throwing them, not rice, at wedding ceremonies. Even King Solomon, in his highly erotic *Song of Solomon*, declares his pleasure in visiting and gazing at his walnut grove!

Almonds also have a rich aphrodisiac reputation. The ancient Greeks esteemed the almond tree for its unique capacity to flower before developing leaves. In *The Perfumed Garden*, Nefzawi encourages men who "feel weak for coition" to partake of a bedtime remedy consisting twenty almonds, a glass of honey, and one hundred pine nuts for three nights in a row.

Much later, during the English Tudor era, almonds were believed to foster fertility, and a marmalade concoction that included almonds was created to help Queen Mary conceive a son.

Cashews owe their aphrodisiac reputation to their dangling under an erotic, pear-shaped cashew apple prior to processing. Although native to Brazil, they made their way to India and Indian lovers especially favored them. When the Portuguese took them to India, they valued them for making brandy and wine. They are considered aphrodisiac in Africa as well.

Archeological excavations have revealed fossils of hazelnuts in China dating back 5000 years, and they were frequently eaten by Romans, according to Pliny, the historian. Among some ancients, they were believed to have mystical powers. In relatively recent times, their aphrodisiac reputation was highly regarded in England. In the 18th century, they are featured in John Gay's poem *Spell*:

Two hazel nuts I threw into the flame,
And to each nut I have
   a sweetheart's name.
This with the loudest bounce
   me sore amazed,
That in a flame
   of brightest colour blazed.
As blazed the nut
   So may thy passion grow
For 'twas thy nut
   That did so brightly glow.

The pecan tree is the only nut native to the southern regions of the United States. They were first eaten by Native Americans, and some tribes believed they represented the Great Spirit. In folk medicine, they were used for a variety of ailments, including the flu, stomach ache, and fever. Thomas Jefferson was a big fan of pecans and planted them at Monticello. Given his well-documented extra-marital proclivities, perhaps some blame should be cast on his nuts.

Lastly, macadamia nuts, with their softly crunchy texture and rich, decadent flavor, are sometimes called the "Queen of Nuts." In my 21st century Aphrodisiac Foods survey, macadamia nuts ranked 2nd as a nut or seed which participants had heard possessed an aphrodisiac reputation. Their voluptuous taste and current association with the exotic allure of Hawaii undoubtedly contributed to the association, though they actually originated in Queensland, Australia. "Aloha" meets "G'Day, Mate!"

Sexy Nutrients
Many nut varieties are simply great for your sex life and sexual health when eaten in moderation. Most are loaded with omega-3s or other healthy fats. They lower bad cholesterol levels and help to protect against both heart disease and diabetes. Nuts provide natural fiber, vitamin E, and several B complex vitamins. They also provide minerals such as potassium, copper, phosphorus, magnesium, and manganese.

Almonds are a very good source of protein and vitamin E. They're specifically recommended by University of Toronto researchers, creators of the "Portfolio Diet" aimed at reducing "bad" (LDL) cholesterol levels. Walnuts are renowned for their high levels of omega-3s, and hazelnuts are particularly high in vitamin E. The US Department of Agriculture has ranked pecans first among all nuts in antioxidants. Cashews have the lowest fat levels, and much of their fat is monosaturated oleic acid, the same heart healthy fat found in olive oil. Macadamia nuts also offer oleic acid, and are an excellent source for thiamine, vitamin B6, and niacin.

For both men and women, major studies offer sexy news about nuts. Harvard's School of Public Health reports that women who eat one serving of nuts or peanut butter two or more times a week gain fewer pounds than women who rarely eat them. As a snack, an ounce of nuts helps you feel full for up to 2 ½ hours, compared to a carb-only snack such as a rice cake that will keep you going for only 30 minutes. Barcelona, Spain researchers also report people who eat nuts twice a week are 31% less likely to gain weight!

For men, the news may be even better. A major, 17-year longitudinal study of

men that controlled for other coronary risk factors and other dietary factors found those who ate nuts two or more times a week significantly reduced their risk of sudden cardiac death or other coronary heart disease death. Keeping your guy alive and healthy has obvious sexual benefits, so the answer is simple and sexy: Grab a handful of nuts!

Oats

Lore and Fun Facts
In the 19th century Dr. John Kellogg created a list of "bland foods that will help you quell your sexual appetite." With his corn flakes at the top of his list, somehow oats managed to escape being included despite their plain color and rather mild flavor. Maybe that's because there's a lot more to oats than meets the eye—or the taste buds!

Wild oats (*avena fatua*) have been gathered around the Mediterranean since 11,000 BCE for various uses. They do a really good job of proliferating—too good a job, really, and can overrun other plant species. That's likely the origin of the widely popular expression, "sow your wild oats," which of course refers to youthful abandon and typically frivolous sexual dalliances before settling down. As Louisa May Alcott in *Little Women* expressed it: "Boys will be boys, young men must sow their wild oats, and women must not expect miracles."

On a more contemporary note, a Scottish fertility clinic in 2010 offered men free oatmeal in exchange for donating sperm. Their posters read: "You give us your oats, we'll give you porridge." Most of us eat domestic oats (*avena sativa*), not wild oats, which permits us the more private though no less sexual privilege of sowing all the oats we want at home!

Sexy Nutrients
One unique and sexy thing about oats is that they retain the bran and germ layers, even when processed. Other grains, such as wheat, lose those healthy parts. Numerous studies have documented that oatmeal and oat bran boost good cholesterol (HDL) and lower the bad kind (LDL). It's the soluble fiber in oats that contributes to their sexy powers, and they're one of the five key foods recommended by the University of Toronto's Portfolio Diet to lower blood pressure and cholesterol.

In addition to providing dietary fiber, oats are an excellent source of manganese and selenium. They also provide significant amounts of magnesium, protein, phosphorus, and vitamin B1. All these great nutrients significantly reduce the odds of developing diabetes and also offer significant protection against breast cancer in pre-menopausal women. In post-menopausal women who have ever used hormone replacement therapy, eating lots of fiber from grains was associated with a 50% reduction in breast cancer risk compared to those consuming the least. As an alternative to many processed and fiber-poor foods so common today, oats keep the girls happy, which of course goes a long way to keeping the boys happy!

Olive Oil

Lore and Fun Facts
Both olives and olive oil were prized by the early Greeks and Romans. Pliny held that the secret to a happy love life was wine "for the inside" and olive oil "for the outside." Members of the Roman army believed it made their limbs supple. We can only imagine where else those randy Romans used it!

The ancient Greek physician Galen, in his treatise *On the Secrets of Women*, asserted that the ingestion of aged olive oil would inspire women to leave their home in search of a good time and sexual satisfaction. I think I'd recommend a little virgin olive oil to cook with, a little more for a sensual massage, and then look no further than your own home and partner for good times and satisfaction!

Sexy Nutrients
Regular use of olive oil in your diet may help lower blood pressure, which is extremely sexy in terms of a longer, healthier love life. A study by researchers at Stanford Medical School of 76 middle-aged men with high blood pressure a few years ago concluded that the amount of monounsaturated fat in three tablespoons of olive oil a day could lower systolic blood pressure about nine points and diastolic pressure about six points. More remarkable, a University of Kentucky study found that a mere two-thirds of a tablespoon of olive oil daily reduced blood pressure by about five systolic points and four diastolic points in men. A happy ticker and a pleasurable sex life are inseparable, so keep the olive oil flowing!

Onions & onion family (chives, green onions, leeks, and shallots)

Lore and Fun Facts
For men especially, all members of the *allium cepa* family—garlic, onions, leeks, chives, green onions and shallots—have long been valued for their aphrodisiac capacities. Throughout many regions of the ancient world, one or another of these pungent plants regularly shows up in recipes to ensure male potency.

The Roman Emperor Nero favored leeks for sexual vigor, and so voluminously devoured them he acquired the nickname, "Borophagus," or "devouring glutton." In the *Art of Love* (43 BCE), Ovid recommended white shallots from

Megara for maximal erotic effect, and Apicius included them in several of his recipes aimed at sexual stimulation.

Similarly, a common translation of Martial's 1st century epigram reads: *"If envious age relax the nuptial knot, Thy food be scallion and thy feast shallot."* On the other hand, a less poetic, more accurate translation of his original Latin speaks more blatantly of curing a devitalized "member" with all manner of onions! *"If your wife is old and your member is exhausted, eat onions in plenty."*

Onions were served at wedding feasts of both the ancient Greeks and Romans to "seek the door of Venus." In a later era, *The Perfumed Garden* provides a love potion of onions and honey, a simplified version of Galen's recipe that also included pine nuts and almonds. To this day several Indian sects prohibit the eating of onions to prevent wanton sexual desire.

To our modern sensibilities, it might seem like women, while not getting the "short end of the stick" in bed, might have found less pleasure in the halitosis coming from their lovers. Of course, that could be remedied by the woman sharing the love potion!

Sexy Nutrients
Onions pack a nutritional goldmine into very few calories. They're a very good source of vitamin C and chromium, which may help to control blood-sugar levels according to animal studies. They also offer heart healthy fiber, vitamin B6, potassium as well as molybdenum, manganese, phosphorus and copper, needed for strong bones.

To further investigate the relationship between onion consumption and bone density, a carefully designed university study controlled for a host of factors, including age (50+), body mass index, exercise levels, smoking status, calcium intake, estrogen use, and serum levels of vitamin D and parathyroid hormone. The results revealed that peri-menopausal and post-menopausal Caucasian women who ate onions at least once a day had a 5% higher bone density than onion-averse women who ate them once a month or less. The researchers also reported that older women who most often eat onions may reduce their risk of hip fracture by more than 20% compared to those who avoid them.

Onions are among the few foods loaded with quercetin, the same antioxidant phytochemical found in apples and tea. Various studies have reported that eating "moderate" amounts of onion, from 1-2 times a week up to 5-6 times a week is associated with lower rates of colon cancer, laryngeal cancer, and

ovarian cancer. Since ovarian cancer and colon cancer are among the deadliest cancers in women and men respectively, reducing those odds can only be good for your sexy future!

Lastly, as mentioned above, onions contain an enzyme aptly named lacrymatory-factor synthase. In the presence of another onion enzyme, alliinase, volatile LF gas is released when you slice and dice. Although literally and figuratively "irritating," the sulfur-containing compounds released provide much of onion's sexy benefits. With just 60 calories to a full cup, it's worth trying one of the gas reducing methods or just putting up with teary eyes to enjoy the sexy benefits of the onion.

Oranges

Lore and Fun Facts
While pomegranates may have more seeds, they aren't the only fruit whose seeds represent fertility.

In certain parts of Europe in the past, a bridal couple was presented with oranges to bless the couple with many children. European folklore also encourages the use of an orange for seductive purposes. The process begins with pricking an orange all over with a needle. Next, the lover in question must sleep with the pricked orange under his or her armpit. Then, if their beloved partakes of the uniquely aromatized orange, they'll find their partner irresistible! Given the great smell of oranges, it's no wonder this "customized pheromone" recipe was concocted to entice a lover!

The Perfumed Garden concurs with the suggestion that orange blossoms are a perfect choice for perfuming a "love-nest."

Despite the wide availability of oranges today, prior to the 20th century they were difficult to preserve and transport without damage. That made them a special, expensive treat enjoyed only on special occasions and holidays such as Christmas. It may help to explain the sexy allure of oranges that, over the millennia, the more rare an item is, the greater its erotic potential. Perhaps even the Victorians got a charge out of furtively peeling a juicy orange and enjoying it, along with their partner, on a chilly Christmas Eve!

Sexy Nutrients
Oranges are renowned for their vitamin C content, and are a popular historical preventive for scurvy. High in dietary fiber, their overall association with good health rivals that of the apple. There's a lot more going on in oranges, though, than vitamin C, which is why taking a supplement is no match the real thing in terms of sexy benefits.

Oranges offer a sexy cocktail of 170+ phytonutrients that include polyphenols, limonoids, carotenoids, anthocyanins and citrus flavonones, including herperidin, which is concentrated in their peel and white pulp. Herperidin has strong anti-inflammatory properties. In animal studies, it lowers high blood pressure and "bad" cholesterol. The folate in oranges has been associated with reductions in cardiovascular risk and even Alzheimer's risk. Since the Renaissance, oranges have been rightly recommended to reduce the odds of kidney stones.

Along with other citrus fruits, recent studies find that citrus limonins offer significant protection against a variety of oral cancers, including the mouth, larynx, pharynx, esophagus, and also stomach cancers. Some research has also suggested a reduced risk of colon, breast and prostate cancer. So in addition to their juicy, tangy-sweet eating experience, oranges can play their part in contributing to a long and robust sex life!

Oysters

Lore and Fun Facts
No summary or history of aphrodisiac food is complete without the queen of aphrodisiacs, the amazing oyster.

Oysters are regarded as the queen of all aphrodisiac foods and are universally recognized aphrodisiacs from 320 BCE Chinese lore, to 17th century Dutch paintings, to the fabulous scene in the classic 20th century film, *Tom Jones*! (to view that wonderfully erotic scene, go online and search "Siskel and Ebert Tom Jones movie eating scene").

Oysters are unique in their representation of the Doctrine of Resemblances, given they evoke both male and female genitals. Their exterior resembles testicles and the interior, in both shape and texture, evokes images of female genitals. Any briny seafood alludes to the smells and tastes of sexual secretions, and their texture is astonishingly similar to the inner female genitalia.

The Romans wrote often of the oysters' hedonistic merits. In one version of the Aphrodite legend, she arose from an oyster shell in the sea. The Roman poet Juvenal, in his *Satire VI*, focuses on the "ways of women" and writes, "What decency does Venus observe when she is drunken? When she knows not head from tail, eats giant oysters at midnight, pours foaming unguents into her unmixed Falerian, and drinks out of perfume flasks, while the roof spins dizzily around, the table dances, and every light shows double!"

Casanova, reputed to have eaten 50 oysters a day, often off the breasts of young women, also wrote in his *The Memoirs of Jacques Casanova de Seingalt, Volume Six:* "I placed the shell on the edge of her lips and after a good deal of laughing, she sucked in the oyster, which she held between her lips. I instantly recovered it by placing my lips on hers." With a sensual, playful serving approach like that, you likely won't need outrageous quantities to appreciate the aphrodisiac effects!

In the early 1700s, Jonathan Swift observed, "He was a bold man that first ate an oyster." That act of courage was rewarded not only with a satisfied palate but with a recharged libido, according to those who believe that the oyster is the ultimate aphrodisiac. And while the psychological impact of oysters on the libido can't be dismissed, its actual physiological impacts aren't just in your head. So sip and slurp, chew and swallow, because this amazing aphrodisiac sets lust and love in motion from first sight to last bite.

Sexy Nutrients
What's sexy about the oyster's nutritional value is that it is a light, protein rich food known for its high zinc content. Zinc is vital to adequate testosterone production, good prostate health and increased sperm count and motility (think speed and mobility in a race to the egg!). Recent research has also found that oysters and other bivalves are loaded with two other unusual kinds of amino acids, NMDA and D-aspartic acid, that also give an immediate boost to testosterone production. The effect is likely maximized when they're eaten raw, a point not lost on Casanova.

Papaya

Lore and Fun Facts
Enjoyed throughout the world, papayas originated in Mexico or Central America, and the word "papaya" is clearly Spanish. The Spanish and Portuguese explorers of the 16th and 17th centuries fell in love with papayas and transported them to Europe, Africa, India and the Philippines. Christopher Columbus reputedly dubbed them "fruit of the angels."

Oddly, they didn't make it to the United States until the 20th century, but we've made up for lost time, with Hawaii as one of the world's largest producers.

For contemporary Cubans, the erotic implications of this succulent fruit are so blatant that the word "papaya" has become slang for female sexual organs and is avoided in polite conversation. Instead, the juicy fruit is called *"fruta bomba,"* which still sounds sexy in a sweet, soft, explosive sort of way!

Sexy Nutrients

It's not surprising that the Center for Science in the Public Interest puts papaya in its list of top five "fabulous" fruits. Papaya boosts the immune system with its excellent level of vitamin C, and it's a very good source of folate and potassium. Dietary fiber, vitamins A, E, and K are also plentiful. All of these nutrients help to keep your cardiovascular system in good shape by lowering homocysteine and LDL "bad" cholesterol levels. Papayas are also high in lycopene, the nutrient associated with prostate health.

They're also anti-inflammatory and reduce the risk of autoimmune disorders and various cancers. A 2002 research study of papaya juice showed a reduction in a specific kind of liver cell proliferation. More recently, in 2010, an American-Japanese research team studied the anti-cancer effects of an extract made from dried papaya leaves. The results demonstrated its effectiveness in attacking lab-grown tumors that included cancers of the breast, cervix, lung, liver and pancreas, especially at higher extract levels. Further, the papaya extract did not have toxic effects on normal cells. Continued research of the restorative powers of papaya extract in animal and clinical trials look quite promising, and in terms of keeping us fit for the deed, very sexy!

Papaya is also well-known for its enzymes papain and chymopaipain that help digest proteins and contribute to colon health. Papain is also used to treat sports injuries, which might come in handy should your bedroom workout tweak a knee or pull a hamstring!

A note of caution: Papayas are one of the more common "latex-fruit allergy" syndrome foods, so if you're allergic to latex, chances are you'll want to avoid papayas!

Pasta

Lore and Fun Facts

It's not clear in the literature, but I have a hunch that part of the aphrodisiac reputation of pasta comes from what it's associated with: Italians, herbs and spices, wine, and romance. Stereotypes aside, Italians are widely known for their love of food as well as their amorous natures.

In her cookbook, big-screen siren Sophia Loren contends that pasta cooked al dente may be what offers "sustaining power" to many a Latin lover. Italians and Turks alike have claimed that various kinds of pasta, from spaghetti to macaroni, increase their fertility.

In my 21st century aphrodisiac foods survey, pasta ranked in the top 10 of "free choice" aphrodisiac favorites. And nearly 20% of participants indicated they had heard that spaghetti or noodles had an aphrodisiac reputation. Whether their instincts are on target or they just have fond memories of a pasta meal cum love fest, pasta has become one of the simplest, sexiest foods on the planet.

Sexy Nutrients

There's a fairly straightforward scientific explanation for pasta's contribution to lovemaking, brought on by an improved mood and relaxation. How does this happen? A high carbohydrate pasta meal releases insulin. The release of insulin in response to raised levels of blood glucose diverts the uptake of most amino acids to peripheral tissues. Simultaneously, it allows tryptophan levels in the blood to rise and head for the brain. There, it becomes the precursor of the neurotransmitter serotonin, which puts you in a relaxed, calm "feel good" mood. The effect is the most pronounced when the carbohydrate is whole grain, and is eaten without protein. The serotonin levels rise gradually and blood-sugar levels remain stable. In contrast, refined grains lead to a blood-sugar rollercoaster and finicky moods, none of which is all that sexy.

Interestingly, though pasta is thought of as a "heavy" food by many, cooked pasta is about 70% water. According to research from the British Nutrition Foundation, eating fluid-rich foods keeps you fuller longer, compared with dry foods. Like bread, the carbs in pasta boost serotonin to help curb overeating. The "Mediterranean" diet is now known to keep weight down and foster heart health, which may explain both the Italians' and pasta's robustly sexy reputation.

Peaches

Lore and Fun Facts

From their sexy scent to their sweet, succulent flesh to their breast-soft outer skin, peaches have been shaking their sexy selves at us for a long time.

As far back as 1100 BCE, peach trees were cultivated and revered by the Chinese. Both the deep cleft of a peach and its sweet juices symbolized female genitals. The peach blossom was a symbol of "easy virtue," and an attractive young bride was called a "peach" (In contemporary China, wreaths of peach blossoms are worn by brides as symbols of fertility).

The peach was unknown in the western world until Alexander the Greek brought it from ancient Persia to Greece. It was known as *percisa*, or "Persian apple," reflecting belief in its exotic Persian origin. That belief likely contributed to its reputation as an aphrodisiac, and only the wealthy could afford the expensive peach.

By the 15th century, the German scholar Konrad von Megenberg's *Buch der Natur* reputedly refers to the peach's ability to boost male sexual performance: "For afflicted men that are impotent because of a cold nature, it is good to induce passion."

By the 16th and 17th centuries of the Renaissance, exquisite foods, not merely expensive ones, were perceived as aphrodisiac and peaches, along with melons, were the most frequently named. In the 17th century, Nicholas Culpeper, in his *Culpeper's Complete Herbal*, succinctly summarized his view: "Venus owns this tree...the fruit provokes lust."

And if that weren't enough, a well known 20th century reference to the sexy fruit comes from The Steve Miller Band, under the guise of the Doctrine of Resemblances, "I really like your peaches, let me shake your tree." So break out the peaches, because the guys just can't leave them alone!

Sexy Nutrients
Peaches are a very good source of vitamins A and C, and of beta-carotene. They're also consistently been prized for contributing to a luxurious "peaches and cream" complexion, with some scientific support. They contain flavonoid polyphenolic antioxidants such as lutein, zeaxanthin and beta cryptoxanthin, which reduce age-inducing free radicals and help protect your eyes from macular degeneration, the most common cause of vision loss in later years. They're a good source of potassium, which helps explain why one study found those who ate peaches and similar fruits (nectarines and plums) had lower blood pressure and kept their waistlines svelte, reducing the risk of developing metabolic syndrome, the precursor to diabetes. Any food that keeps your body supple and your vision clear deserves a welcome place in the kitchen and the bedroom!

Pears

Lore and Fun Facts
Throughout history pears have consistently been associated with the feminine and have often been associated with fertility, children, and prosperity. In many parts of the world a pear tree was planted to celebrate the birth of a female child.

The first pears were domesticated about 5000 years ago in the highlands of Central Asia in what is known as Kazakhstan. Its capital, Almaty, translates as "father of apples." In traditional Chinese medicine, pears are used to tone feminine "yin" energy.

Pears have long been extolled by lovers and glorified in art, song, and poetry. In the *Odyssey*, Homer called them a "gift from the gods." An Old English religious poem suggests that it was a pear that Adam shared with Eve that opened their eyes to each other's sexy body. Over time, their association with the voluptuous feminine form has been consistent, with some likening them to a Ruben's nude.

With all their voluptuous juiciness, pears evoke a feminine sensuality that is best shared with an appreciative lover!

Sexy Nutrients
Both pears and apples, which belong to the rose family, are noted for their pectin levels, a soluble fiber that helps to lower cholesterol levels. Soluble fiber also keeps the colon happily humming along, which lowers the risk of colon cancer. Regular consumption of fruit fiber has also been found to reduce the risk of breast cancer in postmenopausal women. Because few people react to pears, they're often recommended to those with allergies, as part of a hypo-allergenic diet. Pears are a good source of vitamin C, copper, and vitamin E, all of which offer antioxidant activity against free radicals. They offer the most antioxidant boost when eaten fully ripe, a very juicy and highly sexy bit of advice I hope you take to heart soon!

Pineapple

Lore and Fun Facts
Originating in Brazil and Paraguay, pineapples wended their way/traveled north along Indian trade routes to the Caribbean islands where they were a favorite indulgence of the Carib Indians. They featured pineapples in many of their rituals and festivals and also used them to produce a wine.

Christopher Columbus, who knew pineapples as *ananas*, or "excellent fruit," transported them to Europe where they represented a rare delicacy that was coveted and symbolic of royal privilege.

Their English name came about based on their resemblance to a pinecone. King Charles II was so enamored of the pineapple that several of his official portraits show him standing next to one, looking quite pleased and satisfied. Because they were an expensive treat, pineapples were restricted to feasts days, including Christmas, that were celebrated by royalty and the wealthy. During the American colonial era, pineapples were also a high status item and often the "piece de resistance" at feasts.

Much more recently, an episode of *Sex and the City* helped to resurrect the wives tale about how pineapple improves the taste of, how should I say it, bodily fluids. No scientific research exists to support that belief, although one major undergraduate human sexuality textbook produces a chart on which pineapple is listed as a food that helps to produce a "mild" flavor, not a sweet one. That's probably a very healthy result, as well, because "sweet" flavor in this context can be a side effect of diabetes!

Sexy Nutrients
Fresh pineapple's sexy sweet/tart flavor is matched by its nutrients. It's an excellent source of vitamin C and the trace mineral manganese, both of which play a big role in fighting free radicals. It's also a good source of vitamins B1 and B6, copper, and good 'ol super sexy dietary fiber.

What pineapple's most uniquely known for is bromelain, an enzyme. There are many uses for bromelain extracted from the stems of pineapples. Its anti-inflammatory and analgesic properties have been documented in several double blind studies, especially for knee pain. Now that brings up the very sexy possibility that overindulging in pineapple after a rousing romp on your knees might just keep you in better shape to go for round two!

Pine Nuts (also known as pinons, pignola nuts or Italian nuts)

Lore and Fun Facts
Pine nuts might be misnamed—they're technically seeds of certain pines—but they enjoy a long aphrodisiac history in many parts of the world. In Ancient Rome they were associated with life force and vitality. In *Ars Amatoria, The Art of Love*, the Roman poet Ovid includes "the nuts that the sharp-leaved pine brings forth" in his list of aphrodisiacs. For stimulating male performance, Apicius (a real person and also the name for the earliest known collection of Roman recipes) recommends adding pine nuts to a concoction of cooked onions, white mustard and pepper. Galen recommends a more appetizing mixture of honey, almonds and pine nuts.

The Perfumed Garden gives credit to a savant named Djelinouss for getting really specific: "He who feels that he is weak for coition should drink before going to bed a glassful of very thick honey and eat twenty almonds and one hundred grains of the pine tree. He must follow this regime for three days."

During the Renaissance, Benedict continued this "male enhancement" tradition by listing pine nuts as one of the "heating" foods, and in Daoist tradition, pine nuts are believed to confer eternal life. On our own continent, the Western Shoshone Native American tribe prized pine nuts and used them in dancing festivals. Wouldn't it be fun to know what they did in their teepees after all that dancing and eating of pine nuts?

Sexy Nutrients
The tiny pine nut has an oversized nutritional punch with excellent levels of vitamin E, a super-charged anti-oxidant that fights free radicals and helps prevent a variety of chronic diseases. Pine nuts are also an excellent source of vitamin K, needed for healthy bones and blood-clotting. They're a good source of a variety of B complex vitamins, including thiamine, riboflavin, niacin, and folate, which is good for cell metabolism and may also help arrest mild cognitive impairment, according to a recent double-blind study. As for minerals, they're a good source of copper, zinc, and magnesium. They also contain twice the levels of phytosterols as walnuts; phytosterols help to block the absorption of "bad" cholesterol.

Other double-blind research suggested the natural oil pressed from Korean pine nuts may be useful as an appetite suppressant when eaten before a meal. Let's face it: overeating is not sexy on a number of levels, especially when a heavy meal sends blood coursing to your digestive system, as opposed to your sexy parts. A light aphrodisiac meal is far better preparation for a horizontal tango!

Pomegranate

Lore and Fun Facts
As the "apple of many seeds," pomegranates are a fruit whose historical aphrodisiac recognition hasn't necessarily followed into modern times. As we've seen before, many ancient and pre-modern cultures viewed a food's physical characteristics as an indication of what it could do for them. Thus the pomegranate's many, many seeds were an obvious nod to fertility.

They were native to Persia and then spread to Egypt, the Near East, and Greece. As with the pear and certain other fruits, some suggest it was not the apple, but the pomegranate, that tempted Eve in the Garden of Eden.

In mythology, both the love goddess Aphrodite and the Phoenician goddess Astarte revered the pomegranate as a symbol of fertility. The most famous Greek myth revolves around Persephone, the beautiful daughter of Zeus. In the myth, Hades, Zeus's brother and Lord of the Dead, abducts Persephone to the underworld to become his bride. Everyone gets upset, and Zeus demands his daughter's return. Sneakily, Hades gets Persephone to munch some pomegranate seeds which, by the laws of the underworld, compels her to return there. But Zeus strikes a deal with Hades so that Persephone can spend 2/3 of a year with her mother in the upper world, and just 1/3 of the year with her husband in the underworld. Both pomegranates and Persephone's return each year in the spring came to symbolize fertile renewal. Pomegranates still figure in Greek wedding ceremonies to bless the newlyweds with a fruitful union.

The Egyptians favored them as the "fruit of life" and made wine from them. Pomegranates are painted on the tomb of the Egyptian Pharoah Ahkenaton and other Egyptian tombs, most likely as an offering for the afterlife.

In Tang dynasty of ancient China, pomegranate trees were cultivated, and symbolized wealth and a large, healthy family. At weddings, pomegranate seeds were mixed with powdered sugar to be offered to guests and today, a picture of a pomegranate is a common wedding gift.

The history of pomegranates also reflects the relationship between health and sexuality. In addition to their sexy reputation, pomegranates have long been valued for their medicinal benefits, from ancient times to the present. Dioscorides wrote not only of their use for gastrointestinal difficulties, but also included ulcers "in ye mouth and in ye Genitalls," among other conditions. By the 16th century, the Royal College of Physicians of London included a pomegranate in their coat of arms, based on their symbolic representation of fertility, regeneration and "persistence of life."

Despite this huge symbolism of pomegranates, very few participants in my 21st Aphrodisiac Foods Survey were aware of their sexy reputation, though that awareness may be changing. The current status of pomegranate juice as healthy drink is very well deserved despite being exaggerated by marketing. But I'm thinking it might be more fun to brush up on Greek mythology for a sexy verification of the pomegranate—unless your name is "Octomom!"

Sexy Nutrients
Pomegranates are a very good source of dietary fiber, which contributes to cardiovascular health. They're also a good source for vitamins C and K, and potassium, all of which keep you in good shape for love action.

University-based research on rats in 2005 reported that an extract made from pomegranate juice might play a role in reducing prostatic cancer cells. Another double-blind pilot study conducted in 2007 looked at the benefits of pomegranate juice versus a placebo in helping men with mild to moderate erection difficulties overcome the problem. The research managed to get published in a professional journal, but there's a slight problem. Although the results favored pomegranate juice, presumably for its nitric oxide-boosting and vaso-dilating effects, they did not reach the level of statistical significance required for scientific research. Oops!

Another note of caution: Pomegranate juice, like grapefruit juice, can interact with certain medications, and it's worth asking a physician if this is problematic for any prescribed medications. One of these days, the sexy benefits of pomegranate juice, despite its high sugar content, may one day be legitimately documented. In the meantime, enhancing the visual and crunchy taste appeal of a salad or sauce with pomegranate seeds, or squeezing some of its sweet juice into a cocktail, will allow you to enjoy its sexy mysteries and wonderful flavor with your favorite earth god or goddess!

Pumpkin Pie Spice & Pumpkin

Lore and Fun Facts
Pumpkin on its own is among the newest sexy food in this list, with no long-standing reputation as a lust booster. In the United States, most of us associate pumpkin with fall holidays, from Halloween to a delicious pie served at Thanksgiving. In other parts of the world, pumpkin is a common ingredient in many savory dishes. Pumpkin pie spice, which may really be the star of this show, is generally made with cinnamon, cloves, ginger, nutmeg and allspice.

Some fascinating double-blind randomized studies reveal the effects of different smells on male sexual arousal. In one, each participant was connected to a small blood pressure cuff to measure blood flow to the penis. The participant was then blindfolded, and soft music...not really, but it does start to sound really kinky! Next, one at a time, a surgical mask scented with one specific scent was placed over the participant's nose and left in place for one minute. At that time, penile blood flow was measured for each of the many scented masks worn. An interval of three minutes separated exposure to each new smell, during which participants did not wear a mask.

In the first study, baked cinnamon smell was used as a control scent, but ironically it wound up creating the most blood flow to the penises of young and middle aged men. A second study included men aged 18-64 and tested 30 scents, including both perfume and food. Some scents were actually combinations, resulting in 46 scents being tested. This time the pumpkin pie spice/lavender mixture triggered the greatest measurable penile response. Blood flow was increased by an average of 40% in all but the oldest men (who responded more to vanilla). So if you want to get the blood flowing to your special guy's manhood, spritz a little lavender under your blouse and bake up a pumpkin pie!

Sexy Nutrients

Like so many simple, sexy foods, pumpkin is a winner nutritionally. It's loaded with beta-carotene, which helps keep your skin and eyes healthy and vibrant, and is a good source of vitamin C, vitamin E, and lots of B vitamins—thiamin, niacin, B6 and folate. B-complex vitamins are essential for keeping your nervous system happy. Adequate levels of folate during pregnancy significantly reduce the odds of various birth defects such as spina bifida or other neural tube deficits. Pumpkin also provides potassium, which keeps body fluids regulated, as well as manganese, and copper. It's also an excellent source for dietary fiber for keeping your digestive and circulatory systems in good shape. What's more, it has just 40 calories in a full cup, so it won't weigh your man down to nibble your pie!

Quail Eggs (also see eggs)

Lore and Fun Facts

In Ancient Greece, around, around 800 BCE, quail and their eggs were the primary egg source. That means when the Greek poet Ovid sang the praises of eggs as aphrodisiac, he was likely referring to quail eggs. In Indonesia, quail eggs are singled out for their erotic potential. They've long been considered a delicacy, in part based on their smaller size.

Sexy Nutrients

The nutrients in quail eggs are similar to chicken eggs. High in protein, they're also packed with choline, essential during pregnancy and while nursing. What's more, many people allergic to chicken eggs have no allergic reaction to quail eggs. That puts the aphrodisiac pleasures of eggs back on the menu for those who've avoided them in the past. And think of the sexy visual appeal and elegance of topping a dish with quail eggs, or popping a delicate deviled quail egg into your lover's mouth! It's sure to give him or her wings!

Raspberries

Lore and Fun Facts

Raspberry tea made from raspberry plant leaves has long been recommended to help morning sickness. In the 17th century, *Culpeper's Complete Herbal* also recommended raspberry tea for "getting the womb back in place" as part of postpartum recovery. In modern terms, it will get you back in the sack quickly after childbirth!

Raspberries themselves were overlooked as an ancient aphrodisiac food, perhaps because they are quite perishable. Today, it's hard to ignore this tasty member of the rose family for its magnificent aphrodisiac appeal—the intense, sexy color and sweet juiciness beg to be enjoyed as part of an aphrodisiac meal. They are equally enticing used in salads or for making a luscious, vibrant sauce to drizzle over a sumptuous pear—or anything else you may want to put in your mouth!

Sexy Nutrients
Raspberries are an excellent source of antioxidants, from classics like vitamin C and manganese, to ellagic acid, a phenolic compound contained in only a few fruits. A variety of laboratory studies on tumor cells in animals have highlighted its antioxidant and anti-carcinogenic properties, including cancers of the skin, lung, and colon. Tissue culture research on breast cancer cells has also found that ellagic acid seems to counter the cancer-promoting effects of estrogen on the cancer cells. None of this research has documented that these effects extend to humans, but it's safe to say that consuming raspberries is a sexy, healthy thing to do.

Raspberries are a great source for another class of antioxidants, anthocyanins. They are the source of the bright red color of raspberries and are also associated with lower risks of cancer as well as various inflammatory disorders, diabetes, and macular degeneration.

Raspberries also are a good source of the B vitamins riboflavin, niacin (good for keeping you calm), and folate, which reduces homosysteine levels and contributes to cardiac health. It also contains magnesium, potassium, and copper. They offer lots of dietary fiber and with their low gylcemic index, keep blood sugar levels stable.

Rice

Lore and Fun Facts
Rice has grown wild for millennia, including in the Americas, but was first cultivated in India and other far eastern regions. It probably didn't reach Greece until after Alexander the Great and his conquests.

In the mythological traditions of many Asian cultures, a Rice Goddess is revered as a symbol of fertility, abundance, and life itself. The sexiest among them is doubtless the Cambodian Goddess of Fertility, Po Ino Nogar, perceived as the source of rice. With her 97 husbands and 38 daughters this polyandrous goddess kept herself quite busy providing for the people as well as reproducing! No wonder rice has long been thrown at weddings in many cultures to bless newlyweds with a fertile and abundant life.

Celsus, a 2nd century Roman philospher, suggested that rice "stimulated the senses." Centuries later, the Indian love manual, *The Ananga-Ranga*, continued the same theme in a recipe that included wild rice and honey. It was to be eaten at night to provide a man with "enormous vigour and the enjoyment of a hundred women." If it can help a guy handle one hundred women, imagine what it might do if he was just "handling" you!

Sexy Nutrients
If you haven't experienced the rich taste of brown rice before, give it a try. It's always been considered healthier than white rice because of its higher fiber and vitamin B content. Further, very recent data reported from nearly 200,000 participants in three studies revealed that eating white rice for or more times a week increased the risk of diabetes 17%, whereas eating brown rice twice a week or more decreased the diabetic risk 11%. That makes brown rice the sexy winner!

And for an even greater taste experience and possibly greater nutritional punch, consider wild rice. Its nutty flavor is a great compliment to many sexy dishes. Wild rice is high in protein, the amino acid lysine, dietary fiber, and very low in fat. Like true rice, it does not contain gluten. It is also a good source of the minerals potassium and phosphorus, and the vitamins thiamine, riboflavin, and niacin. Wild rice (a grain, actually) is grown across northern latitudes in North America, and is available in many whole foods and specialty shops.

Salmon-See seafood

Seafood

Lore and Fun Facts
Ever since Aphrodite rose from sea foam, the bounty of the sea has accounted for many of the most revered aphrodisiacs. The sea's vastness, its salty, fertile abundance, and even its mysterious depths contribute both fact and fantasy to the lore. Regardless, the sea's contributions to sexy food are many, varied, and swimmingly delicious!

In addition to its great sexy nutrients, seafood has always carried special erotic value due to its relative lightness. Brillat-Savarin's famous 19th century *La Physiologie du Gout (The Physiology of Taste)* recounts an "experiment" reputedly carried out by the 12th century Sultan Saladin, the first sultan of Egypt and Syria. The Sultan is said to have fed two devoted religious anchorites for several weeks on a heavy meat and vegetables diet. He then presented two beautiful odalisques (slaves) from his harem to the dervishes to test their capacity to seduce the anchorites. They failed completely. The anchorites were then fed a diet restricted to fish for several weeks. This time, when presented with the same harem odalisques, the anchorites were enraptured in the presence of the women and helpless in resisting their charms.

In 17th century, a well-known restaurant served fish on a huge platter, in the middle of which lay a nude woman. In 19th century Paris, lusty Parisians fed fish dishes to lovers in boudoir suites.

We've already covered shellfish, caviar and lobster elsewhere, so here are a few more randy seafood treats.

Anchovies

Anchovies are a small pelagic fish abundant in the Mediterranean, although they can be found throughout the world. The ancient Romans ate them raw as an aphrodisiac. In the 3rd century BCE, the Greek king Nicomendes I of Bithynia so craved anchovies when he was inland that his chef, Soterides, carved likenesses of them out of turnips. He then oiled and salted these simulations and sprinkled them with poppy seeds to please his master.

Salmon

Salmon is a game fish known for its bravery and amorous determination, heroically traveling long distances from the sea up freshwater rivers and stream to have sex in the very place they were born, and where they will also die. To put a psychological twist on the Doctrine of Resemblances, the braver and more game-like the fish, the more its ardent virility can be passed on to the willing human.

In the 19th century, a provocatively titled American cookbook, *How to Keep a Husband*, provides a "salmon en papillotte" recipe that calls for little more than salt, pepper, and a nice sautéing of the fish in butter. The power of the salmon spoke for itself, as the following anonymous poem suggests:

Old impotent Alden from Walden
Ate salmon to heat him to scaldin'
  'Twas just the ticket,
  To stiffen his wicket,
This salmon of Amorous Alden.

Scallops

If seafood in general connotes eroticism, members of the mollusca familty, with their very hard shells and soft body, such as scallops, rank at the top. Boticelli's famous 15th century painting, "Nascita di Venere" (Birth of Venus, or Venus on the Half Shell) shows Venus emerging from the sea atop a figurative shell that shares a far greater resemblance to a scallop than an oyster shell. The origin of the word scallop comes from *escalope*, whose original meaning was "shell." In classical antiquity, shells (and presumably the tissue inside pushing out, was a metaphor for the vulva. Even the voluptuous round shape of the scallop itself screams female eroticism!

Shrimp
If mollusks express femininity with their soft bodies, shrimp and other members of the crustacean family have a decidedly masculine feel. One illustrious example is revealed in the records of the famous Captain Cook. During his 18th century travels, the Captain visited a Pacific island on which the king's "duty" was to deflower all of the maidens on the island. He handily succeeded in carrying out his required 8-10 daily conquests. He attributed his virile stamina to a spiced shrimp dish with pineapple that preceded the lucky fellow's daily challenge.

When simply prepared, shrimp are a quintessential finger food. One source claims certain Caribbean indigenous people munch shrimp live during the course of making love. Then there's the scene in *Tampoco* with the poor "drunken live shrimp" bouncing around in sake on the belly of the protagonist's girlfriend.

One survey participant in my 21st century Aphrodisiac Foods Survey fondly shared an experience likely to hold much broader erotic appeal: she brought cooked shrimp into the bedroom where she and her lover fed each other the succulent little love boosters while also feasting on each other.

Tuna
A huge, majestic fish, some members of this amazing predator species cruise non-stop at speeds up to 40 miles an hour. No wonder its aphrodisiac history traces back to ancient times. Their virtues have been described in turn by Aristotle, Pliny the Elder, and Homer.

Recently, tuna is being touted for other sexy properties. A "prosperm" extract featuring docosahexaenoic acid (DHA) extracted from tuna helped two wild boars inseminate sows by significantly increasing their sperm count. Perhaps future research will lead to a legitimate tuna-based elixir for humans. In the meantime, I'd recommend passing on any "Tuna Love Pills" you see being marketed, and opting for an occasional meal featuring tuna. Maybe it'll help you cruise non-stop at a high rate of speed!

Sexy Nutrients
Deep sea, cold water fatty fish such as salmon, tuna, and anchovies are well known for their abundance of Omega-3s; shrimp and scallops are also good

sources. Omega-3s help to control diabetes, and a specific fatty acid, EPA, helps with weight control by stimulating the release of the hormone leptin. Leptin regulates metabolism and reduces appetite to keep you sexy and svelte.

Omega-2 fatty acids also contribute significantly to cardiovascular health. That includes reduction in blood pressure, stroke risk, sudden death (aka dropping dead), lowered levels of triglycerides and "bad" LDL cholesterol. In an animal research model, omega-3s have been found to slow down breast cancer tumors and in epidemiological research, the risk of colorectal cancer is also reduced by more than one-third among those who consume the highest levels of omegas-3s. In population studies, Swedish men who ate salmon at least once a week were 43% less likely to develop prostate cancer than men who never ate salmon.

Omega-3s have significant anti-inflammatory effects, which helps your arteries and your joints, and better permits you to wind up in creative sexual positions. Several populations studies confirm that those who eat fatty fish more than once a week have significantly lower rates of age-related macular degeneration, the leading cause of blindness in older people. Recent brain cell research also links omega-3 fats with a reduction of the beta-amyloid plaques associated with Alzheimer's. So salmon not only tastes great, it helps you bend over backwards to see your lover, whose body you'll never forget!

If that weren't enough, eating lots of omega-3 rich foods and reducing omega-6 consumption may relieve depression by restoring dopamine functioning. During pregnancy, the placenta provides fatty acids to the fetus, thereby depleting the mother's supply. Based on epidemiological studies, not clinical trials, post-partum depression is fifty times higher in countries with low omega-3 intake compared with those having the highest levels. Although recent research has challenged the emotional benefit of omega-3s for pregnant and post-partum mothers, the negative results may relate to insufficient amounts. Overall, routine sensual indulgence in sexy sea foods rich in omega-3s two or three times a week sounds better than popping pills, and certainly will keep your taste buds happy as well.

Seafood offers an abundance of protein, selenium, magnesium, zinc and B-complex vitamins. Zinc is great for prostate health. Vitamin B-12 and niacin are especially associated with helping to reduce total cholesterol in individuals with elevated levels. Vitamin B-12 also reduces levels of the damaging chemical homocysteine. Low levels of homosysteine are associated with a reduced risk of cardiovascular disease, including diabetic heart disease, and a reduced risk of colon cancer, and Alzheimer's disease.

If you have concerns about contaminants such as mercury in fatty fish, choose wild salmon and other smaller-sized fatty fish low on the food chain such as anchovies, sardines or mackerel. For optimal sexual health, eating fatty fish at least a week is a great idea! No matter what the seafood, part of its sexy appeal is its lightness; heavy meals divert blood to the digestive track, and rob your love equipment of what it needs to be ready for action!

Seaweed (sea vegetables or algae)

Lore and Fun Facts
Archeological evidence suggests most regions surrounded by water, from Norway to Japan, have enjoyed the sensual side of seaweed for thousands of years. In ancient Mesopotamia (3000 BCE), women used seaweed as a tint to make their lips more alluring.

Ancient Hawaiians believed eating *limu ko-ele-ele*, a type of seaweed, had aphrodisiac properties when accompanied by a certain chant. One Hawaiian legend refers to the use of seaweed in a love potion. If clever young woman gave her "target" a piece of seaweed, it would make him forever adore her. Among the sexiest sea vegetables today are nori, used in sushi, and wakame, used in Japanese miso soup.

Seaweed holds other sexy qualities, too. An extract made from it, carrageenan, is used in personal lubricants to thicken them. And the Albert Einstein School of Medicine is running clinical trials on a microbicide gel made with carrageenan as a preventive for the sexually transmitted HPV virus. That's a sexy seaweed benefit that would have great ramifications for dealing with a widespread health problem!

Sexy Nutrients
This sexy bounty of Neptune offers the broadest range of minerals of any food. Seaweed is an excellent source of vitamin K and iodine, and a very good source of calcium, folate and magnesium. Folate is essential to avoiding various birth defects, including spina bifida, and in reducing the risk of colon cancer. Magnesium, in addition to helping your bones and cardiovascular system out, also helps reduce migraines—those crippling and very unsexy "headaches"—and also helps to keep your muscles relaxed, a good thing for blood flow before and after a rousing romp! Lignans, another phytontrient in wakame and other seaweed, is credited with reducing the risk of breast cancer in post-menopausal women. Any food that helps us take care of our ta-tas is a very sexy food indeed!

Spinach

Lore and Fun Facts
The modern reputation of spinach is inextricably tied to Popeye, the salty, tattooed version of the Greco-Roman hero of strength, Hercules. On somewhat sketchy historical grounds, Hercules' "steroid" of choice was apparently sniffed garlic, but he switched over to spinach after his archrival, Brutus, chucked him into a spinach patch during a fight. Interestingly, Popeye always got the girl in the end, a willowy woman whose very name appears elsewhere in these sexy pages: Olive Oil! Through the magic of television, many people old enough to remember the cartoon continue to associate this nutritious and tasty vegetable with power.

As an aphrodisiac, the reputation of spinach traces back 2000 years, and a number of cultures have valued it for its amorous qualities. A simple Chinese recipe advises frying it in oil and salt until crispy.

In the 16th century, when the über-sexual Catherine de Medici moved from Florence to marry the king of France, she brought her chefs along with her so that they could prepare her favorite spinach recipes, and insisted on it being served at every meal. This is the same woman who voraciously devoured artichokes as if her (sex) life depended on it. To this day, entrees served over a bed of spinach gain the added flourish, "à la Florentine." Life may not be a bed of roses, but it sure might be rosier on a bed of spinach!

Sexy Nutrients
Spinach is a nutritional powerhouse, and the creator of Popeye, E. Segar, knew that, and what he was really impressed with was its very high vitamin A content. Spinach is definitely high in beta-carotene, lutein, and zeaxanthin (the better to see your lover). It also offers a huge supply of folate, vitamin K (great for your bones), magnesium, and manganese. That's not to mention iron, calcium, potassium, copper, and zinc. Its very high iron content can be released by consuming it with a food high in vitamin C. Spinach is an excellent source of vitamin E and contains a wide range of B complex vitamins and also the antioxidant phytochemical, quercetin.

Spinach is also known for its abundant anti-oxidant and anti-inflammatory nutrients. For example, research has demonstrated that it reduces inflammation of the digestive tract as well as cancers of the digestive tract. Recent studies indicate spinach's very promising results in reducing prostate cancer, with more studies underway. Given the prostate's role in sexual functioning for men, perhaps Popeye was ahead of his time! As he put it, "Shiver me timbers!" "Blow me down!"

Steak

Lore and Fun Facts
While there are some folks who shun it, meat has been highly prized staple of the human diet since we began hunting with tools some 100,000 years ago. Since ancient times, meat, and more specifically beef, has played a part in the amorous lore of many cultures.

Nude priestesses in Dionysian orgies literally tore apart beef with their teeth and bare hands. *The Perfumed Garden* of Sheikh Nefzawi describes a man who demanded a meat and onion dish to sustain him during his arduous assignment to continuously maintain his erection for 30 days (Nefzawi fails to mention how that worked out...). Yikes! Warnings in modern erectile dysfunction medications urge users to head for the emergency room for erections lasting more than four hours. Perhaps our modern men would be better off with a rib eye!

More realistically, the go-to guide for Renaissance era newlyweds, *Tableau de L'amour Conjugal,* recommended beef marrow for fortification and strength in erotic matters. Originally published in 1686, it was so popular that it was reprinted more than 100 years later, in 1814.

In the 18th century, the infamous Louis XV commanded filet of sirloin braised *a la royale* for his *petits soupers.* In that era, *petits soupers,* smaller meals typically consumed later in the evening or even in the middle of the day, were shamelessly erotic. The menu featured aphrodisiac foods of the day, served with fine wine, with the intention of firing up the erotic inclinations of special guests. Petits soupers were often held in a private residence, or even in restaurants, where intimate rooms known as *cabinets particuliers* were dedicated to *petit souper* indulgences. Quite a sensual contrast to "grabbing a quick bite" at a fast food joint!

The French have since made various beef dishes famous for their sumptuous enjoyment, from Chateaubriand to Tournedos Rossini. Contemporary Americans have their own favorite steak dishes, and you'd better prepare them rare! Havelock Ellis, a famous early 20th century British sexologist, pronounced the steak "probably as powerful a sexual stimulant as any food." For many, the deep satisfaction that comes from occasional indulgence in a tender, juicy steak is surpassed only by more frequent indulgence in the tender embrace of a lover.

Sexy Nutrients
What steak has going for it, clearly, is its abundance of essential amino acids, the building blocks of protein.

Protein is vital to the health of your muscles, ligaments, and internal organs. It's also an also a very good source of animal-based *Heme* iron, the most absorbable form of iron. Iron is essential to the production of hemoglobin, the substance that lets you absorb oxygen and gives your blood its vital red color. Oxygen is crucial for sexual health and iron helps to keep you frisky, not fatigued. Steak is also packed with zinc, the ingredient most often associated with prostate health. Scientific research has demonstrated another need of zinc for older men: those with low levels are also at higher risk for osteoporosis. Zinc helps both sexes produce hormones, another sexy prospect!

Steak is also a source of vitamins, especially vitamins B-6 and B-12, and niacin. vitamins B-6 and B-12 help to keep your cardiovascular system humming along by lowering homocysteine levels and reducing the odds of heart attack, stroke, and even the risk of Alzheimer's. With regard to minerals, steak offers high levels of selenium, phosphorus, magnesium, and potassium, all known to help out in the bedroom.

What's more, good, red, juicy meat is a very good source of coenzyme Q10 (Co-Q10). This fat soluble antioxidant is required for the production of ATP, the gas that fuels your heart. Co-Q10 has also been recommended to slow the aging process, for good cardiovascular function, and reduce the symptoms of diabetes. Overcooking steak destroys the Co-Q10—and, I might add, the flavor. Juicy is *good*.

Wait, you say, steak is high in cholesterol and fat. How can that be good? First, those levels can't be determined until you select size and type of steak, and whether you cut off all visible fat—a very good idea. USDA labeling laws indicate that for a 3.5 ounce serving, "lean" beef contains less than 10 grams of total fat, no more than 4.5 grams saturated fat, and 95 milligrams of cholesterol. Happily, the USDA list includes tenderloin (including *filet mignon*), and T-bone. Their guidelines for "extra lean" beef lowers the limits for a 3.5 ounce serving to 5 grams of total fat, 2 grams of saturated fat, and 95 milligrams of cholesterol. Top sirloin steak and mock tender steak also qualify. Double these amounts and a 7-ounce "lean beef" steak remains well below the daily maximum recommended allowances for both saturated fat and cholesterol. Should you eat steak twice a day, every day? No. Can it be included in a healthy, sexy diet? Absolutely!

Steak's often overlooked sexy nutrients, deliciously prepared and in a moderate portion size, make it an ideal occasional choice for an aphrodisiac meal of the highest order.

Strawberries

Lore and Fun Facts

Throughout history, strawberries, a member of the rose family, appear in legend, art, and poetry. Unusual among foods, the strawberry wears its sexuality (seeds) on the outside of its fleshy body.

The early Greeks had a taboo against eating any red foods, except during feasts held in honor of the dead. Red foods such as wild strawberries were believed to possess special powers, which added to their mysterious allure. By contrast, the early Romans valued them for treating many ailments, from various inflammations to that most lamentable of turn offs, halitosis.

During the medieval era of courtly love, strawberries figured prominently as an unabashed flirtatious signal that meant "you intoxicate me with delight" and "you are delicious." In art and literature, the strawberry was usually a symbol of sensuality and earthly desire. The fruit was regarded as an aphrodisiac of the highest quality, due to its prolific number of tiny "seeds." In fact, at wedding breakfasts in provincial France, newlyweds traditionally were served a soup of thinned sour cream, strawberries, borage, and powdered sugar.

In the final stages of the French Revolution, a prominent figure in the court of Napoleon, Madame Tallien, regularly bathed in fresh strawberry juice made of some 22 pounds of fresh berries. Perhaps we can assume that she, like others of her era, bathed only infrequently, but we can also guess at the reason for her indulgence!

In my 21st Century Aphrodisiac Food Survey, strawberries ranked #2 as a free choice aphrodisiac favorite and were in #1 position, outranking chocolate, when selecting from a list of classic aphrodisiacs! I had to resist the temptation of placing an iconic, chocolate-covered strawberry on the cover of my book, though its near overuse by others made it easier to avoid. Throughout the world, strawberries remain the favorite of the berry fruits. They mix well with other foods, and are a bite-sized bit of finger food magic. Sweet and fragrant, juicy and pleasantly textured, strawberries are an extremely popular simple, sexy choice for anyone looking to redden their lips a bit!

Sexy Nutrients

Just eight ripe berries supply 140% of US Recommended Daily Allowance (RDA) for vitamin C, 20% of the US RDA for folic acid and three grams of fiber, making them a very good source. They contain a good amount of potassium—which helps to avoid the retention of excess fluids—iodine, riboflavin, vitamin B5, vitamin B6, vitamin K, and the minerals magnesium and copper.

They even contain omega-3 fatty acids, highly valued for their contribution to a healthy cardiovascular system. With all that, one full cup contains just 55 calories.

Contemporary nutritionists especially tout the antioxidant value of all berries, including strawberries, for their anthocyanins and ellagic acid. They rank right up there with raspberries in both health benefits and pop-in-your-lover's-mouth deliciousness!

Sushi

Lore and Fun Facts
The popularity of these bite-sized morsels of raw fish has soared in recent years; they ranked 6th on the "personal sexy favorites" list of my 21st Century Aphrodisiac Foods Survey.

Interestingly, the 19th century Japanese chef who created the oblong-shaped *nigiri sushi* (hand-formed sushi) did not use raw fish. That came much later, making sushi clearly a contemporary aphrodisiac food. Other forms of sushi in Japan, including the popular *maki sushi*, or sushi rolls, came later still.

A wide variety of sushi rolls created with Western palates in mind, including the popular California Roll, are unknown in Japan. What they all have in common is the rice. The word *"sushi"* means "salted," or "it's sour," and refers to the tartness the rice acquires when seasoned with vinegar. When very fresh seafood is served raw without the rice or seaweed, it's called *shashimi*. Regardless of the name or specific ingredients, sushi is sexy in the minds of many lovers!

Sexy Nutrients
Sushi always offers the sexy nutrients of whatever aphrodisiac seafood is used, plus the sexy benefits of seaweed and the seasoned rice. Sushi is often made with brown rice these days, adding a nutritional punch. When topped with pickled ginger, sushi becomes a lascivious but healthy panoply of sexy nutrients.

Tomatoes

Lore and Fun Facts
The tomato, or "love apple," is something of an accidental aphrodisiac, at least in terms of the historical evolution of its name. It's also an accidental vegetable, given its botanical classification as a fruit.

When the tomato was first brought to Spain from Central America by the Conquistadors in the early 16th century, it was called a *tomate*, but when it reached Italy, it was given the nickname *pomo dei Moro*, or "Moorish apple" because the Italians had imported it from Spanish Morocco. When the French imported the tomato from Italy, they mistranslated *pomo dei Moro* as *pomme d'amour,* or "apple of love," and *love apple* became its popular name in England and America in the 17th century.

On the other hand, it's also a forbidden fruit, in part because of the aforementioned bias against red foods, and in part because it's a member of the nightshade family and was feared poisonous. Thankfully, redness-means-passion has won out over redness-means-death, for the beautiful and delicious tomato is worthy of inclusion in any love feast! Besides, among the many cultivars now in existence, red is just one of the many gorgeous colors represented by the sexy tomato.

There's a remote possibility that the tomato's sexy reputation has been enhanced by its very virility. Anyone who has grown more tomatoes than they know what to do with will appreciate its reproductive capacity.

Part of its popularity is due to its versatility. Raw or cooked, hot or cold, this fruit-cum-veggie is among the most widely dispersed of all foods. Its popularity as a base ingredient in soups and sauces can't be overstated, but it's also hard to beat a slice of garden fresh tomato, lightly salted and peppered, as a sensual delight of the highest order!

Sexy Nutrients
Certain varieties of tomato are ridiculously high in vitamin C, but it's the various antioxidants, especially lycopene, that carry widespread health benefits from a general and a sexual point of view. Lycopene is made more bio-available by the presence of a fat, so drizzling a bit of olive oil on a fresh slab of tomato is sure to do the trick.

A study from Wayne State University in Detroit suggests that lycopene can help prevent the scarring that occurs with endometriosis, a condition occurring in women of childbearing years that, among other troubling impacts, can cause pelvic pain, pain during intercourse, and even infertility. Other studies have indicated relationships between lycopene and prostate health in men, with more research needed. Regardless, diets rich in fruits and vegetables—take your pick, tomatoes can be either one—is the basis for better human health. So you certainly can't go wrong serving your lover a bit of love apple next time you fancy a bit of romance!

Umami

Lore and Fun Facts
The only item in this list that's not actually a food and, in fact, is not a specific ingredient at all, is umami. Rather, it refers to a flavor first described by a Japanese researcher over 100 years ago. It's not one of the classic four flavors: sweet, sour, bitter, or salty. Western scientists refer to it as the "5th flavor," a sensual, earthy sense that roughly translates from the Japanese as "savoriness" or "good flavor."

Foods such as mushrooms, Parmesan cheese, potatoes, soy sauce and red wine are high in umami flavor. So are sea foods such as shrimp, oysters, lobsters, tuna, crab and fresh anchovies, as well as many meats, including beef, pork, and chicken. Specialized cells on the tongue detect a product of glutamic acid that occurs naturally in these foods and creates the deeply satisfying, rich sensation of "savoriness." Some chefs say umami–rich foods create "mouth feel." Whatever you call it—savory mouth-feel, or plain old great flavor—it's a real turn-on for many!

Sexy nutrients
While the specific sexy nutritional value of umami-rich foods varies significantly from food to food, what they all offer with their rich, savory flavor is less need for added salt, which by any measure is a sexy benefit. There's also the possibility of eating a bit less, since foods with umami tend to be calorie and carbohydrate rich, and require small portions to be satisfying. Warning: Like sex, they also offer such deeply enjoyable physical and emotional stimulation that overindulging is always a possibility!

V — See Vanilla-Herbs & Spices

Watercress

Lore and Fun Facts
Watercress is very nearly a so-called "super food," and has been prized from ancient times through the modern era. In fact, it's one of the oldest known leafy vegetables consumed by humans. An aquatic plant, it is native to Europe, North Africa, and Asia, and is cultivated there and in North and South America and the West Indies. In the US and the UK, it now grows wild, especially near the headwaters of certain types of hard water streams.

Pliny noted its Latin name as *Nasus tortus* or "writhing nose," an attribution due no doubt to its spicy flavor and pungent smell. An early Greek writer and military leader, Xenophon, was said to have insisted his soldiers consume watercress as a tonic. Hippocrates prescribed watercress as an expectorant, and it's possible he chose the location of his healing center for its proximity to a stream in which the fresh herb grew.

Egyptians, from ancient times until today, insist on the aphrodisiac qualities of watercress, though more recently, like the rest of the world, they are finding tremendous value in its medicinal use as well. One Egyptian scholar noted, "the (watercress) seed ground, and put in a foamed egg with a little *ashtincosh* (crocodile) salt, and swallowed, shall increase in sperm and add to the erection." Arabs who live in Egypt have gone the Egyptians one better, claiming, "You do not have to eat the Gargir (watercress) to increase masculinity; it is enough to put a bundle of it under your bed, and its intoxicating scent will reach your nose."

Numerous folk references to the sexy power of watercress come to us from the UK, where it has been grown commercially since around 1800. Watercress is mentioned in early Irish poetry from about the 12th century and the shamrock is thought originally to have been watercress. It was introduced commercially to England and France from Germany, where cultivation began around 1700. Worldwide demand for watercress currently widely outstrips its supply, though ever-widening cultivation is attempting to make up for its very short shelf life and unsuitability for drying or freezing.

Sexy Nutrients
Watercress is very nearly in a category of its own when it comes to its nutritional value, both directly and indirectly related to sexual function.

While extremely rich in vitamins and minerals, it has long been considered a "cleansing herb" that purifies the blood and helps clear the lungs. The fresh juice of the plant has both internal and external applications, the latter most notably for skin irritations and the relief of sunburn.

Watercress contains more vitamin C than oranges, lots of vitamin A and beta-carotene, and plenty of vitamins E and B-complex. It boasts a highly absorbable form of calcium, and even more iron than spinach, along with magnesium, phosphorus, potassium, sodium, zinc, copper, manganese, selenium, sulphur, iodine, and manganese, as well as fatty and amino acids.

A strong anti-carcinogenic response has also been discovered in watercress, specifically from the presence of a glucosinolate also found in broccoli and cabbage, and in fact it contains the same arsenal of antioxidants and phytochemicals that help reduce the risk of cancers and heart disease. Extensive research is underway around the world to reveal yet more specific and actionable findings on this amazing plant, but suffice it to say that if it cleanses the blood, loads you up on sexy vitamins, and has strong antioxidant properties, this spicy little green will put a major spring in your next sexy step!

Watermelon

Lore and Fun Facts
Watermelon likely originated in southern Africa, though cultivation evidence exists from around 2000 BCE in the Nile Valley. Watermelon seeds were discovered in the tomb of the Pharaoh Tutankhamen, which may speak to its importance either in ancient Egypt or in the afterlife.

By 10th century CE, the Chinese were actively cultivating watermelon, and continue to be the world's largest producer of the fruit. It was introduced to Europe in the 13th century and to the Americas no later than 1615.

Much more recently, watermelons, most of which are sexy pink in color, have become widely appreciated for both their water and sugar contents. A great finger food, watermelons have the added sexy distinction of containing seeds which are "spit" by blowing them hard off the tongue between pursed lips. Their super sweet yet delicate flavor is perfectly suited to the sexy, slurpy, dripping summertime fun food they have become in the United States and elsewhere.

Sexy Nutrients
Watermelon, like most fruits, is high in several vitamins, especially C, but is also one of the few food sources of lycopene, that type of carotenoid with up to twice the antioxidant power of B-carotenoid. In men, lycopene is protective of the prostate, and for both sexes, it protects the heart and the skin.

Even more promising sexually is the presence of citruline, which produces an amino acid called arginine. The effect of arginine is to relax blood vessels and increase blood flow, which of course is what most of those erectile dysfunction medications do. Two minor issues exist in the research, though. First, the greatest amounts of citruline are found in the rind, which is greedily consumed elsewhere in the world but usually tossed in the garbage in the US. Secondly, one skeptical researcher contends you'd need to consume around 6 cups of watermelon to get the, uh, desired effect. Nutritional botanists are working on boosting citruline in the flesh of the watermelon. As for the high doses needed, six cups of luscious sweetness seems a small price to pay to fortify your lover's manhood. Why not give it a try some hot and sultry summer afternoon?

Wine and Spirits

Lore and Fun Facts
Taken as whole, alcoholic beverages are linked to both food and sex through

the ages. For thousands of years, fermentation was the only process harnessed to make alcohol. In its earliest manifestations, and continuing deep into the 19th century, booze replaced water that was unsafe or unfit to drink.

Prehistoric evidence as far back as 10,000 BCE suggests that Stone Age humans' daily bread may in fact have been daily beer, with additional Neolithic findings from Persia indicating wine consumption at around 5400 BCE. Wine jars from China have been dated to 7000 BCE, where rice, honey and fruits were fermented and widely consumed.

The ancient Egyptians got in on the act via Osiris, a deity they believe invented beer. In fact, they are thought to have enjoyed more than 15 kinds of beer and two dozen varieties of wine. Here, too, is an early connection between alcohol and sex, with recorded warnings about visiting "taverns" where prostitution was rampant.

No ancient cultures seem to have done without alcohol. Fermented beverages were consumed in India and Babylon between 3000 - 2000 BCE.

Yet it's with the Greeks and Romans that we get the first positive connection between alcohol and sex. The Greeks had Dionysus, the Romans Bacchus, those wine gods still mentioned in popular parlance today. It was likely mead, a drink of fermented honey water, that began the Greco-Roman fascination with alcohol, but eventually wine from pressed grapes became more widespread. While the Greeks valued temperance and moderation, alcohol played a role in overriding that mindset. The Cult of Dionysus favored wine-fueled revelry steeped in mysterious rituals deeply associated with notions of life and death and fertility. Bacchanalian traditions were originally connected to agriculture and theater, and involved liberation of oneself through wine and ecstatic behavior. Sexuality was an early byproduct of alcohol consumption. The Romans even had a slogan for it: *sine baccho, venus friget,* or "without wine, love grows old."

Champagne, that most favored of aphrodisiac drinks, was a relative latecomer to the alcohol scene. It wasn't until the 17th century that Dom Perignon began experimenting with sparkling wine. Ironically, he initially went to great lengths to prevent bubbles, which caused the thin bottles and insufficient corks of the day to explode in the cellars. Fortunately, new bottle making and better corking permitted the evolution of the "bubbly" we enjoy today. Not surprisingly, champagne was among the most recognized and appreciated items in my 21st Century Aphrodisiac Food Survey.

Distillation, the process of concentrating ethanol (alcohol) from fermenting plant material, is another relative newcomer. The earliest clear evidence of distilled alcoholic beverages appears around the 12th century BCE in southern Italy, but by the mid-1300s production and consumption had spread throughout Europe, partly in response to the outbreak of the Plague, a decidedly un-sexy killer of millions in the Middle Ages which many thought could be avoided by drinking lots of booze. By the 17th century, most European countries had their own distilled national drink, each based in part on the most readily available plant source.

Wine, beer and spirits are now intricately woven into the cultural fabric of most countries, and their consumption, particularly that of wine, champagne and certain liqueurs, are directly associated in the minds of many of us with sex. At its best, alcohol relaxes the mind and body, deliciously accompanies food, and enhances our appreciation of our senses. With the sensual boost comes a caveat, of course, for many a romantic opportunity has been lost to overconsumption of alcohol, not to mention the lives lost or damaged from its abuse. But as with all the suggestions in this book, a healthy approach to our bodies and minds is the basis for a lifelong enjoyment of that miracle combination of food, drink, and sex. So sip and savor, keep it simple, and let nature take her course!

Sexy Nutrients
Is alcohol a healthy tonic or a poison? Religious and moral strictures aside, the answer is decidedly "dose-dependent." Numerous studies have shown health benefits, particularly cardiovascular benefits, are associated with light to moderate drinking. These benefits include a reduction in heart attack and the most common kind of stroke (ischemic), an increase in HDL, the "good" cholesterol, and improvements in factors that affect blood-clotting. These positive effects are generally associated with increasing age, not youth, a sexy prospect as we age, which is good news for a graying society.

For most people, alcohol in small doses also helps to create a mellow, sexy mood.

On the other hand, we are all very aware that for those who abuse it, its effects are quite toxic, even deadly. Still others must avoid alcohol for various reasons, whether because they have medical conditions, are taking certain medications, or are pregnant.

Although the research on cardiovascular function and alcohol typically reports it's the alcohol itself that confers its positive effects, beer and wine lovers loyal to their own beverage preference are likely to disagree.

Some research supports their view. Although beer is often thought of as "inferi-

or" to wine, as the third most-consumed-beverage in the world, behind water and tea, it's not surprising that various studies support its specific benefits, in light does. For example, beer is a good source of dietary silicon, which is needed both for cardiovascular health and for connective tissue and gone mineral density.

Wines' benefits have been more widely touted for the past 20 years, ever since *60 Minutes* aired a show about significantly lower rates of cardiovascular disease among the French, despite their penchant for dairy foods, pastries, and wine, especially red wine. This phenomenon became known as the "French paradox," which is really no paradox at all, since the French don't actually eat as much as we do, and they eschew trans fats, the real culprits. Researchers were especially inspired to study red wine more intensely, and identified a substance in it known as resveratrol, a polyphenolic compound. Some studies have reported that red wine drinkers, as opposed to beer or spirits drinkers, have lower cardiovascular risks, but other studies have not supported that finding. Despite all the hype, no clinical trials have been run, only short-term in vitro studies. What's more, the beneficial effects specific to red wine may relate more to flavonoids, which are in far higher concentration in red wine than resveratrol.

That said, the Harvard School of Public Health, the Centers for Disease Control, and the Mayo Clinic, among others, all continue to support the idea that light to moderate drinking may well contribute to a healthy sex life (not exactly the way they put it, of course) by reducing the aforementioned cardiovascular risks. On the other hand, it's been well-known for a long time that for women, heavy drinking and breast cancer are linked, and a very recent study has even extended that finding to light drinking, especially between the ages of 18-40. Unsexy, sobering (pun intended) news. Far more women run the risk of getting cardiovascular disease than breast cancer, and it's rare to have to trade one risk for another, but as this book goes to press, the medical experts are leaving this decision in the hands of women.

For those who abstain from alcohol, health care professionals do not suggest taking up the practice, nor do I! As this book highlights, there are plenty of aphrodisiac beverage alternatives, from Sexy Chai to Mango Lassi, to a steaming cup of hot chocolate or a fabulous glass of fruit smoothie!

X-rated foods. Think edible undies for starters...

Yam

Lore and Fun Facts
Yams have been cultivated in Africa and Asia since 50,000 years BCE. They remain a very popular staple food the world over. It wasn't until the Eliza-

bethan golden age of the 16th century, however, that yams were held in high esteem as an aphrodisiac.

The Irish, so famous for white potato consumption, were likely consuming *Ipomeoa batatas*, or sweet potatoes, when promoting their reputation of "restoring the waning vigour of the ageing reprobate." In fact, much confusion remains over the yam-sweet potato identity, with yams being a "root" tuber grown throughout the world except, believe it or not, in North America, while sweet potatoes are "stem" tubers abundantly grown throughout the Americas.

In modern times, the Chinese include yam in extracts given to male livestock to increase the volume of semen and increase their copulation rates. And on an island off Japan, yams and yam products are used in folk-remedies to treat erection difficulties. Likely, their belief in its powers is as much related to The Doctrine of Resemblances as their sexy nutrients. With the equally phallic shape of yams and sweet potatoes, and their sweet, nutrition-packed contents, it seems reasonable to assume that both yams and sweet potatoes hold aphrodisiac appeal.

Sexy Nutrients
Sweet potatoes with red flesh outrank yams and pale-colored sweet potatoes nutritionally. The red varieties are loaded with vitamin A in the form of beta-carotene, something smoking (an unsexy prospect) depletes from the body. Both yams and sweet potatoes are good sources of vitamin C, vitamin B6, manganese, potassium, and dietary fiber. The potassium and fiber are both great for cardiovascular health. And nothing makes for a great romp in the hay quite like a strong and willing heart!

Zucchini

Lore and Fun Facts
As you might have guessed by now, zucchini, (aka courgette) is a Doctrine of Resemblances food rivaled only by the cucumber in its approximation of part of the male anatomy. Perhaps that's why no less a source than the UCLA School of Medicine's training program in human sexuality used to encourage the use of zucchini for certain personal gratifications. That's quite an endorsement for this veggie's erotic potential.

Somewhat ironically, the zucchini fruit is actually the swollen ovary of the female flower, making it ripe for the picking for men or women!

Like all squashes, zucchini originated in the Americas, but was actually reintroduced to the US markets via Italy, where it had become a staple of Italian cooking. It didn't reach widespread consumption in the US until well into the 20th century, beginning, as you might expect, in romantic Italian restaurants.

In my 21st Aphrodisiac Foods Survey, zucchini was recognized as one of the top five sexiest vegetables.

Sexy Nutrients
Zucchini is a very good source of folates, potassium, and vitamin A, as well as a good source of vitamins B6 and C, manganese, phosphorous, magnesium, and zinc. One of its sexiest attributes is its astonishingly low calorie count, just 13 calories in a half cup of raw zucchini. That's a lot of sexy nutrition for those keeping an eye on their—or their lovers'—waistlines!

Herbs/Spices

Introduction
Perhaps no other category of ingredients is as versatile and widely appreciated as herbs and spices. Their reach extends from the depths of recorded history directly into our common fare—and even speech—today. "Spice up your life" means to add flavor and excitement to an otherwise dull pattern of living. In helping you bring new joy and excitement to both your diet and your sex life, herbs and spices are my go-to foods!

Entire civilizations grew up around ancient spice trading routes. Certain spices had more value than gold or money, and even served as "legal tender" in financial transactions. Overall, the role of herbs and spices in ancient history was fairly practical, albeit vital: to preserve food in storage or transport, and to cover up the flavor and odor of spoilage.

There's ample evidence to suggest that both the first circumnavigation of the earth by Magellan and the "discovery" of the Americas by Columbus were driven by the search for spices and a more direct route for their trade to Europe.

By the Middle Ages herbs and spices were associated with both wealth and decadence. And as with so many things that might bring us too much pleasure, the church stepped in to control any excesses. Around the 4th century, saints forbade "sumptuous" dishes prepared from expensive seasonings due to their reputations as potent aphrodisiacs.

The Medieval Christian diet was disseminated in a series of letters to aspiring monks and nuns: They were to abstain from various spices because, "while we folloe after dainties we distance ourselves from Heaven." Due to their expense, "those who seek to be rich (possibly with flavor), fall into temptation and the snares of the Devil."

Today, with the opening of world markets and the availability of otherwise exotic foods as easy as a trip to your local grocer, herbs and spices are experiencing a renaissance of appreciation in North America. As it turns out, science is revealing that these tasty ingredients are more valuable than as simple flavor enhancers.

Research into the health benefits of herbs and spices is preliminary, but very promising. As with other simple, sexy foods, herbs and spices contain powerful compounds that may have sexy side effects. Scientists suggest that the antioxidant, anti-inflammatory, and antibacterial properties in many herbs and spices may contribute to stabilizing blood glucose levels, promoting blood and heart health, improving emotional balance, boosting brain function, and even retarding the growth or organization of cancer cells.

A healthy heart and mind are sexy prospects, indeed. So don't hold off on the chance to spice up your sex life. Variety, flavor, and an occasional surprise are as exciting in the bedroom as in the kitchen!

Basil

Lore and Fun Facts
Basil's name comes from the Greek *basileius*, meaning king, and it is considered a "royal herb" in several cultures. In the Egypt of the Pharaohs, basil was used to assist in childbirth, and was also potted on window sills to keep flies away!

Common basil is native to the Old World tropics of India, Africa and Asia, but now grows all over the world—and likely in your home garden! In India it is believed to hold divine essence. In some Greek Orthodox churches it is used to prepare holy water, as it was found growing around Christ's tomb after the Resurrection.

The prominent English physician and botanist, Nicholas Culpeper, writing in the mid-17th century work called the *Culpeper's Complete Herbal*, praised the powerful aphrodisiac qualities of basil, especially for women. Basil is a token of love in several cultures. Indeed, rarely does the Italian girl pay a visit to her sweetheart without sporting a basil sprig behind her ear.

In Southeastern Europe's Moldova/Romania region, one folk superstition says that if a wandering youth accepts a sprig of basil offered from the hand of a young maiden, he will fall in love with her and remain faithful to her.

In Haiti, Bush Basil is associated with a pagan love goddess named Erzulie, and in Mexico it is used in potions to attract lovers.

Pungent and versatile, aromatic and sensual, basil is an herb whose sexy reputation deserves to be tested at your next love feast!

Sexy Nutrients
Basil contains an abundance of beneficial substances, many of which deliver very sexy health benefits. One, methyl chavicol, shows promise in inhibiting the growth of wicked bacteria such as listeria and E. coli, either of which could seriously dampen amorous intentions!

When eaten fresh, it also provides vitamins A, D, and B2, as well as calcium, iron, and phosphorus. Basil is especially rich in vitamin K, important for proper blood coagulation and bone health. Scientists have recently discovered antioxidant properties in basil, which may turn out to carry numerous benefits to many sexy parts of the body!

Basil contains large amounts of (E)-beta-caryophyllene (BCP), which may be useful in treating inflammatory bowel diseases and arthritis. BCP is the only product identified in nature that activates the cannabinoid receptor, CB2 selectively, effectively blocking chemical signals that lead to inflammation without making you "high."

Cinnamon

Lore and Fun Facts
The spice known as cinnamon is derived from the brown bark of the cinnamon tree, and is available in its dried tubular form, known as a "quill," or as ground powder. The use and appreciation of cinnamon dates back more than 4000 years, with references found on the Temple of Apollo and in the Bible.

Cinnamon is mentioned in the Hebrew *Song of Songs* (or, of Solomon) and in Proverbs. In what is arguably the sexiest, spiciest and most romantic of scriptures, the *Song of Songs* includes it in a list of metaphorically sexy items:

"A garden enclosed is my sister, my spouse; a spring shut up, a fountain sealed.
Thy plants are an orchard of pomegranates, with pleasant fruits; camphire, with spikenard,
Spikenard and saffron; calamus and cinnamon, with all trees of frankincense; myrrh and aloes, with all the chief spices:
A fountain of gardens, a well of loving waters, and streams from Lebanon."

Elsewhere in the Old Testament, an adulteress reveals cinnamon's allure, by saying something along the lines of, "I have sprinkled my bed with myrrh, with aloe and with cinnamon; come let us drink deep of love until the morning, and abandon ourselves to delight."

As with so many spices in ancient times, cinnamon was typically reserved for gift-giving among the very wealthy and as offerings to the gods. By the Middle Ages, however, it came down to earth to grace average folks with its healthful—and sexy—properties.

Despite his famous conversion to Christianity, Emperor Constantine's 4th century CE remedy for impotence was a medicinal paste of spices, which included pepper, ginger, galangal and cinnamon.

By the late 18th century, it was custom for English newlyweds to be served a "posset" shortly before retiring to the wedding bed: a mixture of wine, milk, egg yolk, sugar, cinnamon, and nutmeg.

Today the aroma and flavor of cinnamon graces cuisines around the world. In the US it is primarily a "dessert" spice, though the incursion of world cuisines into American culture has greatly expanded its use in meat and vegetable dishes as well. For many, the smell of cinnamon brings a nostalgic sense of comfort and ease, the perfect preamble to a relaxed and sensual round of lovemaking.

Sexy Nutrients
Anecdotal evidences of the sexy health benefits of cinnamon are many and varied. Its properties have been touted in the treatment of everything from rheumatism, anxiety, and menstrual problems to toothaches and even smoking cessation.

More recently, cinnamon has captured the attention of many researchers. For example, less than a half teaspoon per day of cinnamon has been shown to reduce blood sugar levels for those suffering from Type 2 diabetes, and may also help to prevent its onset.

Cinnamon's antifungal properties help control Candida yeast infections, something any woman and her lover would find to be a very sexy prospect.

Cinnamon is also an excellent source of manganese and a very good source of calcium, iron, and dietary fiber. Last but not least, just smelling the amazing fragrance of this yummy spice boosts brain activity from attention-focused processes to working memory and virtual recognition memory. In other words, a piece of cinnamon toast in the morning might help you retrieve fond memories of last night's romance!

Another series of experiments suggests that the compound *cinnamic aldehyde* may activate an antioxidant response in colon and skin cells and shows promise in treating both colon and skin cancers, the potential for which should give anyone happy goose bumps of arousal!

Cloves

Lore and Fun Facts
Cloves are native to Indonesia, home to the famous "Spice Islands" of old. Their value as a tradable commodity cannot be overstated. Even as recently as the 18th century in Britain, cloves were literally worth their weight in gold, given the expense of importing them.

Roman, Chinese, and Indian sources all make reference to cloves around 2000 years ago. Both the Chinese and Indian texts recommended them for maintaining a fresh, fragrant breath—the better to kiss you with, my dear—while the Roman Pliny emphasized their valued aroma.

Cloves are "hot" or "warm" in character, which may explain why they earned aphrodisiac reputations in later centuries. Anything that would "provoketh sluggish husbands" or "augment the force of Venus," or more specifically (and less poetically), "extenuate the penis mechanically," would be useful in the bedrooms of lovers everywhere!

Sexy Nutrients
Cloves are best known for their pungent aroma, yet there's more to this spice than meets the nose. Cloves are antibacterial, reduce the toxicity of environmental pollutants, and can help reduce joint inflammation.

Cumin

Lore and Fun Facts
Cumin is another hot or warm spice that has been in use since ancient times. Cumin seeds have been found at Syrian and Egyptian archeological digs dating to the second millennium BCE. It's mentioned more than once in the Bible, and was familiar to the tables of ancient Greece and Rome.

To this day, in Morocco, cumin is kept on the table like the more familiar black pepper is elsewhere in the world. It's common in Indian dishes, and can also be found in giving greater depth of flavor to curry mixes and even to good old American-style chili.

As recently as the early 20th century, Italian women living in the countryside fed their lovers cumin seed to "ensure their continued attachment and fidelity." And if her beloved was off to military service or far-away employment, she sent him off with a freshly-baked loaf of bread containing cumin seeds, or wine that had been spiked with cumin powder to encourage his loyalty.

Like the other "hot" foods, cumin has been thought to heat the blood and, well, *inflame* the fires of lust. "Want to heat up the evening, darling? 'Cumin' here and we'll get started!"

Sexy Nutrients
Cumin seeds, or *Cuminum cyminum,* are a decent source of iron, a mineral vital to healthy blood, and which plays a role in energy production and metabolism. Of course it's vital for menstruating women to get enough iron to replace that lost in their cycle, as it is for pregnant or lactating women.

Cumin seeds have traditionally been noted to be of benefit to the digestive system, and scientific research is beginning to bear out cumin's age-old reputation. Research has shown that cumin may stimulate the secretion of pancreatic enzymes, compounds necessary for proper digestion and nutrient assimilation.

Recent research indicates that cumin seeds may also have anti-carcinogenic properties. In one study, cumin was shown to protect laboratory animals from developing stomach or liver tumors. This cancer-protective effect appears to be related to cumin's penchant for hunting down free radicals, and may also be related to its ability to boost enzymes that detoxify the liver. And while it may not sound glamorous, any substance that fights cancer and purifies the body deserves a sprinkle into your next simple, sexy meal!

Mint

Lore and Fun Facts
How sexy is mint? Consider that its original botanical name is *Labiatae*, so called because the flowers fuse into an upper and lower lip, resembling a very sexy part of the female anatomy. In terms of the old Doctrine of Resemblances, mint is right on the money!

Middle Eastern and European research has attempted to document its aphrodisiac effects. As a "hot" herb associated with sexual stamina, its production during wartime was discouraged, lest it distract soldiers from battle. Its use is so widespread, both as a food enhancer and as an additive to various products like cigarettes and room fresheners, that it would be hard to go through a day without encountering it in some form or other.

Mint graces Middle Eastern lamb dishes, and in Britain and the US is commonly found in jellies, sauces, desserts and even drinks. The famously sexy mint julep, an alcoholic drink based on rum, is enjoying a renaissance in the US, but is perhaps most commonly associated with well-dressed, hat-wearing fans of the Kentucky Derby.

In terms of sex appeal, it's hard to deny the breath-enhancing qualities of mint. Historically a teeth whitener and a remedy for halitosis, the taste of mint on a lover's lips has led to unimaginable numbers of sexy encounters, and might just be the secret to post-meal sex appeal!

Sexy Nutrients
The powerful phenols and volatile compounds in mint's aromatic tissues show promise for the treatment of a variety of health issues. Beyond the stimulating effect of its aroma, studies are beginning to reveal answers about the potential impact of mint on gastrointestinal complaints, pain relief and even anti-cancer treatment. More research is needed, and going on every day, but mint holds a healthy and refreshing place in the simple, sexy world of aphrodisiac foods!

Nutmeg

Lore and Fun Facts
Also known as *myristica* or *nux moschata*, nutmeg is another of the old world spices that originated in the Indonesian Spice Islands. It has been used for centuries by Hindus, Arabs, Greeks, and Romans to improve sexual drive. In the Orient it was especially highly priced among women. Indian texts prescribe nutmeg mixed with honey and a half-boiled egg should be taken an hour before the intercourse to prolong the duration of the sexual act.

A rather unappetizing and decidedly unsexy historical event related to nutmeg occurred in 17th century Denmark. A young man was brought to trial for a form of "witchcraft" in which he taught a friend to seduce a young woman using nutmeg. The process, however, involved eating a whole nutmeg (seed of the nutmeg tree), capturing it after it passed through the digestive system, and then grating it into the drink of his beloved, after which she was supposed to become powerless to resist him.

Then there's the far more appetizing and quite sexy practice in the late 18th century of English newlyweds enjoying a mixture of wine, milk, egg yolk, sugar, cinnamon, and nutmeg before their nuptials. Hot, steamy, sweet and creamy, with just a hint of spice and a mild kick of alcohol, now THAT is sexy in any era!

Sexy Nutrients
The active components of nutmeg have many therapeutic applications in traditional medicines, including anti-fungal, anti-depressant, aphrodisiac, digestive, and carminative (preventing gas!) functions.

Nutmeg is known to science as a good source of copper, potassium, calcium, manganese, iron, zinc, and magnesium. Potassium helps control heart rate and blood pressure, while manganese and copper have antioxidant properties. Iron is of course necessary for red blood cell production. Nutmeg is also rich in many B-complex vitamins including vitamin C, folic acid, riboflavin, niacin, vitamin A, and contains many flavonoid anti-oxidants like beta carotene and cryptoxanthins that are known to promote vigorous health. And a healthy, vigorous partner is often all the aphrodisiac a guy or girl could want!

Oregano

Lore and Fun Facts
While most Americans think of Italian food when they think of oregano, its use in Italian cooking was preempted by the Greeks. Legend has it that Venus created the plants, along with their delicious flavor and odor, and that Aphrodite was very fond of the herb.

Some origins give oregano the Greek meaning of "joy of the mountain," from *oros*, meaning "mountain" and *ganos*, meaning "joy." Oregano grew wild and untamed on Greek hillsides, all the better for imparting grazing sheep and goats with tender and tasty meat.

Its associations from ancient times have leaned toward marital "happiness," which I loosely translate as "good sex." Many newlyweds were adorned with crowns of oregano to send them to the marriage bed with sufficient vigor!

There are several cultivars of oregano, including Mexican oregano, which must have been brought to that land by the Spanish. Closely related to and often confused with marjoram, oregano is generally associated with Mediterranean cooking, but as with so many simple, sexy ingredients found in this book, has found its way into world cuisines.

Sexy Nutrients
As with other members of the *Labiatae* family, oregano contains lots of volatile oils like *thymol* and *carvacrol*, both of which have been shown to inhibit the growth of nasty bacteria, including *Pseudomonas aeruginosa* and *Staphylococcus aureus*. In Mexico, researchers have compared oregano to tinidazol, a commonly used prescription drug to treat infection from the amoeba *giardia lamblia*. These researchers found oregano to be more effective against *giardia* than the oft-prescribed tinidazol.

Also like its Labiatae relatives, oregano is a very good source of iron, manganese, and dietary fiber, as well as a good source of calcium, vitamin C, vitamin A (beta-carotene), and omega-3 fatty acids. In laboratory studies, oregano has demonstrated stronger anti-oxidant abilities than either of the two synthetics commonly added to processed food: BHT (butylated hydroxytoluene) and

BHA (butylated bydroxyanisole). Interestingly, oregano has far more antioxidant strength than apples, potatoes, oranges and even blueberries. As an excellent source of fiber, it works well both as a digestive aid and to cleanse the body of toxins. All this, and a flavor straight from the Gods! No wonder the Italians, who may not have originated the use of oregano but have brought it into everyday cuisine, are so well known for their preoccupation with amorous pursuits!

Parsley

Lore and Fun Facts
An ancient plant with a libidinous reputation, parsley is another of the "hot" herbs whose production was discouraged during wartime.

The Greeks crowned winning athletes with parsley at their Nemean and Isthmian games and used the herb as a flavoring.

The bawdy Romans wore curly leafed parsley garlands in their hair because they thought so doing would permit them to down as much wine as they wished without getting hammered. They also fed it to their horses to increase their speed and stamina.

The plant is described by Seneca, who tells how the tempting sorceress Medea gathered parsley and other forbidden herbs by moonlight, while the *Satyricon* of Petronius connects parsley with aphrodisiac foods and mentions that "sacred" parsley was used to cleanse "profane fingers." Both Apicius in his pioneer cookbook and Rabelais in the best of debaucherous books speak of parsley's impact on sexual prowess. Interestingly, their opinions are confirmed in part today by the discovery that parsley is rich in sexually potent vitamin E.

"Parsley grows for the wicked, but not for the just," says an old English proverb. In parts of England, parsley wine is still consumed as an aphrodisiac. In a bow to the Doctrine of Resemblances, the phrase "curly parsley" was once used as British slang for "pubic hair," while "the parsley bed" referred to the female vulva.

The French believe parsley sparks the libido, an idea that comes from the Greek physician Dioscorides, who said parsley "provides venery and bodily lust." In Spain, parsley is fed to sheep to bring them into heat. Bah, ram ewe, indeed!

Sexy Nutrients
Parsley is rich vitamins A and C, potassium and iron, and also contains three phytochemicals: apiloe, apiin, and pinene, which help improve digestion,

eliminate bloating, and decrease blood pressure. Just don't eat too much if you are pregnant. In large amounts, parsley can cause uterine contractions.

In addition to being the most popular culinary herb and one of nature's great breath fresheners, parsley is high in histidine, an amino acid that the body converts to histamine, a molecule that regulates ejaculation and orgasm. Histidine also works as a vasodilator, making blood flow to the sex organs easier. So it's like two herbs in one: it freshens your breath and reduces erectile dysfunction!

Pepper

Lore and Fun Facts

Black pepper has also been used as an aphrodisiac for thousands of years. Peppercorns, or *Piper nigrum*, are spicy berries native to India or Malaysia. Their aphrodisiac reputation runs back thousands of years, receiving mention in both the *Kama Sutra* (2nd century, BCE) and in the 15th century Arabic text, *The Perfumed Garden of Sensual Delight*.

Like sweet peppers, peppercorns' color variations reflect changes with time and treatment. At the time of picking, peppercorns are green. As they dry in the sun, they transform from red, to yellow, to brown, and finally to black. If the black husk is removed after the drying process, the result is white peppercorns, the very spiciest version.

Pursuit, acquisition and trade of pepper, along with several other seminal spices, evolved into the Spice Trade and was responsible for both the development and destruction of entire civilizations.

Pepper was known to the ancient Mediterranean world. Pliny was amazed by its popularity and noted "Both ginger and pepper grow wild in their own countries, yet they are purchased by weight as if they were gold and silver." Pepper was used as a medicine as well as in cooking itself, but it was also a commodity of trade so powerful that it was used as a gift to sovereigns, a bribe to judges, or part of a rich young woman's dowry.

Pepper was a symbol of virility and power, and was used as a coin of the realm, sacks of pepper being traded for goods and commodities.

The Latin variation of "piper" refers to "energy," which applies to the bedroom as well, and that meaning was carried over long periods of history through to today. "Pepper" has referred to energy ever since. In the early 20th century, this was shortened to "pep," and more recently, someone with lots of energy is said to be "peppy."

Pepper was regarded as extremely hot and dry, a perfect booster for performance in the bedroom: "...as impotence was frigid, so lust was hot..." Pepper in all forms stimulates saliva flow, so it's a perfect choice to "whet" your appetite in more ways than one!

Sexy Nutrients
Black pepper is an excellent source of manganese and a very good source for iron and vitamin K. Its primary active ingredient, piperine, stimulates the taste buds, which alert the stomach to increase hydrochloric acid secretion. The hydrochloric acid facilitates digestion and reduces the production of "windy breezes" not well suited to amorous activity. Pepper also has diuretic properties, the better to keep you from bloating, which can be quite unsexy. What's more, it stimulates the sweating process, giving you a head start on feeling hot to trot!

Rosemary

Lore and Fun Facts
Rosemary is deeply connected with sexuality, with many classic aphrodisiac recipes, love potions and perfumes counting rosemary as a key ingredient. Derived from the Latin *ros marinus*, rosemary translates into "dew of the sea." Aphrodite wore a shawl of rosemary when she rose from the sea, and is still associated with it today.

In certain European countries, bridegrooms received a bouquet of rosemary to ensure "manly virtues" and rosemary flowers adorned the bridal beds to wish the newlyweds nuptial bliss.

Rosemary has long been associated with wedding ceremonies, especially in the Middle Ages. Both bride, groom and even guests were adorned with it, and it became a love charm of sorts. Newlyweds planted a branch of rosemary on their wedding day.

Rosemary was even used to divine the future, as it was grown in separate pots and given the name of a lover-to-be. Whichever grew the fastest and strongest revealed the true love. Rosemary was also stuffed into cloth dolls to attract a lover or ward off illness.

Even Napoleon, that General so short in stature but long in ego, ordered large quantities of rosemary-infused Eau de Cologne to bathe in or splash on himself before romancing his wife. We must assume that he wasn't rejected at the ramparts of her love as he was rejected at the outskirts of Moscow!

Sexy Nutrients

Recent research finds rosemary leads the pack, along with turmeric and Chinese ginger (fingerroot), in significantly reducing the formation of heterocyclic amines (HCAs), the cancer-causing compounds produced when meat is barbecued, grilled, broiled or fried. HCA levels are highest in the blackened part of grilled meats, and hamburger patties are thought to be the biggest culprits. Adding a sexy nutrient like rosemary to meats can lower HCA production by up to 40%. Prostate and breast cancer, along with stomach, lung and pancreatic cancers, are all associated with high levels of HCAs. Grilling and chilling with your lover? Better add some rosemary!

The results of another study suggest that carnosic acid in rosemary may lower the risk of stroke and even Alzheimer's disease, and is a potential anti-cancer agent.

With its sexy ingredients, protective qualities and marvelous aromatic flavor and aroma, the "dew of the sea" should have a special place in your kitchen, though consuming it might lead you to a more romantic room in your home!

Saffron

Lore and Fun Facts

The origins of saffron are not perfectly clear, with scholars split between Chinese and Assyrian beginnings. What is clear is that it is a cultivated—not wild—plant selectively bred by humans from a wild plant.

It is associated with a dizzying number of positive health attributes, having been used as a treatment for everything from depression to battle wounds. Its sexy history includes many references from various cultures, and it remains to this day the most expensive spice by weight in the world.

Ancient Phoenicians gave moon-shaped, saffron-flavored love cakes to their fertility goddess Astoreth to endure reproductive health and crop success. One ancient Greek legend held that eating saffron for a week would render a girl unable to resist a lover. Yet another Arabic sex recipe calls for boiling saffron along with dates, anise, wild carrots, orange blossoms and egg yolks in water mixed with honey and dove blood. I know, it sounded great right up to the dove blood part.

Its use is widespread in ethnic cuisines, from Spanish Paella to French Bouillabaisse to Milanese (Italian) risotto, but is also popular in Asian, Turkish, Pakistani, Indian and Iranian cooking. "I'm just wild about Saffron, and she's just wild about me."

Sexy Nutrients

While saffron has a deep and long history in traditional remedies, modern medicine has revealed, and in some cases confirmed, its healthy benefits. Both the petal and sought-after stamen of saffron have shown potent antidepressant effects in several studies. In fact, a few studies found that 30 milligrams of saffron was just as effective as commonly prescribed fluoxetine (*Prozac*, *Sarafem*) and imipramine (*Tofranil*) for treating mild-to-moderate depression. Other research has uncovered anticarcinogenic (cancer-suppressing) and anti-oxidant-like properties. Very recent studies show that saffron may protect the eyes from the direct effects of bright light and retinal stress, and may help slow down macular degeneration, a very widespread condition among older people resulting initially in the loss of peripheral vision that gets worse over time. So if you want to keep the titillating effect of seeing your lover coming toward you out of the corner of your eye, keep saffron in your spice rack!

Sage

Lore and Fun Facts

Another member of the *labiatae* family, sage (or *salvia officinalis*) was used by the ancient Egyptians as a fertility enhancer. The Romans used it widely for treatment of various ailments, and remained popular throughout the Middle Ages as an antiseptic. It was an ingredient in a popular anti-plague remedy of the day, and sage was one of the "strewing herbs," aromatic plants "strewn" about to cover the nauseating stench of urban life, a problem that would surely dampen lusty pursuits.

Over the centuries sage has been used to treat various menstrual and menopausal symptoms in women. But it is perhaps most respected for its anti-anxiety, memory-enhancing, diuretic, and perspiration-reducing qualities, all of which would be helpful in the bedroom!

"He that would live for aye
Must eat sage in May."
–Old English Proverb

Sexy Nutrients

The name for sage, or salvia, derives from the Latin, *salvere* (to save), which hints at the known healing properties of this delicious herb. Modern studies have identified its anti-sweating effect, and also its uses as an antibiotic, anti-fungal agent, and more.

Research has identified three compounds in sage—flavanoids, phenolic acids, and enzymes—team up for a strong antioxidant impact that prevents cell damage. Another well-designed study determined that sage was effective in managing mild to moderate Alzheimer's disease, a sexy prospect for older folks who still enjoy a healthy romp with their partners!

Thyme

Lore and Fun Facts

Thyme is among the most ancient of human-cultivated plants, most likely originating in the Mediterranean civilization of Greece and Rome. Though thyme is thought to have received its common name in part from Theophrastus, the 3rd century BCE philosopher and naturalist, its name origin isn't clear, and in any case it was already well known and loved by that, well, time.

Ancient Egyptians valued it as a pain reliever, while Greeks appreciated it as an energy booster, purifier and fertility enhancer.

In the Middle Ages Europeans thought it encouraged lust and sexual potency. Even the famous Benedictine monks got in on the act, and thyme is still an ingredient in their decadent liqueur.

Thought to have mind-clarifying properties, thyme was an ingredient of various love potions, including this St. Luke's Day (October 18th) prescription for young maidens:

"Take marigold flowers, a sprig of marjoram, thyme, and a little wormwood; dry them before a fire, rub them to powder, then sift it through a fine piece of lawn; simmer these with a small quantity of virgin honey, in white vinegar, over a slow fire; with this anoint your stomach, breasts, and lips, lying down, and repeat these words thrice:

'St Luke, St. Luke, be kind to me,
In dream let me my true love see!'

This said, hasten to sleep, and in the soft slumbers of night's repose, the very man whom you shall marry shall appear before you."

Today thyme is among the most widely used herbs in the world's cuisines. The herb is a basic ingredient in Middle Eastern, North African, Indian, Caribbean, and the Romance countries of Europe all heavily include thyme.

It's found in *les herbes de Provence* and in *bouquet garni,* and its flavorful character is perhaps best suited to meat, stew, and soup. Many cultures flavor lamb with thyme, while others use it as a table condiment.
Easy to grow, sensual and aromatic, thyme is a must-have staple in your garden, and also in your simple, sexy kitchen!

Sexy Nutrients

Another member of that astonishingly sexy plant family *labiatae*, thyme possesses many of the same properties as its "cousins," basil, rosemary, and oregano. Strong antioxidants all, this family is tough in the fight against cellular damage! The source of this power is typically from flavonoids, in thyme's case including *apigenin, naringenin, luteolin*, and *thymonin*. In addition, thyme's a very good source of manganese, another antioxidant booster.

The primary volatile oil in thyme is thymol, named after the herb, a conspicuously healthy compound with scientific and commercial credentials. Antiseptic and antifungal, thymol is used in a wide variety of natural and processed products, including most famously as the active ingredient in Listerine® mouthwash! Ever use a natural, alcohol-free hand sanitizer? Chances are its active ingredient is thymol.

In studies on aging in rats, thymol has been found to protect and significantly increase the percentage of healthy fats found in cell membranes and other cell structures. In particular, the amount of DHA (docosahexaenoic acid, an omega-3 fatty acid) in brain, kidney, and heart cell membranes was increased after dietary supplementation with thyme. In other studies looking more closely at changes in brains cells themselves, researchers found that the maximum benefits of thyme occurred when the food was introduced very early in the life-cycle of the rats, but was less effective in offsetting the problems in brain cell aging when introduced late in the aging process. So get to nibbling that thyme, and you might just find you're gifted with more time for lovin' on this earth!

The volatile oil components of thyme have also been shown to have antimicrobial activity against a host of different bacteria and fungi. *Staphalococcus aureus, Bacillus subtilis, Escherichia coli* and *Shigella sonnei* are a few of the species against which thyme has been shown to have antibacterial activity.

As we've mentioned, since ancient times, herbs and spices have been used to preserve and protect food from microbes (spoilage). Science has picked up on this, of course, and there are exciting developments on the natural food preservative front. A 2004 study reported in *Food Microbiology* revealed that both thyme and basil can not only prevent microbial contamination, but can actually de-contaminate food as well. A very small amount of essential thyme oil reduced bacteria on lettuce to undetectable levels.

Now, I don't want you to start ignoring good food (or sexual) hygiene, but it may not be a bad idea to include more thyme and basil in your recipes, especially accompanying uncooked, raw foods! Many bacteria are seriously unsexy, and a thyme-infused vinaigrette on that romaine may just help keep your sights set on sensual pursuits rather than on the quickest way to the emergency room!

Turmeric

Lore and Fun Facts
Turmeric is a tropical plant of the ginger family, which grows wild primarily in South and Southeast Asia, and in India. Its aphrodisiac history isn't as detailed as some herbs and spices, but it has been a vital part of Indian ceremonies for thousands of years.

Even today it is used in every part of India during wedding ceremonies and religious ceremonies. In southern India, dried turmeric tuber is an appropriate substitute for the Mangalsustra, or sacred thread of love similar to our wedding rings. In Europe in the Middle Ages it was called Indian Saffron, an inexpensive substitute for that very pricey spice.

Today it is a mainstay in many of the hundreds of varieties of curry, and is used throughout Asia as both a flavoring and a coloring agent. Note: This spice will stain your skin and clothes! So, if your lover fancies you with a natural, golden body paint you can cook in the buff; otherwise, you might want to wear an apron, and not much else, while cooking with turmeric.

Sexy Nutrients
In Ayurvedic medicine, the Indian "alternative" practice meaning "the complete knowledge for a long life," turmeric has been used as an anti-inflammatory agent and treatment for digestive problems. Raw turmeric is thought to strengthen cartilage and bone structure. Turmeric is also used as a topical antiseptic for cuts and bruises.

Western science has determined that turmeric contains the compound *curcumin*, a powerful anti-inflammatory and antioxidant compound that studies have found offers protection against diabetes, cancer, Alzheimer's, and arthritis. Since healthy and sexy go hand in hand, a little turmeric is just what the doctor—or healer—ordered!

Vanilla

Lore and Fun Facts
Vanilla is one of those spices that is a bit difficult to categorize, not because it is vague or that little known about it, but because of its very complexity and long and luxurious history. It is second only to saffron in cost, and there's a richness and decadence to its flavor and aroma that's worthy of the gods.

Native to Central America, vanilla is derived from the seed pod of a tropical orchid, and named by Spanish Conquistadors for its resemblance to the sword sheaths (Sp. *vaina*) or *vanilla*, meaning "little sheath."

Before the Spanish washed out the "pagan" beliefs of the indigenous people in that region, vanilla's legend had a sexy component, albeit a violent one. The orchid originated when a Totonac Princess took off into the woods with her mortal lover. They were captured, naturally, and beheaded, and in the place where their blood touched the ground grew the tropical orchid. Talk about dying for something sweet!

One thing about vanilla: you can't really separate its smell from its flavor. Jean-Paul Guerlain, the famous perfumer, once revealed that all of their successful perfumes included vanilla. Not surprisingly, research has documented its scent helps to trigger erections in men, especially mature men.

In 18th century France, Madame DuBarry, the last mistress of Louis XV, is said to have used vanilla pods "to keep her lovers perpetually ready."

Around the same time, vanilla was the basis of a German impotency "study." It's claimed that all 342 test subjects were "cured," causing not only a furthering of vanilla's sexy reputation, but also no doubt a great deal of smiling and satisfaction among the subjects!

Nowadays vanilla's primary use is in ice cream, though its use in desserts, baking and sweets of many kinds is also widespread. Utterly unique, at once sweet and spicy, deliciously scented and a pleasure for the taste buds, vanilla is one of the sexiest spices available. It's not just for ice cream, anymore!

Sexy Nutrients
Vanilla extract contains small amounts of B-complex group of vitamins such as niacin, pantothenic acid, thiamin, riboflavin and vitamin B-6. This complex of vitamins helps in enzyme synthesis, nervous system function and regulating body metabolism.

This spice also contains small traces of minerals such as calcium, magnesium, potassium, manganese, iron, and zinc. We know the value of these minerals in our health, though the concentrations in vanilla are not large.

In what is perhaps the most interesting research on vanilla and sexual health, it's not the compounds in vanilla reacting in the body that turns us on, but the odor of vanilla acting on our olfactory senses and memory that does it. Research into scents and sexuality has shown that vanilla triggered more erectile response than any other scent in older, mature men ages 55 and up. It also worked for younger men, but not to the same degree as donuts and pizza! Regardless of age, nothing sets a sexy stage like the sweet, spicy smell of vanilla wafting through your kitchen, love nest, or both!

Part I
Tease Me Anytime
(appetizers, soups, salads, quickies)

Introduction

For many people, nothing says "sexy" like a delicious appetizer or some fun little finger food. This may be due to the manner of eating—think fingers—or the intensity of flavor or aroma, the appearance, or shape or texture of certain appetizers.

Webster's Dictionary defines an appetizer as *"a small portion of a tasty food or a drink to stimulate the appetite at the beginning of a meal, or a bit of something that excites a desire for more."* Indeed!

Appetizers are the foreplay of the food world, tantalizing and fun. Their endless varieties and the fact that they lend themselves to experimentation and improvisation make them the ideal partners for sex. Along with your elixir of choice, an appetizer may be all you need or want to get the home fires burning.

It's also true that our busy lives don't always lend themselves to a sit-down dinner, whether due to the prep time, clean up, or the fact that a meal might last one to three hours, cutting into what already may be limited time for other physical pleasures! Please know that, while I encourage you to try to slow down and appreciate both food and sex, I also recognize that "some" is better that "none," and a quickie nibble followed by a quickie tumble might be just right for your needs.

For convenience' sake, the recipes in this sex-ion are those you can enjoy on their own as a prelude to sex or in combination with other recipes, as part of a formal dinner with your lover.

For that reason I've included soups and salads in this section. These mainstays of the American diet are often consumed as appetizers anyway, but are also sexy, and can be enjoyed anytime, even as a complete meal. From the deep down comfort of a savory soup to the varied and sometimes exotic combination of flavors in a great salad, you may be tempted to look no further for your simple, sexy food of choice.

Soups and salads are all-in-one foods, gaining their appeal both by the seemingly limitless combinations of ingredients that give them life, and by their simplicity. Soups of all kinds deserve the sexy label, especially those whose ingredients are sexy to start with, but including those whose aroma, color, or texture is sexy. Soup is comfort food, and comfortable is often sexy. Salads too, allow the distinct flavors of their ingredients to be appreciated on their own, or in delectable combinations in the mouth. Salads are healthy and pleasantly filling without being too much food.

It's also true that smaller portions of food may be better for our bodies. This isn't a health book per se, but it's undeniable that healthy is sexy—and sex is healthy—on so many levels. Whether we eat a bit less to avoid feeling tired afterwards and thus diminish our sex drive, or consciously take better care of ourselves so that we live longer and thus give ourselves more and better years of lovemaking, healthy choices can be sexy choices. Lovemaking itself is physically, mentally, and spiritually healthy, and it could be argued that being in good physical condition creates more and varied opportunities for sexual enjoyment.

My hope for you is that you find both food and sex to be healthy contributors to the quality of your life, and that you enjoy both to their fullest without losing a sense of balance and gentle control over their impact on your well-being.

Survey Secrets: Fresh cut fruit and champagne are an ideal combination for teasing up a bit of sensuality. In my survey, strawberries not only placed #1 in aphrodisiac fruits, but were also the #1 most appealing personal aphrodisiac! Champagne, of course, was the #1 aphrodisiac beverage. If you add chocolate (#2 personal aphrodisiac) and a bit of whipped cream to the mix, you may never leave home!

Eggplant Crostini

A great hors d'oeuvres for an intimate supper or when dining al fresco.
A softer, fruity red wine would be a good accompaniment.

SEXY FOODS: eggplant, onion, garlic, parsley, pepper
2 TO 4 SERVINGS

1 large eggplant (about 1 pound)
2 tablespoons olive oil
1/2 cup finely chopped onion
1 tablespoon finely chopped garlic
Scant 1/3 cup crème fraîche
2 tablespoons chopped fresh parsley
3 tablespoons fresh lemon juice
1/4 teaspoon salt
1/4 teaspoon freshly ground black pepper
1/8 teaspoon Tabasco sauce
4 to 6 sun-dried tomatoes, cut into slivers
Crostini or crackers for serving

1.   Preheat oven to 400 degrees. Wash & dry eggplant and pierce skin
with fork in several places. Place whole eggplant on baking sheet & bake for
about an hour, until skin has blackened & wrinkled and fleshy interior is soft.
Remove from oven, cover with clean kitchen towel, & let cool 5-10 minutes.
2.   While the eggplant is cooling, heat the oil in a medium skillet over
medium heat, and sauté the onion and garlic until softened but not browned,
about 5 minutes. Set aside.
3.   Cut off the stem and then peel the skin from the eggplant. Cut eggplant into large chunks and place in a food processer and pulse to a coarse
purée. Or mash the eggplant with a potato masher in a nonreactive bowl.
4.   Transfer the eggplant purée to a bowl and add the onion-garlic mixture, crème fraiche, and parsley. Stir to blend well.
5.   Add lemon juice, salt, pepper, & Tabasco. Adjust if desired.
6.   Spread dip on crostini & garnish with 2 slivers of sun-dried tomato.

Simple Sexy Kitchen Tip: Reduce the cooking time for the eggplant by using
a microwave. Cut several deep slits in the skin and place the whole eggplant
in a baking dish. Cook on high about 6-8 minutes. Half way through the
cooking time turn the eggplant over. Remove from the microwave and set it
aside, covered, for several minutes before removing the skin.

Aphrodite Says: The Kama Sutra (2nd century, BCE) offers a remedy to
"weakened sexual power" that includes rubbing an eggplant along the length
of the lingam (penis) to produce a "swelling" said to last up to a month!

113

Bagna Cauda (Hot Bath)

With this simple, colorful appetizer, you and your lover dip your own favorite array of raw vegetables into a shared fondue pot of bold, bubbling butter and oil. The amazing flavor of the "bath" comes from the addition of anchovies and garlic.

SEXY FOODS: seafood (anchovies), garlic, a variety of vegetables with aphrodisiac reputations—asparagus, artichoke, carrots, mushrooms, tomatoes, zucchini
SAUCE FOR 8 SERVINGS

1 to 2 cups bite-sized pieces of assorted fresh vegetables per serving, such as thin asparagus; mushrooms with stems (for easy dunking); grape or cherry tomatoes with stems (eat just the juicy red portion!); broccoli and cauliflower florets; red or white cabbage chunks; small carrots; thin green beans; cooked and cooled artichoke leaves; zucchini; yellow crookneck squash; bell peppers
8 tablespoons (1 stick) butter
1/4 cup olive oil
2 large cloves garlic, finely chopped
1 (2-ounce) can flat anchovy fillets, drained and finely chopped
1 fresh baguette, cut on the diagonal into 1/4-inch slices

1.   Wash, dry, and cut the selected vegetables as needed. Attractively arrange them on a large platter or lazy Susan. (If desired, you may prepare the vegetables up to 8 hours in advance; store them in plastic bags or wrap with plastic wrap, and refrigerate. Just before using, sprinkle lightly with water.)
2.   In a fondue pot or similar heatproof pot, mix the butter, oil, garlic, and anchovies. Place the pot on a stove burner, and heat and stir the mixture until it bubbles.
3.   Set the pot over fondue holder with lighted candle or canned heat, such as Sterno. Keep the flame low enough that the mixture does not overheat and burn.
4.   Place the vegetable platter and sliced bread next to the fondue pot.
5.   To eat, use one hand to swirl a piece of vegetable through the hot sauce. In the other hand, hold a piece of bread and use it like a napkin under the vegetable to catch sauce drips as you lift it from the sauce. With repeated use, the bread piece, infused with sauce drippings, becomes another tasty morsel.

Simple Sexy Kitchen Tip: Refrigerate any leftover Bagna Cauda. It can be reheated for a second use, tossed with cooked pasta, or used for a great variation to traditional garlic bread.

Love Skills: Heat up the conversation between you and your lover as you dip raw veggies into a shared, hot bubbly bowl of Bagna Cauda. Take this opportunity to feed each other while brushing up on your flirtatious love talk.

Aphrodite Says: Ever since Aphrodite rose from sea foam, the bounty of the sea has accounted for many of the most revered aphrodisiacs. The sea's vastness, its salty, fertile abundance, and even its mysterious depths contribute both fact and fantasy to the lore. Regardless, the sea's contributions to sexy food are many, varied and swimmingly delicious!

Guacamole

Serve with chips and an assortment of raw vegetables.

SEXY FOODS: avocado, chilies, black pepper, green onion, cumin, cilantro
4 TO 6 SERVINGS

2 cups roughly mashed ripe avocado (about 2 medium)
1/2 cup chopped fresh cilantro leaves
1 teaspoon crushed red chili flakes
1 clove garlic, minced
2 tablespoons fresh lemon juice, or more to taste
4 green onions, finely chopped (include both white and some green parts)
1/4 teaspoon ground cumin
1/8 teaspoon cayenne pepper, optional
1/2 teaspoon salt, or to taste
1 teaspoon freshly ground black pepper, or to taste

1.   In a medium bowl, mix the avocado, cilantro, chili flakes, garlic, lemon juice, green onion, cumin, and cayenne pepper, keeping the mixture somewhat chunky.
2.   Season with salt and pepper.

Simple Sexy Kitchen Tip: If not serving immediately, cover with a piece of plastic wrap placed directly on the surface of the guacamole, and refrigerate. Serve at room temperature.

Love Skills: If you've never tried cooking in the nude, here is your recipe! Give your partner a visual to stimulate the senses and increase his/her sexual appetite. Note: Most Mexican chefs will mash the avocados with their bare hands. Try gently squeezing them yourself!

Lobster Guacamole (or "Lobster Guac")

If your honey loves guacamole, surprise him or her with this special version. It's guaranteed drive you both wild!

SEXY FOODS: lobster, avocado, chili, ginger
1 1/2 CUPS, 2 GENEROUS STARTER SERVINGS

1 cup diced avocado (about 1 large)
2 tablespoons fresh lime juice (about 1 to 2 limes)
1/2 teaspoon finely chopped fresh cilantro
1/2 teaspoon finely chopped red onion
1/2 teaspoon seeded, minced fresh Anaheim chili
1/8 teaspoon salt
2 to 3 grindings black pepper, or to taste
2 ounces cooked lobster meat, chopped
Pickled ginger slices (gari) for garnishing
Sesame rice crackers

1.   In a medium, nonreactive bowl, combine the avocado, lime juice, cilantro, onion, and chili, and carefully mix together with a spoon.
2.   Add the salt and several grindings of pepper, or to taste, mix gently, then fold in the lobster.
3.   Serve in chilled large martini glasses and garnish with a little of the pickled ginger on the rim of each glass. Or use other decorative bowls and garnish with a few pieces of ginger in the center of each serving. Accompany with the crackers.

Simple Sexy Kitchen Tip: If the guacamole isn't finished in one sitting, place a piece of plastic wrap directly on the surface, cover tightly, and refrigerate. Then finish it up within 24 hours.

Love Skills: One of the best "tools" in the seduction kit is surprise. If your lover loves guacamole, he or she is liable to do back flips when you serve this ridiculously sexy dish.

Grand Marnier Orange Spice Pâté

SEXY FOODS: chicken livers, onion, spices, liqueur
ABOUT 2 CUPS, 4 TO 6 SERVINGS

1/2 pound fresh chicken livers
1/4 cup sliced yellow onion
1 small clove garlic, minced
1/4 California bay leaf or 1/2 Turkish bay leaf
1/2 teaspoon salt
1/2 cup water
12 tablespoons (1 1/2 sticks) butter, cut up
1 teaspoon Chinese five-spice powder
2 tablespoons Grand Marnier liqueur
Orange zest strips or orange blossoms for garnishing
Fresh French bread, sliced

1.   In a small heavy saucepan, combine the livers, onion, garlic, bay leaf, salt, and water. Bring to a boil, cover, reduce heat to low, and simmer for 10 minutes.
2.   Drain well, discarding the liquid. Discard the bay leaf and transfer the solid ingredients to a food processor.
3.   Add the butter, a few pieces at a time, pulsing to incorporate after each addition. Add the five-spice powder and liqueur, and process until completely incorporated and mixture is smooth and creamy.
4.   Place the mixture in a serving dish or mold, and smooth the top with a spatula. Cover tightly with plastic wrap and refrigerate for at least 24 hours before serving.
5.   Let sit at room temperature for 30 to 45 minutes before serving. Garnish top of the pâté with crisscrossed orange zest strips or orange blossoms. Serve with French bread slices.

Simple Sexy Kitchen Tip: This is a wonderful make-ahead dish for a special occasion or a picnic . . . or a midnight snack. The pâté can be kept tightly covered and refrigerated for up to 5 days.

Deviled Eggs

SEXY FOODS: egg, celery, green onion, parsley, pepper
2 SERVINGS

5 large eggs, at room temperature
1 tablespoon minced green onion (white part only)
1 tablespoon finely chopped red sweet pepper
1 tablespoon finely chopped celery
3 tablespoons mayonnaise
1 tablespoon sweet hot mustard
1/4 teaspoon salt
1/8 teaspoon white pepper
Chopped fresh parsley, paprika, minced anchovy, or capers for garnishing

1.   Place the eggs in a non-aluminum saucepan just large enough to hold all the eggs without touching. Cover with cold water to 1 inch above the eggs.
2.   Tightly cover the pan and place over medium heat. Bring the water just to a boil, then immediately remove the pan from heat and let sit for 30 minutes.
3.   Transfer the eggs to a bowl of ice water and let cool for 15 minutes, adding more ice as necessary.
4.   Peel the eggs and cut in half lengthwise. Remove the yolks carefully and place in a medium bowl. Set the eight best egg white halves aside for stuffing and discard the remaining two or reserve for another use.
5.   With the back of a fork, mash the yolks, and then add the onion, sweet pepper, celery, mayonnaise, mustard, salt, and white pepper. Mash and mix with the fork until all ingredients are thoroughly combined. Stir to a smooth, fluffy paste.
6.   Gently spoon the yolk mixture into the egg white halves. Garnish and serve immediately.

Love Skills: Many people enjoy stripping. What better time for a little prelude to the main course than you shedding some layers for your partner? Let go of the long day and appreciate your body and hard work. Stripping to some music is a great way to get in a little fitness, relieve a ton of tension, and shift to an erotic mood.

Spicy Tuna Sushi Rolls

SEXY FOODS: tuna, chili sauce, seaweed, rice
4 ROLLS OR 24 PIECES

2 cups cooked brown short-grain rice or sushi rice, cooked according to
package directions, at room temperature
1/4 cup unseasoned rice vinegar
1 teaspoon sugar
Pinch of salt
4 tablespoons mayonnaise
1 teaspoon Sriracha or other Asian hot chili sauce
1/2 pound very fresh sushi-grade ahi tuna, cut into rough 1/4-inch cubes
4 sheets nori (dried seaweed)
2 teaspoons white sesame seeds
A bamboo sushi rolling mat
Soy sauce for dipping
Pickled ginger, optional

1.   In shallow glass or pottery dish, spread cooked rice in an even layer.
2.   In a small nonreactive saucepan, combine the vinegar, sugar, and
salt, and warm over very low heat, just until sugar dissolves. Let cool to
room temperature.
3.   Sprinkle the vinegar mixture evenly over the rice and toss with a
spatula to mix well.
4.   In a medium bowl, mix the mayonnaise and chili sauce, then lightly
mix in the tuna; set aside.
5.   For each of the sushi rolls: Place a nori sheet on the bamboo rolling
mat. Spread nori evenly with 1/2 cup of sushi rice, leaving a 1/2-inch margin
on the edge away from you. Sprinkle with 1/2 teaspoon of sesame seeds.
Place one quarter of the tuna mixture lengthwise on the rice. Roll up the
bamboo mat, pressing forward to shape the sushi into a cylinder. Press the
bamboo mat firmly and remove it from the sushi.
6.   Cut each roll into 6 pieces. Serve with soy sauce for dipping and
ginger on the side.

Simple Sexy Kitchen Tip: Cutting sushi calls for a very sharp knife. After
each cut, wipe the knife blade with a damp cloth before the next cut.

Sexy Survey Secrets: Sushi ranks in the top ten most recognized aphrodisiac
foods, and #6 on the free-choice personal favorite list. It seems young people
are especially familiar with sushi's reputation, while older folks were less
likely to have heard of its sexy qualities.

Melon and Prosciutto Wraps

In my opinion, this is one of the sexiest light meals ever! Use fancy picks to feed the melon balls to each other.

SEXY FOODS: melon
2 SERVINGS

1/2 ripe cantaloupe, seeded
1/2 ripe honeydew melon, seeded
9 thin slices prosciutto de Parma (dry-cured Italian ham)
3-ounce piece Romano cheese

1.   Using a melon baller, scoop the flesh of each melon into balls. Refrigerate, covered, until ready to use.
2.   With a sharp knife, cut the prosciutto slices into 2- to 2 1/2-inch lengths, or pieces long enough to wrap a melon ball. Throughout the process, keep the prosciutto covered with plastic wrap to prevent it from drying out.
3.   Position a melon ball in the middle of a slice of prosciutto, fold over all the sides of the prosciutto, enclosing the melon. Place, seam side down, on a serving dish and cover with plastic wrap. Repeat with the remaining prosciutto pieces and melon balls. Refrigerate, tightly covered, until ready to serve.
4.   To serve, use a vegetable peeler to shave long slices of cheese onto a serving platter. Arrange the melon balls over the bed of cheese.

Love Skills: No peeking! Try covering your partner's eyes before seating him or her at the table with a blindfold. Sensually feed your lover each delicious morsel and see what senses become aroused!

Waldorf Salad

I love this variation of the classic salad. Nourishing, satisfying, light and refreshing...a great preamble!

SEXY FOODS: apple, dates, walnuts, celery, cinnamon, honey
2 TO 4 SERVINGS

1/2 cup (2 ounces) walnut halves
1/2 cup plain nonfat yogurt
2 tablespoons reduced-fat mayonnaise
1 teaspoon honey
1/2 teaspoon grated lemon zest
1/4 teaspoon freshly ground black pepper
1/4 teaspoon ground cinnamon, or more to taste
2 large crisp apples, such as Fuji or Gala
1 tablespoon fresh lemon juice
2 ribs celery
1/3 cup chilled pitted dates
Lettuce leaves, optional
Ground cinnamon for garnishing

1.   Preheat an oven to 350°F.
2.   Spread the nuts on a baking sheet and toast for 8 minutes. Let cool. Break the halves into small pieces and set aside.
3.   Meanwhile, in a medium bowl, mix the yogurt, mayonnaise, honey, lemon zest, pepper, and cinnamon. Set aside.
4.   Wash and dry apples, halve and core, or use apple corer, leaving skin on. Cut into 3/4-inch pieces, sprinkle with lemon juice, and add to the bowl.
5.   Halve the celery ribs lengthwise then cut into 1/2-inch slices. Chop the cold dates into 1/4-inch pieces. Add the celery and dates to the bowl.
6.   Fold the fruit and celery into the dressing, stirring carefully. Cover and refrigerate if not serving immediately.
7.   Just before serving, add the walnuts and toss well. (For two servings, toss half of the walnuts into half of the apple mixture.)
8.   Arrange the lettuce leaves, if using, on salad plates, and place a salad serving on each. Sprinkle with additional cinnamon if desired.

Simple Sexy Kitchen Tip: Although they grow only in hot climates, dates are easier to chop when cold.

Aphrodite Says: Honey is used in numerous recipes in both the *The Perfumed Garden* and in *The Kama Sutra*, in some cases to ward off premature ejaculation, and in others as a topical application on the penis to help with erectile dysfunction.

Marinated Mushrooms

The perfect accompaniment to a light picnic, perhaps including some cold leftover chicken or some sandwiches.

SEXY FOODS: mushrooms, onions   *   4 TO 6 SERVINGS

2/3 cup tarragon vinegar or tarragon wine vinegar
1/2 cup canola oil
1 tablespoon sugar
2 tablespoons water
1 1/2 teaspoons salt
Dash of Tabasco sauce
1 medium onion (about 4 ounces), sliced into rings
1 pound fresh white mushrooms, sliced

1.   In a large, nonreactive dish, mix the vinegar, oil, sugar, water, salt, and Tabasco sauce.
2.   Separate the onion rings and add onions and mushrooms to the dish.
3.   Mix gently, cover, and refrigerate. Let marinate for 12 to 24 hours before serving.

Love Skills: If you can't find a private picnic spot outdoors, throw a blanket on the living room floor and have at it!

*****

Watermelon–Pineapple Salsa

SEXY FOODS: watermelon, pineapple, onion, mint, chilies, honey, cilantro
ABOUT 2 1/2 CUPS, 4 TO 6 SERVINGS

2 cups 1/2-inch-diced watermelon
2 cups (12 ounces) 1/2-inch-diced fresh pineapple
1/3 cup chopped red onion
2 tablespoons coarsely chopped fresh cilantro
2 tablespoons coarsely chopped fresh mint
1/2 to 1 jalapeño chili, seeded and minced
1 1/2 tablespoons fresh lime juice
1 tablespoon honey

1.   Gently mix all ingredients and chill for at least 1 hour, or up 4 hours, before serving.
2.   Serve with Jamaican Chicken Breasts or with tortilla chips.

Aphrodite Says: A great finger food, watermelons have the added sexy distinction of containing seeds which are "spit" by blowing them hard off the tongue between pursed lips. Their super sweet, yet delicate flavor is perfectly suited to the sexy, slurpy, dripping summertime fun food they have become in the US and elsewhere.

Ceviche

An absolutely classic love food packed with libido-enhancing ingredients and enough flavor to keep the love fires burning long and hot.

SEXY FOODS: scallops (seafood), chilies, onions, tomatoes, olives, cilantro, fortified wine
2 TO 3 SERVINGS

3/4 pound scallops or mild fish, cut into thin slices
6 tablespoons fresh lime juice
2 tablespoons dry white vermouth
1/4 cup minced red onion
1 large vine-ripened tomato, juiced, seeded, and cut into pieces (2/3 cup)
1/2 teaspoon salt
1/8 teaspoon dried leaf oregano
2 tablespoons olive oil
1/4 cup sliced California ripe olives, drained well
1 canned green chili, minced
1/2 cup chopped fresh cilantro
Avocado, canned green chili strips, pimiento, or chopped cilantro for garnish
Tortilla chips, optional

1.   In medium saucepan, bring just enough water to cover scallops to low boil. Add scallops. Poach at low simmer for about 1 minute; do not overcook. Immediately remove scallops from the pan and let cool. Discard water.
2.   In a medium, wide, nonreactive dish, place the scallops in one layer.
3.   Add the lime juice and gently stir to coat scallops. Cover and refrigerate for 2 hours, stirring gently after 1 hour.
4.   Add the vermouth, onion, tomato, salt, oregano, oil, olives, and chili to the mixture. Stir carefully to mix, and refrigerate for 2 hours more to allow flavors to blend.
5.   Just before serving, stir in the cilantro.
6.   Garnish as desired and serve very cold with tortilla chips on the side.

Aphrodite Says: Both olives and olive oil were prized by the early Greeks and Romans. Pliny held that the secret to a happy love life was wine "for the inside" and olive oil "for the outside." Members of the Roman army believed olive oil made their limbs supple. We can only imagine where else those randy Romans used it.

Simple Sexy Survey: Chilies. These humble pods of potency have an educated following. Survey respondents possessing graduate degrees were significantly more likely to have heard of the chilies' reputation for sexiness than people with less education.

Kokoda

Kokoda is a sexy, Asian version of Ceviche. Try it when you're feeling a bit adventurous. You might find it helps bring a bit of adventure and exploration to your love life!

SEXY FOODS: seafood, coconut, green and red onion, chilies, tomato
2 TO 3 SERVINGS

10 ounces very fresh, boneless, skinless raw white fish, such as halibut, cod, mahi-mahi, or red snapper, cut into 1-inch cubes (or use a mix of white fish and small, very fresh, raw shrimp or scallops)
3 to 4 tablespoons freshly squeezed lime juice
1/2 medium red onion, chopped
1 serrano or other hot chili, finely chopped
1/2 red bell pepper, chopped
1 clove garlic, pressed
1 large green onion, including green part, finely sliced
1 medium tomato, seeded, juiced, and diced (about a heaping 1/2 cup)
3/4 cup canned unsweetened coconut milk
1/4 teaspoon salt, or more to taste
1/8 teaspoon white pepper, or more to taste
Large leaves Boston or red lettuce, 1 for each serving
Lime slices for garnishing
Additional chopped fresh hot chili, optional

1.   Place the fish in a nonreactive dish with a lid or in a zip-style plastic bag. Add the lime juice and mix until the fish is well coated.
2.   Cover the dish or seal the bag, and refrigerate for at least 4 hours, or overnight, stirring or turning at least once while the fish marinates.
3.   Add all the remaining ingredients and carefully mix together until well blended.
4.   Line serving plates with lettuce, and spoon each serving of kokoda onto lettuce.
5.   Garnish with lime slices. Serve a side dish of chopped fresh hot chili if you like things really hot!

Simple Sexy Kitchen Tip: For this special, sexy treat, use only the freshest seafood. If you have any concerns about eating seafood "cooked" in this manner, whether it's a general concern or because you are pregnant or have a medical condition, please consult with your health care provider. If only part of the kokoda is served, drain the liquid into a separate container. Immediately refrigerate the liquid and solid parts, separately, tightly covered; recombine and use the next day.

Chilled Asparagus with Lemon Sauce

This recipe needs just a few simple ingredients and a deft hand. Egg yolk and lemon complement the taste of the asparagus.

SEXY FOODS: asparagus, egg
2 TO 3 SERVINGS

1 1/2 pounds asparagus, tough ends removed, spears tied in a bundle
1 tablespoon cornstarch
2 egg yolks
2 tablespoons fresh lemon juice
Salt to taste
1/4 teaspoon sugar, optional

1.   Set up a large bowl half full of ice and cold water.
2.   Bring a large pot of lightly salted water to a boil and cook the bundled asparagus until just tender-crisp, 5 to 7 minutes.
3.   Drain the asparagus, reserving 1 scant cup of the cooking liquid. Immediately immerse the asparagus in the ice bath to arrest further cooking. Drain the asparagus and set aside.
4.   In a small saucepan, mix the cornstarch with a tablespoon or two of the reserved cooking liquid and blend well. Stir in the remaining cooking liquid and bring to a boil, stirring constantly. Reduce the heat to low and cook until the sauce thickens slightly. Remove from heat and allow to cool slightly.
5.   In a small bowl, beat the egg yolks thoroughly with the lemon juice then gradually stir into the cooled sauce.
6.   Cook the sauce over very low heat, stirring constantly, until fairly thick. Be careful not to overheat the sauce or it may curdle. When thickened, remove from heat and continue stirring for 1 minute.
7.   Season to taste with salt, and if you prefer a slightly less tangy sauce, stir in the sugar. Allow the sauce to cool slightly.
8.   Stir cooled sauce and drizzle over the cooked asparagus. Cover asparagus and remaining sauce separately. Refrigerate both for at least 2 hours.
9.   To serve, attractively arrange asparagus on individual plates and serve the lemon sauce alongside.

Aphrodite Says: There's an old Roman saying, "As quick as cooking asparagus," meaning something accomplished rapidly. And you've got to appreciate its prolific growth: Some will grow 10" per day and must be harvested twice a day! Hey honey, about we cook up some asparagus over our lunch hour, and then again for dinner?
Survey Secrets Quote: "My sexiest food experience was being hand fed asparagus by a tall, thin naked lady. Wow! That sounds almost bisexual."

Gravlax (Cured Salmon) with Mustard Sauce

I like to serve moist dark pumpernickel or another rye bread or crackers with the salmon. Gravlax can also be served on blinis with a little sour cream.

SEXY FOODS: salmon (seafood), pepper, dill, honey
4 SERVINGS

Salmon

3/4 pound frozen, skin-on salmon fillet
1/2 cup sugar
1/4 cup kosher salt
1 tablespoon white peppercorns, crushed
1 large bunch fresh dill, chopped (use entire plant except root)

Sauce

1 tablespoon sweet-hot mustard
1/2 teaspoon Dijon mustard
3/4 teaspoon honey
3/4 teaspoon cold espresso
2 1/4 teaspoons white wine vinegar
Pinch of salt
Pinch of freshly ground black pepper
6 tablespoons canola oil
1/4 cup chopped fresh dill

1.   To cure the salmon: Thaw the fish in the refrigerator. Remove any small bones from the fillet.
2.   In a small bowl, mix the sugar, salt, and peppercorns. Working over a large cookie sheet or tray, pat some of the sugar mixture onto the salmon on both sides. Then pat the chopped dill onto both sides.
3.   Put the fish in a large zip-style plastic bag. Sprinkle in any remaining dry rub and dill, covering both sides of the fish well. Seal the bag.
4.   Lay the bag in a flat dish in the refrigerator, and let the salmon cure for 1 1/2 to 2 days, turning the bag from time to time to thoroughly coat all sides of the fish with the accumulating liquid.
5.   To make the sauce: In a medium bowl, whisk together both mustards, honey, espresso, vinegar, salt, and pepper. Gradually whisk in the oil, emulsifying the sauce. Stir in the dill.
6.   Cover and refrigerate for at least 4 hours, or up to 24 hours, to allow the flavors to blend.
7.   When ready to serve, remove the gravlax from the bag and scrape off seasonings.
8.   Slice the salmon on the bias into thin slices. Serve with the mustard sauce.

Simple Sexy Kitchen Tip: Any leftover gravlax can be refrigerated, tightly wrapped, for up to 1 week. When chopped, it makes a delicious addition scrambled eggs . . . as part of a luxurious Champagne breakfast.

Survey Secret: According to my data, people who report having sex 2-4 times a week are significantly more likely to select salmon from a list of aphrodisiac foods.

Aphrodite Says: In the 19th century, a provocatively titled American cookbook, *How to Keep a Husband*, provides a "salmon en papillotte" recipe that calls for little more than salt, pepper, and a nice sautéing of the fish in butter. The power of the salmon spoke for itself, as this anonymous poem suggests:

Old impotent Alden from Walden
Ate salmon to heat him to scaldin'
*   'Twas just the ticket,*
*   To stiffen his wicket,*
This salmon of Amorous Alden.

Vietnamese Marinated Shrimp

SEXY FOODS: shrimp, garlic, chili flakes, mint, green onion, cilantro
2 TO 4 APPETIZER SERVINGS

1/2 teaspoon minced fresh garlic
2 tablespoons whole fresh cilantro leaves
2 tablespoons whole fresh mint leaves
2 tablespoons minced green onion (white part only)
2 tablespoons canola or other mild vegetable oil
2 tablespoons Asian fish sauce (see Simple Sexy Kitchen Tip)
1/4 cup fresh lemon juice
4 teaspoons sugar
1/4 teaspoon crushed red chili flakes
1/2 pound peeled, cooked medium-large shrimp
Whole leaves of Boston lettuce or Belgium endive

1.   In a medium, wide, nonreactive dish, mix the garlic, herbs, green
onion, oil, fish sauce, lemon juice, sugar, and chili flakes.
2.   Gentle mix in the shrimp, then spread out to one layer.
3.   Cover the dish tightly with plastic wrap and refrigerate for at least 4
hours, or up to 12 hours. Stir the shrimp once or twice while marinating.
4.   When ready to serve, drain the shrimp well. Arrange them on the
greens so that you can eat the dish as fun "finger food." Just fold the leaves
over the shrimp—no utensils needed. Or, spear the shrimp with picks and
arrange on a bed of lettuce.

Simple Sexy Kitchen Tip: Asian fish sauce is available in Asian markets or
the specialty section of most supermarkets. Called nuoc mam in Vietnam and
nam pla in Thailand, both are made with water, salt, and a Southeast Asian
species of anchovy. For best quality, look for a label that reads nuoc mam
nhi, which means that it comes from the first draining of liquid. Golden Boy
and Squid Brand are especially good.

Aphrodite Says: More "shrimp" tales! One of my participants wrote fondly
of eating shrimp in bed while making love, and in the Caribbean, some locals
eat them live while doing so!

Survey Secrets: Shrimp were particular favorites for the under 50 participants, with one in four including shrimp in their top five favorite sexy
seafood choices. When asked why, taste and manner of eating were most
often cited as their reasons.

Vichyssoise with Caviar

SEXY FOODS: caviar, leek, cucumber, pepper, chives
4 TO 5 SERVINGS

4 tablespoons (1/2 stick) butter
2 large leeks, white part and some tender green part, cleaned, coarsely chopped
1/2 medium onion, coarsely chopped
2 medium thin-skinned potatoes, peeled and cut into chunks
3 cups homemade or canned beef or chicken stock
1/2 English cucumber, peeled and cut into chunks
1/2 teaspoon salt, or to taste, depending on whether you used unsalted stock
1/2 cup plain nonfat yogurt
1/2 cup sour cream
1/4 teaspoon white pepper, or to taste
Pinch of freshly ground nutmeg, or more to taste
1 1/2 tablespoons red or black caviar, or to taste
Whole chives for garnishing

1.   In stockpot over low heat, melt butter. Cook the leeks and onion, stirring frequently, for about 10 minutes, or until wilted and soft but not brown.
2.   Add the potatoes, stock, cucumber, and salt. Bring to a boil, reduce the heat, and simmer, partially covered, for about 25 to 30 minutes until potatoes are very tender. Uncover and let cool.
3.   In food processor or blender, purée leek and potato mixture in batches until smooth and no lumps remain. Transfer each batch to a large bowl.
4.   Before transferring the last batch, add yogurt, sour cream, white pepper, and nutmeg, & blend just until ingredients are well combined. Pour into the bowl and mix well. Adjust the seasoning with salt and pepper to taste. Cover the bowl with plastic wrap, and refrigerate the soup until well chilled.
5.   Serve the soup in individual wide bowls. Place 1 to 2 teaspoons of caviar in the center of each serving, and garnish with chives.

Survey Secrets Results and Quote: 26% of participants put caviar on their top five sexy seafood favorites! Yet it's clearly for special occasions. A 35 year-old male survey participant noted: "My partner surprised me with 4 ounces of beluga caviar for my birthday. When I arrived home from work, candles were lit, music was playing... and caviar was well-chilled and ready!"

Aphrodite Says: After Alexander the Great brought Beluga caviar to the west, Romans so lusted for it, they had their servants bring live sturgeon from the Caspian Sea, while Greeks began their "cocktail" parties (aka orgies) with a plate of hors d'oeuvres including caviar, oysters & roasted grasshoppers.

Velvety Asparagus Soup

The optional garnish for this sublime soup adds tasty, sexy visual appeal to the soup. Include it for a special occasion or if cooking together with your lover.

SEXY FOODS: asparagus, leek, potato, white pepper, spirits (fortified wine)
2 GENEROUS MAIN-DISH SERVINGS

Soup

2 pounds asparagus
2 tablespoons butter
1 tablespoon vegetable oil
3/4 cup chopped leeks, white part and a little of the green
5 1/2 cups water
2 teaspoons salt
1/3 cup chopped, peeled, white boiling potato
1/2 cup dry white vermouth
1/2 cup half-and-half
1/2 teaspoon white pepper, or more to taste

Garnish, optional

4 spears asparagus
Vegetable oil, for frying
1/2 cup Keebler Club cracker crumbs
1 egg

1.   To make the soup: Cut off and discard the bottom 1/2 inch of asparagus spears. Using a vegetable peeler, remove the scales and a bit of the tough outer layer of the stalks. Cut off the top 3 to 4 inches; set the tips and lower portions aside separately.

2.   In a large, heavy soup pot over medium heat, melt the butter and add the oil. Sauté the leeks until softened but not browned, about 3 to 5 minutes.

3.   In another large pot, bring the water to a rapid boil. Add the salt and reserved lower portions of asparagus stalks. Adjust heat and cook at a slow boil for five minutes, uncovered.

4.   Reserving the liquid, remove the asparagus stalks and add them to the leeks along with the chopped potato.

5.   Cover the mixture and cook over low heat while you complete the next step.

6.   Bring the reserved cooking water back to a boil. Add the asparagus tips and boil slowly, uncovered, for about 5 minutes, or until just tender. Remove immediately from heat. Drain the asparagus tips and set aside, again reserving the cooking liquid.

7.   Add the cooking liquid and vermouth to the leek mixture and simmer, partially covered, until the asparagus stalks are very tender, about 25 minutes. Stir in the half-and-half and remove pot immediately from heat.

8.   Working in small batches, add some of the soup mixture with the asparagus stalks plus some of the reserved asparagus tips to a food processor or blender and blend at high speed until very smooth. Transfer to a warm soup tureen or other covered container. Continue until all the soup is blended. Add the white pepper and additional salt if desired. Keep warm until ready to serve.

9.   To make the garnish, if using: Snap off and discard the asparagus ends where they naturally break, rinse the spears, and dry thoroughly.

10.   In a pot just wide enough to accommodate the asparagus, add oil to a depth of 3 inches and heat to 375°F.

11.   In an oblong dish long enough to hold the asparagus, whisk the egg to mix yolk and white well. Spread the cracker crumbs on a plate.

12.   Dip each asparagus spear in egg and then coat with cracker crumbs.

13.   Fry the asparagus in the hot oil, removing when nicely browned, about 2 minutes. Drain on paper towels.

14.   Ladle the soup into individual, warmed bowls and garnish with 1 or 2 fried asparagus, suggestively placed across the upper edge of each bowl.

Simple Sexy Kitchen Tip: Store any leftover soup in the refrigerator for 2 to 3 days.

Aphrodite Says: In *Culpeper's Complete Herbal* (1652), Nicholas Culpeper suggests, "A decoction of asparagus roots boiled in wine and being taken fasting several mornings together, stirreth up bodily lust in man or woman, whatever some have written to the contrary."

Cold Fresh Strawberry Soup

SEXY FOODS: strawberries, white wine, nutmeg
2 SERVINGS

1 pint fresh strawberries, washed, hulled, and quartered
1/3 cup sugar
1/4 cup sour cream
1/4 cup plain yogurt
2/3 cup half-and-half
1/3 cup Riesling or other fruity white wine
1/2 lime
Freshly grated nutmeg
2 thin slices lime
1 fresh strawberry, washed, hulled, and sliced lengthwise, for garnishing

1.	Purée the strawberries and sugar in a blender.
2.	To remove seeds, pour the purée through a fine-mesh sieve into a chilled bowl. Set aside.
3.	In a small bowl, whisk together the sour cream and yogurt until well combined. Whisk in the half-and-half to blend thoroughly. Whisk in the wine.
4.	Whisk the cream mixture into the strawberry purée until thoroughly blended. The soup can be made ahead to this point then refrigerated for up to 12 hours.
5.	To serve, pour into chilled cups. Add a squeeze of lime juice and a grating of nutmeg to each cup.
6.	Garnish each serving with slices of lime and strawberry.

Survey Secrets: In my survey of aphrodisiac knowledge and preferences in the US, I found interesting differences between what foods respondents identified as having a sexy reputation, what they chose as their personal favorites from a list, and what they preferred "free choice" without any list or suggestions. The overall winner, however, placing first in two categories and second in one category, was strawberries! (Reputation: 62%; preference chosen from list: 72%; free choice: 2nd place)

Aphrodite Says: During the medieval era of courtly love, strawberries figured prominently as an unabashed flirtatious signal that meant "you intoxicate me with delight" and "you are delicious." In art and literature, the strawberry was usually a symbol of sensuality and earthly desire. The fruit was regarded as an aphrodisiac of the highest quality, due to its prolific number of tiny "seeds."

Spicy Black Bean Soup

SEXY FOODS: bean, avocado, chilies, garlic, onion
2 MAIN-DISH SERVINGS

Soup
1 1/2 tablespoons olive oil
1/2 cup chopped onion
2 large cloves garlic, finely chopped
2 (15-ounce) cans black beans, with their liquid
1/2 cup Mexican salsa verde (green chili sauce)
1/4 teaspoon salt, or to taste
1/2 teaspoon freshly ground black pepper, or to taste

Garnishes
Guacamole chopped fresh cilantro, red salsa, chopped onion, sour cream or
Mexican crema, grated queso añejo or Cotija or cheddar

1.   In a large soup pot, heat the oil over medium-high heat and sauté the
onion, stirring occasionally, until soft and golden, about 3 to 5 minutes.
2.   Add the garlic and sauté, stirring constantly, until softened but not
browned, about 1 1/2 to 2 minutes.
3.   Add the beans and their liquid, and bring to a boil over high heat.
Reduce heat and simmer for 5 minutes to blend the flavors.
4.   Stir in the salsa verde and remove from heat. Season to taste with salt
and pepper.
5.   Let cool slightly. Then, working in batches, transfer the soup to a
food processor or blender, filling just half full to avoid spattering the hot
liquid, and purée the soup until smooth. Or, use an immersion blender to
purée the soup in the pot.
6.   Serve the soup in warmed soup bowls. Accompany with side dishes
filled with garnishes of your choice.

Simple Sexy Kitchen Tip: If you love voluptuous, smooth soups and other
blended foods, investing in an immersion blender saves hassle, prep time,
and clean-up time (since there's no need to transfer food to a blender)... and
lets you direct your attention to sexier things on the agenda!

Crab Cakes with Herb Salad

SEXY FOODS: seafood (crab), onion, cilantro, egg
4 STARTER SERVINGS, OR A NICE, LIGHT "NOONER"

Vinaigrette
1/2 cup mild salad oil, such as canola
1/4 cup fresh lemon juice
1 tablespoon minced green onion
1 tablespoon minced fresh dill
1 tablespoon minced fresh tarragon
1 tablespoon minced fresh cilantro
1/2 teaspoon Dijon mustard
Salt and freshly ground black pepper

Crab Cakes
2 tablespoons mayonnaise
1 large egg
1 tablespoon fresh lemon juice
1 1/2 teaspoons finely grated lemon zest
1 1/2 teaspoons Dijon mustard
2 tablespoons minced green onions
2 teaspoons minced fresh cilantro
2 teaspoons minced fresh dill
2 teaspoons minced fresh tarragon
1/8 teaspoon freshly ground black pepper
1 cup panko (Japanese breadcrumbs)
1/2 pound crabmeat, such as blue or Dungeness
1 tablespoon butter
1 to 2 tablespoons vegetable oil

Salad
5-ounce container herb salad mix
Fresh herb sprigs, such as cilantro, dill, tarragon, for garnishing
Lemon wedges for garnishing

1.   To make the vinaigrette: In a small bowl, whisk together all vinaigrette ingredients except salt and pepper.
2.   Season to taste with salt and pepper. Set aside.
3.   To prepare the crab cakes: Line a baking sheet with waxed paper and set aside.

4.   In a large bowl, whisk together the mayonnaise, egg, lemon juice and zest, mustard, onions, cilantro, dill, tarragon, and pepper until thoroughly blended.

5.   Using your fingers to find and remove any remaining pieces of shell and cartilage, sort through the crabmeat and break it up a bit, then add the crab to the mayonnaise mixture.

6.   Sprinkle half of the panko into the mixture, and mix in. Let stand 10 minutes.

7.   Spread the remaining panko in a wide, shallow dish.

8.   Using a scant 1/4 cup of the crab mixture for each, form 8 crab patties, about 2 inches in diameter. Press both sides of each patty into the panko to coat well then transfer patties to the lined baking sheet. Cover and chill for at least one hour, or up to 24 hours.

9.   To finish and serve the dish: In a large heavy skillet, melt half of the butter and oil over medium-high heat.

10.   Add the crab cakes and cook until golden on both sides, about 2 to 3 minutes per side, adding more oil as needed. Cook in batches if necessary so as not to crowd the pan.

11.   Meanwhile, to make the salad: In a large bowl, toss the herb salad mix with 1/4 cup of the vinaigrette. Arrange on individual serving plates.

12.   Top with the hot crab cakes and garnish each serving with herb sprigs and lemon wedges. Serve the remaining vinaigrette on the side.

Simple Sexy Kitchen Tip: The vinaigrette can be made ahead 24 hours, covered, and refrigerated. Bring to room temperature before serving.

Curry Soup

This soup is simple to prepare and will heat you up. Its 30- to 40-minute simmering time lends itself to sexy intermezzo moments.

SEXY FOODS: curry (a blend of aphrodisiac spices), onion, zucchini, onion, garlic
6 SERVINGS

2 1/2 cups low-fat evaporated milk
2 cups reduced-sodium chicken broth or stock (I like Perfect Addition unsalted frozen broth.)
2 cloves garlic
1/2 medium onion, chopped (about 1/2 cup)
1/2 large green bell pepper, cored and cut in chunks (about 3/4 cup)
1/2 large sweet yellow pepper, cored and cut in chunks (about 3/4 cup)
1/2 large sweet red pepper, cored and cut in chunks (about 3/4 cup)
1 medium-large zucchini, cut in chunks (about 2 cups)
1/2 cup broccoli florets
1/2 cup cauliflower florets
1/2 cup quartered white mushrooms (about 1 1/2 ounces)
1/2 Russet potato, peeled and cut in chunks
1 to 2 tablespoons Madras curry powder
2 teaspoons salt, or less if using salted chicken broth
1/8 teaspoon white pepper, or more to taste
6 to 8 ounces cooked chicken or crab pieces, optional, warmed

1.   In soup pot, combine evaporated milk, broth, garlic, and vegetables.
2.   Stir in the curry powder, salt, and pepper, and bring to a boil.
3.   Reduce heat, cover, and simmer for 30 to 40 minutes, or until all the vegetables are very tender.
4.   Remove from heat and cool for a few minutes. In batches in a blender, or with an immersion blender, purée the soup until smooth. (Use caution handling the hot soup.)
5.   Add chicken or crab, if using. Taste, and correct seasoning if needed.
6.   Serve in warmed soup bowls.

Simple Sexy Kitchen Tip: If you think your time and energy is better spent on sexy maneuvers than breaking off cauliflower florets and cutting up vegetables, head for your supermarket's salad bar section to pick up as many of the vegetable ingredients for this yummy soup as you can.

Aphrodite Says: Cumin is a main ingredient in curry. Like the other "hot" foods, cumin has been thought to heat the blood and, well, inflame the fires of lust. "Want to heat up the evening, darling? 'Cumin' here and we'll get started!"

Miso Soup

SEXY FOODS: seaweed, green onion
2 TO 3 SERVINGS

4 cups water
4-inch piece daikon radish, cut into long thin slices
1 1/2 tablespoons Japanese-style red miso paste
1 tablespoon Japanese-style yellow miso paste
2 teaspoons wakame seaweed flakes
5 ounces firm tofu, cut into 1/2-inch cubes
1 green onion, white and light green parts only, thinly sliced

1.   Bring the 4 cups of water to a boil in a small pot.
2.   Add the radish, reduce heat to simmer, and cook for about 1 minute to soften the radish a bit.
3.   Adjust heat if needed so that mixture continues to simmer but does not boil. Scoop about 1/4 cup of the hot cooking liquid into a separate bowl, add the two miso pastes, and mix to blend.
4.   Add the miso mixture to the pot then add the seaweed and tofu. Simmer for about 3 minutes, until the seaweed has expanded and softened.
5.   Ladle the soup into warm bowls and sprinkle with green onion.

Simple Sexy Kitchen Tip: Miso, daikon radish, and packaged wakame seaweed flakes can be found at well-stocked supermarkets, Asian markets or natural food stores.

Aphrodite Says: Ancient Hawaiians believed eating *limu ko-ele-ele,* a type of seaweed, had aphrodisiac properties when accompanied by a certain chant. One Hawaiian legend refers to the use of seaweed in a love potion. If clever young woman gave her "target" a piece of seaweed, it would make him forever adore her. As an added plus, this sexy bounty of Neptune offers the broadest range of minerals of any food.

Spiked Cold Mango Soup

SEXY FOODS: mango, pineapple, honey, spirits (rum)
4 SERVINGS

3 cups diced mango (about 2 mangoes)
1 1/2 cups unsweetened pineapple juice
2 tablespoons fresh lime juice
1/8 teaspoon freshly ground black pepper
1/2 cup dark rum, such as Myers's
2 tablespoons honey
Lime slices, strawberries, or lime sherbet for garnishing

1.   In a blender jar, combine the mango, pineapple juice, lime juice, pepper, rum, and honey, and blend until smooth. Add more honey if desired.
2.   Chill thoroughly.
3.   Pour 2 bowls of soup and garnish with a slice of lime, whole strawberry, or tablespoon of lime sherbet on top.
4.   Refrigerate any remaining soup in a tightly closed container. Use within 2 days.

Variation: Fill 2 tall glasses with ice cubes. Pour 1/2 cup of soup into each glass then fill with chilled Champagne or club soda.

Aphrodite Says: The mango is mentioned in *The Kama Sutra* at least 6 times, including a recommendation to drink the tropical juice before sexual play. Another sexy reference to the mango comes courtesy of an anonymous Arabic poet, who, though acknowledging the practice of cunnilingus, cannot bring himself to describe it in proper mouth-watering detail:

Her breath is like honey spiced with cloves,
Her mouth delicious as a ripened mango.
To press kisses on her skin is to taste the lotus,
The deep cave of her navel hides a store of spices,
What pleasure lies beyond, the tongue knows,
But cannot speak of.

Butternut Squash Soup with Red Pepper Mousse

This is a delicious, make-ahead, special-occasion soup.

SEXY FOODS: winter squash, carrot, cumin, onion, garlic
ABOUT 7 CUPS, 4 TO 5 SERVINGS

Mousse
One-half 12-ounce jar roasted red peppers, drained, rinsed, and patted dry
1 1/2 teaspoons extra-virgin olive oil
1/2 teaspoon sherry vinegar
1/8 teaspoon Hungarian hot paprika
1/8 teaspoon salt
1/4 teaspoon unflavored gelatin (from a 1/4-ounce envelope)
1 tablespoon water
1/4 cup chilled heavy cream

Soup
3/4 cup chopped carrot
1/2 cup chopped onion (about 1/2 large onion)
1 clove garlic, minced
1/4 California bay leaf or 1/2 Turkish bay leaf
1 1/2 tablespoons extra-virgin olive oil
2 to 2 1/4 pounds butternut squash, seeded, peeled and cut into 1-inch pieces
(9 cups)
1/2 teaspoon salt
1/4 teaspoon ground cumin, or more to taste
1/8 teaspoon freshly ground black pepper
2 1/2 cups reduced-sodium chicken broth
1 3/4 cups water

1.   To make the mousse: In a blender or food processor, purée the peppers, oil, vinegar, paprika, and salt until very smooth.
2.   In a 1-quart heavy saucepan, sprinkle the gelatin over the water and let stand 2 minutes to soften. Heat the mixture over low heat, stirring, just until gelatin is dissolved. Remove from heat and whisk in the pepper purée, 1 tablespoon at a time.
3.   With an electric mixer, beat the cream at medium speed until it just holds soft peaks. Fold in the pepper mixture gently but thoroughly, then cover surface of mousse with plastic wrap and chill until set, at least 2 hours.
4.   To make the soup: In a 6- to 8-quart heavy pot over medium heat, cook the carrot, onion, garlic, and bay leaf in the oil, stirring occasionally,

until vegetables are softened, 5 to 6 minutes. Add the squash, salt, cumin, and pepper, and cook, stirring occasionally, until squash begins to soften around the edges, about 15 minutes. Stir in the broth and water and bring to a boil. Reduce heat and simmer, covered, until vegetables are very tender, 35 to 45 minutes. Discard the bay leaf.

5.　　　Working in batches, blend the soup in cleaned blender until smooth. (Use caution when blending hot liquids.)

6.　　　If not serving immediately, cool and refrigerate (see Tip). Just before serving, reheat the soup over low heat.

7.　　　Ladle into bowls and top each serving with 1 1/2 tablespoons of mousse.

Simple Sexy Kitchen Tip: The mousse can be chilled for up to 2 days. The soup can be made up to 3 days ahead and cooled, uncovered, then chilled, covered. Reheat as indicated. The soup can also be made with pumpkin or another winter squash instead of the butternut squash if you prefer.

Love Skills: This is a special-occasion soup so satisfying, and so packed with love-inducing ingredients, it can easily be the main course to accompany you as the main event! Use your imagination for the warm-up show and the encore!

Oyster Stew

Oyster stew is traditionally served with oyster crackers but I love it with whole-wheat crackers.

SEXY FOODS: oysters, parsley
2 SERVINGS

2 tablespoons unsalted butter
16 freshly shucked oysters or about 8 to 10 ounces fresh-pack jarred oysters, oyster liquor strained and reserved
1/4 cup clam juice
2 teaspoons Worcestershire sauce
1 teaspoon paprika
1/4 teaspoon celery salt
1 cup half-and-half
1 cup milk
Butter pats and chopped fresh parsley for garnishing

1.   Put about 2 inches of water in the bottom of a double boiler. Insert the top part, making sure that the water does not touch it. Bring the water to a boil and melt the butter in the top part. Add the oysters, strained oyster liquor, clam juice, Worcestershire sauce, paprika, and celery salt.
2.   Stir the mixture for about 1 minute, until the oysters are just starting to curl.
3.   Add the half-and-half and milk and, stirring frequently, bring just to a boil. Turn off heat.
4.   Serve in warmed soup bowls and garnish with butter and parsley.

Survey Secrets: Oysters. These remarkable fruits of the sea were the 3rd most recognized aphrodisiac food in my survey. This decadent delicacy also showed a mature, manly preference. Significantly more likely to find oysters sexy were mature men (age 50+, 37%). Also more likely to choose oysters were people with at least some college education (31%).

Oysters on the Half Shell with Mignonette Sauce

SEXY FOODS: oysters, shallots, parsley, chives, pepper
2 TO 4 SERVINGS

3/4 cup white wine vinegar or Champagne vinegar
1 teaspoon sugar
3 tablespoons finely chopped shallots
1 teaspoon coarsely ground black pepper
1 tablespoon finely chopped mixed fresh parsley and chives
Crushed ice
24 very fresh raw oysters, scrubbed under cold running water
3 lemons, cut into wedges

1.   In a small nonreactive saucepan, combine the vinegar, sugar, and shallots, and boil for 1 minute, just to dissolve the sugar.
2.   Remove from heat and let cool to room temperature.
3.   Just before serving, stir in the pepper and herbs, and transfer the sauce to a serving dish.
4.   Fill a serving platter or individual plates with crushed ice.
5.   Shuck the oysters (see Tip) and arrange them decoratively on the ice.
6.   Garnish with lemon wedges. Serve the sauce on the side.
7.   Place a large bowl nearby for the discarded shells.

Simple Sexy Kitchen Tip: To shuck oysters, place a thick kitchen towel (or towel folded over several times) on a clean surface (or use shucking gloves). Put the oyster, deeper shell downward, on the towel with the oyster hinge (pointed end) toward you. With your free hand on top of the oyster, insert the tip of an oyster knife between the shells close to the hinge. When the knife is in, twist it until the hinge "pops." Keeping the knife close to the flatter shell, work the knife back and forth through the slit, all around the shell, to free the oyster from the upper shell. Keeping the oyster level so as not to lose the liquor when the shell opens, carefully pry the shell halves apart. Cut the top shell at the hinge and discard. Insert your knife under the oyster, cut the hinge to free the oyster from the shell but leave the oyster in place. Remove any shell fragments and place the oyster on the crushed ice.

Aphrodite Says: Oysters are unique in their representation of the Doctrine of Resemblances, given they evoke both male and female genitals. Their exterior resembles testicles and the interior, in both shape and texture, evokes images of female genitals. Any briny seafood alludes to the smells and tastes of sexual secretions.

Rainbow Fruit Salad

This is a wonderful recipe for a steamy summer night.

SEXY FOODS: watercress, papaya, avocado, raspberries (strawberries), ginger
3 SERVINGS

Dressing
1/8 teaspoon sweet Hungarian paprika
1 tablespoon chopped crystallized ginger
1 tablespoon plain (unsweetened) yogurt
1/4 cup white Zinfandel or white grape juice
1 1/2 tablespoons red wine vinegar
1/4 teaspoon salt
1 1/2 teaspoons canola oil or other mild salad oil

Salad
1 medium ripe papaya or mango
1 medium ripe avocado
2 to 2 1/2 cups raspberries or strawberries (about 3/4 pound)
1/2 bunch watercress, rinsed and dried
1 tablespoon slivered almonds, toasted, optional

1.   To make the dressing: In a small bowl, mix together the paprika, ginger, and yogurt until thoroughly combined.
2.   Whisk in the wine or grape juice, vinegar, and salt until thoroughly mixed.
3.   Gradually drizzle in the oil, whisking constantly. Set aside.
4.   To assemble the salad: Peel the papaya and cut into 1/4-inch-thick wedges.
5.   Peel and pit the avocado and cut into 1/2-inch-thick slices.
6.   If using strawberries: Hull them and halve lengthwise.
7.   Arrange half of the watercress sprigs on each serving plate.
8.   Attractively arrange papaya and avocado slices, alternating colors, on each bed of watercress. Place raspberries or strawberry halves around and on top of the other fruit.
9.   Scatter the salads with toasted almonds if desired.
10.   Re-whisk the dressing and drizzle a little over each salad. Serve the remaining dressing on the side.

Simple Sexy Kitchen Tip: This can be a make-ahead salad (up to 4 hours in the refrigerator) if you brush the fruits lightly with lemon juice. Add the dressing just before serving.

Aphrodite Says: For contemporary Cubans, the erotic implications of this succulent fruit are so blatant that the word "papaya" has become slang for female sexual organs and is avoided in polite conversation. Instead, the juicy fruit is called *"fruta bomba,"* which still sounds sexy in a sweet, soft, explosive sort of way!

Love Skills: Role playing is a great way to add flavor to your love life. While making this recipe, have one partner become head chef while the other partner is sous-chef. Bring those desires to life!

Part II
Daytime is the Right Time
(breakfast, brunch, lunch, afternoon delight)

Introduction

From breakfast in bed to a leisurely weekend brunch to a re-energizing meal after some vigorous afternoon delight, eating and loving during daylight hours has a magic all its own.

Perhaps it's the fact that the sun is shining on us, revealing nuances and preferences that are hidden in the dark. Perhaps it's the fact that being in bed—or on the floor or couch—during the day is an infrequent extravagance reserved for those times when our lives permit such luxury. Or maybe it's the sometimes illicit, furtive nature of daytime lust, a seizing of the moment and of each other at times when one "should" be doing something else.

Spontaneous as these moments may be, a bit of forethought might make your daytime coupling not only more likely, but also more enjoyable. This is certainly the case for actual daytime sexy food choices, but it also applies to the setting and even your clothing choices!

For lovers with children, consider a "sleepover swap" with other parents. You might entertain the troops one weekend night into the next morning, then let another family do it the next time so you can have both an evening and a morning alone with your partner.

Another factor in the enjoyment of food and sex during the day is our modern society's nemesis, fatigue. Whether you're a busy, professional person with little energy left for sex at night, or a soccer mom juggling multiple demands on your time and attention, getting quality "twogether" time where the focus is solely on you and your partner can be a challenge.

The recipes in this section, like all those in this book, can be prepared solo or together with your partner. You might find that surprising your lover with breakfast in bed creates an aphrodisiac effect on both of you, for both serving and being served is sexy. You might even switch off roles from week to week. Still, many couples enjoy preparing food together, whether as a prelude or "postlude" to sex.

The principles of Simple Sexy Food include reducing stress and increasing opportunities for you and your partner to relish each other, aided by the aphrodisiac qualities of food. For some couples, preparing food together is sexually stimulating in itself. Sharing space, bumping into each other, chatting, feeding each other tidbits, anticipating, all can lead to emotional closeness that makes eventual sexual connection so much more satisfying.

On the other hand, your partner might not share your kitchen savvy, in which case it could be stressful to include him or her in your food preparation. For those folks, taking small steps toward including your partner in the kitchen— like handing you some utensil or ingredient—can lead to more interest and participation. And there will always be those times where it's nice to crank up something delicious and serve to your lover without any expectation of reciprocity or assistance. The key is knowing what works for you, and what makes the most sense in that moment.

Love Skills: Research into human sexuality confirms that the demands of modern society produce stressors and fatigue that diminish the sex drive. Our fast-food, over-processed diets, too, can contribute to diminished interest in sex. A return to simple, sexy food is a great way to counter those trends.

Survey Secrets: Of the food-related events which are considered most romantic or sexually appealing, a "surprise, home-cooked meal" ranked #2, with 63% of respondents in favor. Added to the luxury of being served by your lover, a bit of breakfast in bed might just be the ideal morning pick-me-up for your love life.

French Toast with Grand Marnier

SEXY FOODS: egg, orange, cinnamon, spirits
2 SERVINGS

1 orange
5 large eggs
1/4 cup whole milk
3 tablespoons Grand Marnier liqueur
1/2 teaspoon ground cinnamon
Dash of nutmeg
1 teaspoon salt
6 slices light rye bread (unseeded) or good-quality French or sourdough bread
(sliced about 3/4-inch thick)
3 tablespoons unsalted butter
Confectioners' sugar for garnishing
Pure maple syrup, warmed, with a dash of Grand Marnier liqueur if desired

1.   Preheat an oven to 200°F.
2.   Wash & dry orange and grate 1 teaspoon orange zest. Set aside.
3.   Cut the peel off the orange, removing all white pith. Cut the fruit in
half vertically then cut into thin slices. Flick out seeds. Set slices aside.
4.   In shallow bowl or pie plate, combine eggs, milk, liqueur, cinnamon,
nutmeg, orange zest, and salt. With a fork, beat the egg mixture until frothy.
5.   Soak the bread in the egg mixture, one or two pieces at a time. Turn
the slices carefully so that both sides are saturated but not falling apart.
6.   In large skillet or griddle over medium heat, melt 1 tablespoon butter.
7.   Letting excess egg mixture drip off, add as many pieces of bread as
will fit without crowding. Cook until crisp and golden brown on the under-
side, about 2 to 3 minutes.
8.   Cut a tablespoon of butter into several pieces and add to the pan,
distributing evenly. Flip the bread with a spatula and brown the other side,
another 2 to 3 minutes.
9.   Keep the finished toast warm in a single layer in the oven. Repeat the
procedure until all the bread has been cooked.
10.   Place the toast on warmed plates. Use a small, fine-mesh sieve to
lightly dust each serving with confectioners' sugar. Surround the toast with
the orange half-moon slices. Serve with the syrup.

Aphrodite Says: By the late 18th century, it was custom for English newlyweds to be served a "posset" shortly before retiring to the wedding bed: a
mixture of wine, milk, egg yolk, sugar, cinnamon, and nutmeg. In one study,
baked cinnamon smell was used as a control scent, but ironically wound up
creating the most blood flow to the penises of young and middle aged men.

Spiced Pumpkin Pancakes

SEXY FOODS: pumpkin, pumpkin pie spice, vanilla, eggs, pecans
ABOUT TEN 4 1/2-INCH PANCAKES

1/4 cup plus 2 tablespoons whole-wheat pastry flour
1/4 cup unbleached all-purpose flour
1 1/2 tablespoons sugar
1 teaspoon baking powder
3/4 teaspoon pumpkin pie spice
1/4 to 1/2 teaspoon salt
2 large eggs, separated (let egg whites come to room temperature)
1/4 cup plus 2 tablespoons puréed cooked pumpkin (plain, not pumpkin-pie filling)
2/3 cup nonfat milk
2 tablespoons canola oil or other mild vegetable oil
1/2 teaspoon vanilla extract
1/2 cup chopped pecans, optional
1/2 cup pure maple syrup
2 tablespoons butter
1 tablespoon dark rum, optional

1.   In medium bowl, sift together flours, sugar, baking powder, pie spice, and salt.
2.   In another medium bowl, whisk the egg yolks slightly. Then whisk in the pumpkin, milk, oil, and vanilla to blend well.
3.   Add the pumpkin mixture to the dry ingredients, whisking just until smooth. (The batter will be thick). Mix in the pecans if using.
4.   In a small, deep, clean dry bowl (not aluminum or plastic), beat the egg whites with an electric mixer until stiff but not dry. Fold the egg whites into the batter in two additions.
5.   Brush a large nonstick skillet with oil then heat over medium-high heat until a water droplet dances in the pan before evaporating.
6.   Working in batches, pour the batter by 1/4 cupfuls into the pan. Quickly spread batter to form 4 1/2-inch rounds; do not crowd the pan. Cook until bubbles form on the surface and bottoms are light brown, about 2 minutes. Flip the pancakes and cook until done. For each new batch, brush the pan with oil to coat, and reheat to medium-high before adding more batter.
7.   Place cooked pancakes on a warm plate and cover to keep warm.
8.   Meanwhile, in small saucepan, warm syrup, butter, and rum if using.
9.   Serve the pancakes with the syrup.

Love Skills: Breakfast in bed will never go out of style! Sneak out of the sheets and whip up this scrumptious recipe. If you have work, be sure to keep an eye on the clock since morning "sessions" are sure interrupt your schedule!

Coconut Pumpkin Nut Bread

SEXY FOODS: coconut, pumpkin, nutmeg, cinnamon, walnuts
Two 8-by-4-inch loaves

2 cups all-purpose flour
1 1/2 cups whole-wheat pastry flour
2 cups dark brown sugar, packed
2/3 cup granulated sugar
1 (15-ounce) can pumpkin purée (plain, not pie filling)
2/3 cup coconut milk, stirred before measuring
1 cup canola oil or other mild vegetable oil
2 teaspoons baking soda
1 teaspoon salt
1 teaspoon freshly grated nutmeg
1 1/2 teaspoons ground cinnamon
1 cup (4 to 5 ounces) toasted walnuts
2/3 cup unsweetened, finely grated coconut

1.   Preheat an oven to 350°F. Grease two 8-by-4-inch loaf pans with vegetable oil and dust with flour, shaking out any excess flour. Set aside.
2.   In a mixing bowl of an electric mixer, combine the flours, sugars, pumpkin, coconut milk, oil, baking soda, salt, and spices. Mix on low speed, then raise speed to medium and mix until well blended.
3.   Fold in the walnuts and coconut, then scrape the batter into the pre-pared pans, being sure to fill the corners. Rap the pans on a counter to release any air bubbles.
4.   Bake for about 1 1/4 hours, or until a toothpick comes out clean.
5.   Remove the pans from oven, set on a cooling rack, and immediately cover each loaf tightly with aluminum foil. Allow the loaves to steam in their own heat for 10 minutes.
6.   Remove foil and let the loaves cool, in the pans, on a cooling rack.

Simple Sexy Kitchen Tip: The addition of whole wheat pastry flour gives this bread a wonderfully sexy, lighter texture! To freeze one of the loaves for later use, let cool completely, then wrap air-tight and freeze for up to 4 months.

Baked Eggs over Creamy Leeks

SEXY FOODS: egg, leek, sage
2 SERVINGS

1 tablespoon butter
1 teaspoon olive oil
8 ounces leeks, white part and a little tender green part only, cleaned and thinly sliced (about 6 leeks)
5 to 6 tablespoons whipping cream
1/4 teaspoon salt, or to taste
1/16 teaspoon white pepper, or to taste
4 large eggs
Chopped fresh sage for garnishing

1.   Preheat oven to 375°F. Spray four 6-ounce ramekins or custard cups with cooking spray or oil, and set aside.
2.   In large skillet over medium heat, heat butter and oil and sauté leeks for about 4 to 5 minutes, stirring frequently, until softened but not browned.
3.   Reduce heat to low, add 3 tablespoons of the cream, and cook for 5 minutes, until leeks are very soft and cream is absorbed. Season with salt and white pepper.
4.   Divide the leek mixture among the ramekins and place in a baking dish large enough to hold them without touching.
5.   Break an egg into each ramekin and spoon the remaining cream over the eggs. (If you prefer a scrambled-egg texture, mix each egg individually with two teaspoons of cream and pour the mixture over the leeks.) Season lightly if desired.
6.   Pour boiling water into the baking dish to halfway up the ramekins. Bake for about 10 minutes, until just set, or until eggs are done to your liking.
7.   Sprinkle with chopped sage and serve immediately.

Love Skills: Tired of having sex with your partner at the same time of day? After whipping up this recipe, bring the meal back to bed and surprise your partner by switching up the routine. This sumptuous dish can be enjoyed as a breakfast in bed, a midday quickie, or a late dinner, whenever the time seems right!

Aphrodite Says: The Venetian Casanova, arguably the historical figure most known for his sexual escapades, made egg the primary ingredient in his secret, egg salad "love recipe" to assure his "stamina" throughout the night. Humpty Dumpty might not have been so lucky, but Casanova knew to crack a few eggs to hold up his part of the sexual bargain!

Herb Crêpes

These crêpes are a perfect marriage with caviar (see accompanying recipe), or tuck Chilled Asparagus with Lemon Sauce into these crêpes and sprinkle with a cheese such as Gruyère or Parmesan.

SEXY FOODS: egg, parsley, basil, chives
ABOUT 8 CRÊPES

1 egg
1/2 cup milk
3 tablespoons water
1/2 cup all-purpose flour
1/8 teaspoon salt
2 tablespoons minced fresh herbs, such as flat-leaf parsley, basil, or chives, or a mixture
1 tablespoon butter, melted, plus more for cooking the crêpes

1.   In a blender jar, combine the egg, milk, water, flour, salt, herbs, and 1 tablespoon melted butter. Pulse for about 10 seconds, or until smooth. Scrape down and repeat if needed.

2.   Cover and refrigerate the batter for at least 2 hours, or up to 24 hours.

3.   When ready to cook the crêpes, gently stir the batter if it has separated. Batter should be just thick enough to coat a wooden spoon. If batter seems too heavy, gently beat in water, 1/2 teaspoon at a time, until desired consistency is reached.

4.   Heat a 6- to 7-inch nonstick crêpe pan or skillet over medium-high heat until hot. Brush with melted butter to coat evenly.

5.   Put 2 to 3 tablespoons of batter into the pan and swirl until bottom of pan is completely covered with batter.

6.   Cook the crêpe until almost dry on top and lightly browned on the edges, about 30 to 60 seconds.

7.   Loosen the edges, flip the crêpe over, and cook for 10 to 15 seconds, or until lightly browned on second side.

8.   Transfer crêpe to a warmed plate and cover with aluminum foil.

9.   Repeat steps 4 through 8 with the remaining batter, stacking the cooked crêpes with foil between each. Keep warm in a warming drawer or 200°F oven.

Simple Sexy Kitchen Tip: If making in advance, let crêpes cool completely, then wrap in foil. Store, refrigerated, for up to 3 days. To reheat, preheat an oven to 325°F and warm the crêpes in the foil packet on a baking sheet for 5 to 10 minutes, or until heated through.

Herb Crêpes with Caviar

SEXY FOODS: caviar, onion (chives), basil
2 SERVINGS

Herb Crêpes or eight 6- to 7-inch-diameter savory crêpes
1/2 cup light sour cream or plain yogurt
1 1/2 ounces golden, black, or red caviar
1 1/2 teaspoons minced fresh chives, or substitute finely minced green onion tops
8 whole chives, about 7 to 8 inches long, or substitute green onion tops

1.   Prepare the crêpes. Cover them with aluminum foil and keep them warm in a 200°F oven. (Or, if the crêpes have been made ahead, reheat them, wrapped in foil, on a baking sheet in a preheated 325°F oven for 5 to 10 minutes, or until heated through.)
2.   Working quickly to assemble the purses, lay out the crêpes on a clean work surface. Spoon a tablespoon of sour cream and a teaspoon of caviar onto the center of each crêpe, and then sprinkle with minced chives.
3.   Gather each crêpe into a bundle the shape of a drawstring purse and tie at the "neck" with a whole chive. Serve immediately.

Aphrodite Says: Jackie Kennedy indulged in caviar frequently (because she could—at about $140/ounce!) Her favorite meal at the Four Seasons in New York was a baked potato heaped with caviar and a glass of champagne.

Survey Secrets: An appreciation for caviar seems to come with age. According to my survey, people 36 years old and older were more likely to select caviar as sexy from a list of possible choices, and people 50 years old and older were significantly more likely to have heard of its sexy reputation.

Fish Tacos

SEXY FOODS: seafood, cilantro, tomato, chilies
2 SERVINGS

Tacos
6 crisp taco shells or 6 flour or corn tortillas
1/4 cup low-fat sour cream
1/4 cup mayonnaise
3/4 cup chopped fresh cilantro
1/2 serrano or jalapeño chili, finely chopped
1/4 cup (half of 1-ounce packet) taco seasoning mix
1/2 pound halibut, cod, or other white fish fillet, cut into 1-inch pieces
1 tablespoon fresh lime juice
1 tablespoon canola or other vegetable oil

Garnishes
Shredded cabbage
Chopped tomatoes
Chopped red or green bell peppers
Crushed red chili flakes
Lime wedges

1.   Preheat an oven to 300°F and warm the taco shells or tortillas, wrapped in foil, on a baking sheet.
2.   In a small bowl, mix the sour cream, mayonnaise, cilantro, chilies, and 2 tablespoons of the taco seasoning. Set aside until ready to serve.
3.   In a separate bowl, gently mix the fish, lime juice, oil, and remaining 2 tablespoons taco seasoning.
4.   Heat a skillet over medium-high heat and add the fish mixture. Cook, stirring constantly, for 4 to 5 minutes, or until the fish is just opaque throughout. Do not overcook the fish.
5.   Fill the warmed taco shells or tortillas with the fish mixture.
6.   Serve the tacos accompanied with the garnishes and reserved sauce.

Love Skills: Switch up the dress code tonight for your romantic meal at home. No shoes, shirts or pants required! Dining partially nude will keep you hungry for more.

Simple Sexy Kitchen Tip: Many kinds of fish can be substituted for halibut. Generally, the less oily, more delicate and flaky fish do better when pan fried. If your partner is a freshwater angler, this is a great recipe for panfish, walleye, and pike!

Artichokes Stuffed with Shrimp

Eating an artichoke takes time...a great metaphor for sensual lovemaking.

SEXY FOODS: artichoke (or avocado), shrimp
2 SERVINGS

2 medium to large artichokes
2 1/2 tablespoons fresh lemon juice
10 cups water
2 teaspoons vinegar
1 3/4 teaspoons salt
1/3 cup mayonnaise
1/4 cup sour cream
1/2 teaspoon freshly grated lemon zest
1/4 teaspoon chopped fresh tarragon
1/4 teaspoon Dijon mustard
1/4 pound peeled, cooked small shrimp
Lemon wedges for garnishing

1.   Remove coarse outer leaves from the artichokes and trim the stems even with the bases so artichokes stand upright. With a sharp knife, cut off the top third of each artichoke. With scissors, trim thorns from tips of remaining leaves. Rub the cut surfaces with about 1 teaspoon of the lemon juice.

2.   In a 3-quart or larger non-aluminum pot, combine the water, vinegar, and 1 1/2 teaspoons of the salt. Bring to a boil over high heat. Add the artichokes, cover, and boil gently until the stem ends pierce readily with a fork, about 30 minutes. Drain.

3.   Let cool slightly, then pull out and discard center leaves, and scrape out fuzzy centers with a spoon. Drizzle the cavities with about 2 teaspoons of the lemon juice and let the artichokes cool thoroughly. Wrap and refrigerate for 1 hour or until the next day.

4.   Meanwhile, in a small bowl, mix the mayonnaise, sour cream, lemon zest, tarragon, mustard, remaining 1 1/2 tablespoons lemon juice, and remaining 1/4 teaspoon salt. If making ahead, refrigerate the sauce until needed.

5.   When ready to assemble, mix the shrimp with 1/4 cup sauce in a small bowl, then spoon the mixture into the artichoke cavities.

6.   Serve the remaining sauce in individual dishes for dipping the artichoke leaves. Garnish with lemon wedges.

Variation:
Substitute a large avocado, halved, for the artichokes. You can scoop out a little of the avocado flesh to make more room for filling. Stuff each half with shrimp mixture. Serve the remaining sauce on the side.

Simple Sexy Kitchen Tip: When grating citrus zest, do not go too deep. You want to avoid the underlying bitter, white pith.

Love Skills: Get the prep work out of the way, and make some time for a little foreplay!

Aphrodite Says: In centuries past, French street vendors cried out: "Artichokes! Artichokes! Heats the body! Heats the spirit! Heats the genitals!"

Lobster Tail and Watermelon Salad

Quite simply, this is an amazing combination of aphrodisiac foods!

SEXY FOODS: lobster, avocado, papaya, watermelon, honey, coconut, cilantro

2 MAIN-DISH SERVINGS OR 4 TO 6 STARTERS

2 (6-ounce) lobster tails, cooked, or about 1 1/2 cups sliced, cooked lobster meat
1/4 cup fresh lemon juice
1 tablespoon honey
1 1/2 teaspoons dry jerk seasoning
3/4 cup canola or other mild salad oil
1/4 teaspoon salt, or more to taste
1/4 teaspoon freshly ground black pepper, or more to taste
1 cup 1/2-inch-cubes watermelon
1 avocado, cut into 1/2-inch cubes
1 papaya, cut into 1/2-inch cubes
1/4 cup chopped fresh cilantro
1 head red lettuce, shredded
1/4 cup coconut flakes, optional

1.   If using lobster tails, remove meat from shells and cut in half lengthwise; devein. Cut the lobster meat into 1/2-inch slices. Set aside.
2.   In a large bowl, whisk together the lemon juice, honey, and jerk seasoning. Gradually whisk in the oil, and then stir in the salt and pepper.
3.   Add the watermelon, avocado, papaya, cilantro, and reserved lobster. Toss gently to coat the ingredients evenly with dressing.
4.   Refrigerate for 1 hour, stirring occasionally.
5.   To serve, create a bed of shredded lettuce on each plate, arrange the lobster mixture on the lettuce, and sprinkle with coconut.

Simple Sexy Kitchen Tip: This recipe calls for dry, not wet, Jamaican jerk seasoning. The most authentic version has a real kick to it and includes Scotch bonnet chilies, similar to habanero. See the Resources page for a great one. Other variations are available in supermarkets.

Aphrodite Says: Recent research suggests that a lobster's fertility actually increases with age. Some scientists point to "negligible senescence" as evidence that, barring injury or disease, a lobster could live indefinitely!

Spinach Salad with Mango Chutney Dressing

It's like having all the delicious condiments of a main-dish curry in a salad! I think you'll find this recipe makes a spicy prelude to afternoon delight.

SEXY FOODS: apple, cashew, turmeric, pepper, garlic, cumin, ginger, green onion, spinach

2 GENEROUS MAIN-DISH SERVINGS OR MORE AS A SIDE

Dressing

1/4 cup canola or other mild salad oil
1 1/2 teaspoons finely chopped mango chutney, such as Major Grey's
Scant 1/2 teaspoon curry powder
Scant 1/2 teaspoon dry mustard
Scant 1/2 teaspoon salt
Pinch of white pepper
Dash of Tabasco sauce

Salad

1 red apple
5 ounces baby spinach, washed and dried
1/3 cup golden raisins
1/4 cup unsalted, roasted cashews
1 green onion, thinly sliced
2 teaspoons toasted sesame seeds, optional
3 ounces lean bacon, cut into 1-inch pieces and cooked until crisp

1.   To make the dressing: In a blender jar, combine the oil, chutney, curry powder, mustard, salt, white pepper, and Tabasco sauce, and blend at medium speed until emulsified.

2.   Set the dressing aside at room temperature for 2 hours or more to let flavors blend.

3.   When ready to serve salad: Core and cut the apple into thin slices.

4.   In a large bowl, toss together the apple slices, spinach, raisins, cashews, green onion, sesame seeds, and bacon.

5.   Drizzle with the reserved dressing and toss again until dressing is evenly distributed. Serve immediately.

Variation: Add tiny bay shrimp to make this a main dish.

Aphrodite Says: In the 16th century, when the über-sexual Catherine de Medici moved from Florence to marry the king of France, she brought her chefs along with her so that they could prepare her favorite spinach recipes, and insisted on it being served at every meal.

Part III

Love-Feasts, or Dine-In, Dine-On
(sit-down dinners, pampering your lover, complete meals)

Introduction

Somewhat surprisingly, most people find the evening meal to be the most sexually appealing event combining food and sex.

In fact, if one wanted to generalize, an evening, candle-lit dinner prepared as a surprise and consisting of oyster appetizers with champagne, followed by a seafood main course (shrimp or lobster) and wine, and finished off with chocolate-dipped strawberries, whipped cream and a snit of high-end liqueur would be the ultimate, modern-day aphrodisiac meal, according to my survey data.

When it comes to pampering your lover, nothing compares to the elegance and atmosphere of an evening meal. The lighting can be adjusted to perfection, the music can play lightly in the background, and there's time to truly appreciate the sensuality of the moment. The array of potential food choices is nearly limitless, as are the combinations of courses, beverages, table settings and venues.

That limitlessness has drawbacks, of course. You can spend a king's ransom on a three or four course meal with beverages, but what if your partner doesn't like what you've done? Part of what I hope to convey in these pages is the sense that your own style, preferences and circumstances should dictate your sexy food choices. Your body will respond with arousal based both on the food you're ingesting, and also on the way you feel about the food, the setting, and more. Research into human sexuality and into the mind-body connection with food reveals that the aphrodisiac effect of a given food has both physiological and psychological components. As for the psychological aspect, if it makes you feel sexy, or contributes to your sexual arousal or satisfaction, it's an aphrodisiac.

The same can be said for how you feel about yourself. As I point out in my book, *Love Skills*, a healthy self-image is vital to thoroughly enjoying sex. If you feel sexy, you will be sexy. In the same vein, if you're stressed out over money, the kids, problems at work, your schedule, your in-laws, whatever, you're less likely to be in the mood for a romp in the hay.

All of this is to say that if preparing a formal, sit-down meal complete with mood lighting and music is a stretch right now, don't worry about it. Your love life may not need the added complication, and I would suggest you try one of the appetizers (Part I), or perhaps just some divine chocolate-covered strawberries (Part IV), delivered in a slinky negligee or silk sarong with a bottle of champagne, to get started. Remember, if it feels sexy, it is sexy.

Survey Secrets: Of all the sexually stimulating food events preferred by respondents, 82% chose "an evening, candlelight dinner at home" the most sexy!

Simple Sexy Kitchen Tips: Wherever possible and appropriate I've made suggestions for substitute ingredients in these recipes. If you can't find exactly what you need at your local grocer, there are likely to be perfectly good alternatives you will be able to find.

But if you and/or your partner is a "foodie" and you have the time, money and desire to whip up one of the incredible meals in this section, by all means, do it. On the money side of things, you'll find that even the most decadent home-prepared meal will cost significantly less than dining out, plus you'll be close to whatever room of your home will find you in your lover's arms, enhancing your precious time together.

The point is to have the food and sex fit in with your lifestyle. I've tried to make ease of preparation a feature throughout, for it will contribute to less stress, greater confidence, and more time to savor your partner and the moment.

Roasted Cornish Game Hen with Red Grapes

This elegant and succulent dish may take a bit of time to prepare, but is well worth the effort. The sweetness of the grapes melds beautifully with the savory game hens, especially with the Cognac to draw the flavors together. The leftovers from this meal also make a great midday snack or picnic treat!

SEXY FOODS: red grapes, spirits, pepper
2 SERVINGS

6 tablespoons butter, softened
1 1/2 teaspoons coarsely ground or cracked black pepper
1 teaspoon salt
2 Cornish game hens, 1 to 1 1/2 pounds each
30 red seedless grapes, halved lengthwise
5 tablespoons Cognac
1/4 cup sherry
1 cup chicken broth
1 tablespoon cornstarch
1 teaspoon grated lemon zest
1 tablespoon fresh lemon juice

1.   Preheat an oven to 350°F.
2.   Mix 4 tablespoons of the butter with pepper and salt and set aside.
3.   Rinse the birds and pat dry, inside and out, with paper towels.
4.   Put 1 tablespoon of butter and 15 grape halves in each bird's cavity.
5.   Sprinkle 1 1/2 teaspoons of Cognac inside each cavity and 1 table-spoon over the outside of each bird.
6.   Truss the birds with string or small skewers to hold the legs together.
7.   Rub the outside of the birds generously with the reserved butter mixture. Place the birds, spaced apart and breast up, in a small roasting pan. Roast, basting as described below, for about 1 1/4 hours, or until done.
8.   To make the basting sauce, in a small saucepan, combine the sherry, broth, remaining grape halves, and remaining 2 tablespoons Cognac, and heat gently for about 3 minutes. Remove from heat and keep warm. About every 15 to 20 minutes, baste the birds with the liquid. About 5 to 10 minutes before they are done, use slotted spoon to transfer grapes to the roasting pan.
9.   Cook the birds to an internal temperature of at least 165°F at the thickest part of the inner thigh (not touching the bone). Transfer them to a warm serving platter and tent with aluminum foil, or use a warming drawer, and keep warm. Place the roasting pan, with the pan juices, over a low burner.
10.   In a small dish, mix the cornstarch with a 2-3 tablespoons of the basting sauce until thoroughly blended. Set aside.

11.   Add the remaining basting sauce to the roasting pan, raise heat to medium, and deglaze the pan, scraping up all the brown bits on the bottom. Add the lemon zest and juice and pour in the cornstarch mixture. Stirring constantly, simmer the sauce until slightly thickened.

12.   To serve, remove the skewers and string. Drizzle some sauce over the birds and serve the remaining sauce on the side.

Survey Secrets: Historically, grapes are central to the sex/food continuum. Their sexy credibility remains strong today, as evidenced by their placing high in my survey: in the top ten for reputation, choice-from-a-list and free choice. Champagne grapes and red grapes held a sexy edge over others types. Sweet and juicy, with a pleasant pop when bitten, grapes are the perfect finger food for lovers of any era.

Roast Rosemary Chicken with Lemon and Onion

Leftovers from this delicious bird are wonderful cold or reheated.
Great anytime, at home or for a picnic!

SEXY FOODS: apple, onion, celery, rosemary, lemon, garlic
4 SERVINGS PLUS LEFTOVERS

1 whole roasting chicken, about 4 pounds
2 tablespoons fresh lemon juice
1 teaspoon onion powder
1 tablespoon dried rosemary, crushed
1 clove garlic, pressed or minced
1 small apple, quartered
1 small onion, quartered
1 stalk celery, halved crosswise

1.   Preheat an oven to 350°F.
2.   Remove giblets, if present, from the chicken and discard. Wash and dry the chicken and set aside at room temperature for 30 to 45 minutes (not longer) before preparing.
3.   Brush the outside of the chicken with lemon juice.
4.   Mix together the onion powder, rosemary, and garlic, and sprinkle the mixture over the chicken skin and into the cavity.
5.   Put the apple, onion, and celery pieces into the cavity, including the neck cavity if pieces remain.
6.   Close the cavities with poultry lacers and string and set the chicken on a rack in a roasting pan.
7.   Bake the chicken, uncovered, for about 1 1/4 to 1 1/2 hours, until a leg joint moves freely and juices run clear, or a meat thermometer gives an internal temperature reading of 165°F.
8.   Remove the chicken and let it rest for 5 to 10 minutes before carving. Remove the cavity stuffing and discard or use for garnish.

Simple Sexy Kitchen Tip: Julia Child, that maven of sensuality and succulence, suggests allowing the uncooked chicken to sit out for a while (e.g., 30 minutes) to take some of the chill off. This does add additional time to the preparation, but perhaps that interlude might allow time for some pre-meal warm-up activities. Once the bird's in the oven, there's a second opportunity to chill with your lover and bask in the aromas of the meal you're about to share!

Aphrodite Says: Rosemary has a lively and prominent history of sexy influence. Napoleon, that General so short in stature but long in ego, ordered large quantities of rosemary-infused Eau de Cologne to bathe in or splash on himself before romancing his wife. We must assume that he wasn't rejected at the ramparts of her love like he was rejected at the outskirts of Moscow!

Love Skills: Chicken legs are a perfect "finger food," and might present you with an opportunity to hand-feed your lover. Allow yourself to be fed, as well. It reduces the space between you and creates an instant intimacy you can't reproduce from across a table!

*****

Chile Relleno Casserole

You'll note the spelling of this dish differs from other references to chilies in this book. While either spelling is acceptable, I've used the more common "chili" to refer to members of the capsicum family. "Chile Relleno" is the name of a dish, not a particular pepper species.

SEXY FOODS: chilies, egg, mushroom
4 TO 6 SERVINGS

1 1/2 cups (about 11 to 12 ounces) canned diced green chilies, such as Ortega
8 ounces low-fat Cheddar cheese, grated
8 ounces low-fat jack cheese, grated
2/3 cup (2 ounces) sliced white mushrooms, slices cut in half if very large
2 eggs, separated
2 tablespoons all-purpose flour
3/4 cup nonfat evaporated milk
1/4 teaspoon salt
1/4 teaspoon Mexican seasoning
Tomato salsa of choice, optional

1.   Preheat an oven to 325°F. Lightly oil an 8-inch-square glass baking dish or spray with cooking spray. Set aside.

2.   Drain the chilies of excess liquid, if needed, and scatter half of the chilies evenly in the baking dish.

3.   With a light hand, evenly mix the cheeses in a medium bowl.

4.   Sprinkle half of the cheese mixture and all of the mushrooms over the chilies. Layer on the remaining chilies and then the remaining cheese. Set aside.

5.   In a medium bowl, whisk the egg yolks until light, then sprinkle the flour over the yolks and whisk in. Whisk in a third of the evaporated milk, mixing well. Add the remaining evaporated milk, salt, and Mexican seasoning, and whisk well to make a batter. Set aside.

6.   In a small, deep, clean, and dry glass, ceramic, or steel bowl, beat the egg whites, using an electric mixer, until stiff peaks form.

7.   Fold some of the egg whites into the batter to lighten it. Then gently fold in the remaining egg whites. (Do not stir.)

8.   Pour the batter over the chili–cheese layers, spreading it edge to edge to form an even layer on top.

9.   Bake for 1 hour, or until the top is rich golden brown.

10.   Remove from the oven and let cool for a few minutes before cutting.

11.   Serve with salsa if desired.

Simple Sexy Kitchen Tip: Using high-quality block cheeses and shredding them together in a food processor maximizes the delicious flavor of this dish. If you're pressed for time, and play-time is at a premium, go for high-quality, low-fat pre-grated cheeses.

Love Skills: Not feeling frisky tonight? Try spicing up your mood by turning on some Latin music and shedding layers. Dancing is an excellent way to add some cardio to your day and will be sure to raise both the temperature and your interest in each other.

Orange Beef Stir-Fry

SEXY FOODS: oranges, ginger, chili flakes, cilantro, rice
4 SERVINGS

2 cups fresh orange juice
Zest of 2 oranges, grated or finely minced
3 tablespoons dry sherry
3 tablespoons low-sodium soy sauce
1 1/2 teaspoons canola oil or other mild vegetable oil
1 pound stir-fry beef sirloin
1 1/2 ounces fresh ginger, peeled and minced
1/4 teaspoon crushed red chili flakes
1 1/2 cups (6 ounces) bean sprouts
1 1/2 cups (6 ounces) snow peas, stems and strings removed
Steamed brown or white jasmine rice
1 teaspoon sesame oil
2 to 3 tablespoons chopped fresh cilantro for garnishing

1.   In a small bowl, stir together the orange juice and zest, sherry, and soy sauce. Set aside within reach of the stove.
2.   Heat wok or large nonstick skillet over high heat until very hot. Add canola oil, then quickly add beef, ginger, and chili flakes, and stir-fry until the beef is browned, about 3 to 4 minutes. Remove the beef and keep warm.
3.   Add orange juice mixture to oil left in the wok, & bring to a simmer.
4.   Add the bean sprouts and pea pods, and stir-fry for about 1 minute, or just until pea pods turn bright green.
5.   Return the beef and any accumulated juices to the wok just long enough to reheat.
6.   Serve over steamed rice, drizzle with the sesame oil, and sprinkle with the cilantro.

Variation: This recipe is also delicious made with chicken-breast strips.

Simple Sexy Kitchen Tip: This makes really good leftovers . . . say, for a lazy weekend brunch for the two of you.

Aphrodite Says: By the 14th century in England, ginger was second only to pepper as the most common spice, and by the Tudor era, it was a key ingredient in both hippocras and gingerbreads, said to "provoketh sluggish husbands." Consider that the next time your lover needs a little "ginger" in his get-me-up!

Saffron Rice

If you are turned on by bold flavors, try this colorful, spiced rice with Moroccan Honey Chicken. Any leftover rice can be refrigerated, tightly covered, for up to 3 days then sprinkled with a few drops of water and gently reheated.

SEXY FOODS: saffron, nutmeg, onion, rice
2 GENEROUS SERVINGS FOR RICE LOVERS

1 tablespoon butter
1/4 cup yellow onion, chopped
1 cup basmati or long-grain white rice
2 cups boiling water
Pinch of saffron threads or 1/8 teaspoon powdered saffron
1/4 teaspoon freshly grated nutmeg
1/2 teaspoon salt, or more to taste
1/4 to 1/2 teaspoon freshly ground black pepper

1.   Preheat an oven to 400°F.
2.   In an ovenproof heavy saucepan, melt the butter over medium heat and sauté the onion until softened but not browned, about 1 minute.
3.   Stir in the rice and sauté until shiny and coated with butter. Add the boiling water, increase heat to high, and bring to a boil, stirring once or twice. Add the saffron, nutmeg, salt, and pepper; cover with a tight-fitting lid; and transfer to the oven.
4.   Bake the rice until liquid is absorbed and rice is tender, about 18 minutes.
5.   Remove from the oven and set aside, covered, for 5 minutes. (Do not peek!)
6.   Fluff the rice with a fork, and serve immediately.

Simple Sexy Kitchen Tip: Flavored rice, or rice in general, is among the most companionable of side dishes. Saffron-flavored rice can be served with seafood, chicken, and various meats.

Aphrodite Says: Ancient Phoenicians gave moon-shaped saffron-flavored love cakes to their fertility goddess Astoreth to endure reproductive health and crop success. One ancient Greek legend held that eating saffron for a week would render a girl unable to resist a lover. Yet another Arabic sex recipe calls for boiling saffron along with dates, anise, wild carrots, orange blossoms and egg yolks in water mixed with honey and dove blood. I know, it sounded great right up to the dove blood part.

Pepper-crusted Ahi Tuna Steaks with Spinach

SEXY FOODS: tuna (seafood), pepper, spinach, onion (shallots)
2 SERVINGS

1/2 pound spinach, cleaned
1/2 teaspoon canola oil
3 tablespoons fresh lemon juice
2 ahi tuna steaks, 1 to 1 1/2 inches thick, 4 to 6 ounces each
2 teaspoons "rainbow" peppercorns, crushed (see Tip)
2 tablespoons butter
1/2 cup minced shallots
1/4 teaspoon salt
1/2 lemon, cut into wedges

1.   Preheat an oven to 400°F. Lightly oil a baking sheet and set aside.
2.   Blanch the spinach for 5 seconds in boiling water; drain and set aside.
3.   In a small bowl, stir together the oil and 1 1/2 teaspoons of the lemon juice. Brush the tuna with the mixture.
4.   Put the crushed peppercorns in a small flat dish. Dip both sides of the tuna into the peppercorn mixture, pressing lightly, and place the steaks on the baking sheet.
5.   Bake for about 8 to 12 minutes, depending on thickness, or until the fish is browned and cooked to rare to medium rare, or to desired doneness.
6.   Meanwhile, melt the butter in a medium sauté pan. Add the shallots, and cook over medium heat until soft, about 3 to 4 minutes. Add the spinach and sauté quickly, just to heat through. Season with the salt and remaining 1 1/2 tablespoons lemon juice.
7.   Divide the spinach between serving plates and arrange the tuna steaks on top. Serve immediately with the lemon wedges.

Simple Sexy Kitchen Tip: Packages of "rainbow" peppercorns are available at most good grocery retailers or markets. To crush peppercorns, spread them in an even layer in a well-sealed zip-style plastic bag. Place the bag on a solid surface, such as a cutting board, and whack the peppercorns with the bottom of a heavy pan. Or use a mortar and pestle.

Aphrodite Says: Tuna is a huge, majestic fish. Some members of this amazing predator species cruise non-stop at speeds up to 40 miles an hour. No wonder its aphrodisiac history traces back to ancient times, having been reviewed in turn by Aristotle, Pliny the Elder, and Homer. Maybe this dish will get you going at top speed!

Curry with Shrimp, Clams, and Pineapple

SEXY FOODS: pineapple, curry, shrimp, clams, rice, chile, cilantro
2 SERVINGS

1 1/4 cups coconut milk
1 tablespoon red curry paste
1 tablespoon Asian fish sauce
1 1/2 teaspoons sugar
1/2 pound clams, scrubbed
1/4 pound shelled and deveined, raw jumbo shrimp
2/3 cup crushed or finely chopped fresh pineapple (3 ounces)
2 to 3 kaffir lime leaves, torn (if unavailable, use 1 tablespoon finely chopped lemongrass)
Hot cooked brown or white jasmine rice, optional
2 fresh Thai red chilies, finely chopped, or substitute red jalapeños
Fresh cilantro leaves for garnishing

1.   Put half of the coconut milk in a large saucepan, bring to a boil over high heat, and cook, stirring, for 2 to 3 minutes.
2.   Reduce heat to medium, add the curry paste, and cook until fragrant, 1 to 2 minutes. Add the fish sauce and sugar, and cook and stir the mixture for 1 minute.
3.   Add the remaining coconut milk and return to a boil. Add the clams and cook for 5 minutes, then add the shrimp, pineapple, and lime leaves, and return to a boil.
4.   Reduce heat and simmer for about 3 to 5 minutes, until the clams have opened and the shrimp are pink and fully cooked. Discard any un-opened clams.
5.   Serve over rice if desired. Sprinkle with chopped chilies and garnish with cilantro.

Survey Secrets: Shrimp. These delectable crustaceans ranked in the top ten of both the free-choice and choose-from-a-list categories of favorite aphrodisiac foods. Interestingly, folks with a high school-only educational background were significantly more likely (35%) to have heard of its reputation than those with college or more.

Love Skills: Try duet cooking wherever possible or appropriate. With this dish, one of you can prepare the ingredients; the other can oversee the cooking pot. The prep cook will likely enjoy "overseeing" the pot-watcher, too, so be prepared for some "assistance" while your hands are otherwise occupied!

Lobster and Pasta in Rich Tomato Sauce

Guaranteed to light your fire! This recipe combines two 21st Century Aphrodisiac Foods Survey favorites: lobster and pasta. Lobster ranked in the top 10 of choose-from-a list favorites (and 2nd as seafood), while pasta made it in the top 10 on the write-in list of personal favorites!

SEXY FOODS: lobster, pasta, tomato, onion, garlic, chilies, parsley, spirits (wine)
2 SERVINGS

1 1/2 teaspoons salt
3 tablespoons extra-virgin olive oil
2 uncooked lobster tails, 3 1/2 to 4 ounces each, in the shell, thawed if frozen
2/3 cup finely chopped onion
2 tablespoons finely chopped garlic
1/3 cup finely chopped flat-leaf parsley
1/2 cup dry white Italian wine
1 1/2 cups (1 14 1/2 ounce can) imported Italian plum tomatoes, cut up, with their juice
1/2 to 1 chopped fresh serrano chili or other hot chili
4 ounces high-quality imported Italian dried spaghettini or thin spaghetti

1.   In a large pot, bring 2 quarts of water to a boil over high heat. Add 1 teaspoon salt and 1 1/2 teaspoons olive oil, cover the pot, and adjust the heat to maintain a simmer.

2.   Using a cleaver, cut each lobster tail in half lengthwise, devein if needed, and then cut each half into thirds crosswise. You should have 6 pieces per tail. Set aside.

3.   Select a skillet or sauté pan that can later contain all the lobster pieces without overlapping. Heat 2 tablespoons olive oil in the pan over medium heat. Add the onion and sprinkle with 1/4 teaspoon salt. Sauté the onion until softened and translucent, about 3 minutes. Add the garlic and cook 1 minute more, or until aromatic.

4.   Stir in the parsley and add the wine. Simmer for several minutes, until the scent of alcohol subsides.

5.   Add the tomatoes, chili, and 1/8 teaspoon salt, and simmer for about 10 minutes, or until the consistency of marinara sauce.

6.   While the sauce is simmering, return the pot of water to a boil and drop in the pasta.

7.   When the sauce is the desired consistency, add the lobster pieces and 1/8 teaspoon salt to the skillet and coat them in the sauce. Cook the lobster for about 2 to 3 minutes on one side, then turn the pieces and cook for another 2 to 3 minutes, until just cooked through. Using a slotted spoon, lift

the lobster pieces from the sauce and transfer them to a large plate or bowl.

8.   Meanwhile, check the pasta. Drain the spaghettini when it is still firm to the bite (al dente), transfer to a very warm serving bowl. Drizzle in 1 1/2 teaspoons olive oil and toss to coat the pasta.

9.   As soon as the lobster is just cool enough to handle (you can wear kitchen gloves), remove the meat from the shells, and return the meat to the sauce.

10.   Pour the lobster mixture over the pasta and toss thoroughly. Serve immediately.

Simple Sexy Kitchen Tip: You can prepare the sauce an hour or so in advance, through Step 5. (Refrigerate the lobster until ready to use.) When ready to proceed, bring the sauce to a steady simmer before adding the lobster pieces. This special dish warrants a special setting. Let yourself be inspired!

Aphrodite Says: The ancient Egyptians filled King Tutankhamun's tomb with massive amounts of garlic, perhaps in the hope of sending their leader to the next world with a big smile on his face. You could say this gives a whole new meaning to rising from the dead!

*****

Thai Chicken with Basil and Coconut Sauce
Double the cooking sauce recipe if you like lots of sauce!

SEXY FOODS: basil, ginger, mushroom, coconut, chili flakes, rice, garlic, onion
2 SERVINGS

Sauce
1/2 cup coconut milk
2 tablespoons soy sauce
2 tablespoons unseasoned rice vinegar
1 tablespoon Asian fish sauce *(nam pla)*
1/8 to 1/4 teaspoon crushed red chili flakes
2 teaspoons all-purpose flour or cornstarch
2 teaspoons water

Chicken

3 (2- to 3-inch-diameter) fresh shiitake mushrooms
10 ounces boneless, skinless chicken breast
1 to 2 tablespoons canola or other high-temperature vegetable oil
1/2 medium onion, cut into thin slices and separated into rings
2 cloves garlic, minced or pressed
1 1/2 teaspoons minced fresh ginger
2 small green onions, both white and green parts, cut into 1-inch pieces
1/3 rounded cup lightly packed, thinly sliced fresh basil leaves
Hot cooked rice

1.   **To make the sauce:** In a medium saucepan, mix the coconut milk, soy sauce, vinegar, fish sauce, and chili flakes, stirring well. Bring to a boil, stirring frequently, and let sauce reduce by about 1/3.

2.   Meanwhile, in a small bowl, make a slurry by mixing the flour or cornstarch with the water until smooth. Set aside.

3.   When the sauce is reduced, remix the reserved slurry and gradually add it to the sauce, boiling and stirring constantly for about 2 minutes, to thicken. Set aside and keep warm.

4.   **To prepare the chicken:** Cut the chicken crosswise into 1/2-inch-thick strips and set aside.

5.   Cut off and discard the mushroom stems, then cut the caps into 1/4-inch-thick slices and set aside.

6.   Heat a large skillet or wok over high heat then add and heat 1 tablespoon of the oil.

7.   Add the onion rings, garlic, and ginger, and stir-fry until the onion rings are lightly browned. Use a slotted spoon to transfer the onion mixture to a plate and set aside.

8.   Add a third of the chicken to the pan and stir-fry for about 3 minutes, until the meat begins to brown and is just cooked through. Lift out the cooked chicken and add to the onion mixture. If needed, add a bit more oil to the pan and cook the remaining chicken, in two batches, as before.

9.   Return the onion and chicken mixture to the pan. Add the reserved mushrooms, green onions, and basil, stir-frying until just heated through.

10.   Pour the reserved sauce into the pan and bring to a boil.

11.   Serve immediately over hot rice.

Simple Sexy Kitchen Tip: For added authenticity, try Thai basil, which is a bit sweeter than its Western counterpart, and Thai ginger, which is also a bit milder. Both are typically available at Asian markets.

Love Skills: While preparing a meal, keep in mind that you are the main course. Dressing up in what makes you feel sexy and confident will enable you to become a master in the kitchen and in the bedroom.

Jamaican Chicken with Salsa

Jamaicans use the hottest chili on earth, the Scotch bonnet, to create the flaming deliciousness of jerk recipes. If that much heat sends you running for a fire extinguisher instead of into each others' arms, feel free to substitute with habanero, which is only slightly less hot, or the relatively tamer jalapeño or serrano chilies.

SEXY FOODS: allspice, garlic, thyme, nutmeg, ginger, onion, chilies, black pepper
2 TO 4 SERVINGS

2 teaspoons dry Jamaican jerk seasoning
1/4 cup finely chopped green onion, both white and green parts
1 hot chili, seeded, such as Scotch bonnet, habanero, jalapeño, or serrano
2 tablespoons olive oil
2 tablespoons low-sodium soy sauce
6 tablespoons distilled white vinegar
1/4 cup orange juice
1 teaspoon fresh lime juice
1 teaspoon dark Jamaican rum
1 pound boneless, skinless, chicken breast halves
Watermelon–Pineapple Salsa
Hot cooked rice, optional

1. In a nonreactive small bowl, mix the jerk seasoning, green onion, chili, oil, soy sauce, vinegar, orange and lime juices, and rum.
2. Pat the chicken dry with paper towels and place in a nonreactive bowl. Pour the marinade over the chicken and turn the chicken in the marinade to coat well. Cover and refrigerate for at least 4 hours, or overnight. Turn chicken pieces once or twice while marinating.
3. When ready to cook the chicken, prepare the salsa and cook the rice if using.
4. Heat a large nonstick skillet over medium-high heat, and sauté the chicken for about 4 minutes on each side, or until done.
5. Serve immediately with the salsa and rice.

Simple Sexy Kitchen Tip: The chicken can also be grilled—hot and fast over direct heat. Be sure your grill grate is clean and lightly oiled, and take care not to overcook the chicken.

Love Skills: Who says you need to restrict your rendezvous to the bedroom? Set up an impromptu table for two with a blanket on the floor, on the balcony, or in a private garden. No reservations required!

Couscous

SEXY FOODS: onion, garlic, black pepper
2 TO 3 SERVINGS

1 tablespoon olive oil
1 cup chopped onion
1 tablespoon plus 1 teaspoon minced garlic
1 red bell pepper, finely chopped
1 3/4 cups chicken stock
1 1/2 cups quick-cooking whole-wheat couscous
1/4 teaspoon salt
Freshly ground black pepper to taste
1/2 pound broccolini

1.   In a large skillet over medium heat, heat the olive oil. Add the onion, 1 tablespoon garlic, and bell pepper, and sauté until tender, about 3 minutes. Add 1 1/2 cups chicken stock and bring to a boil. Stir in the couscous, cover, remove from heat, and let stand for 5 minutes.
2.   Meanwhile, in a medium skillet, heat the remaining 1/4 cup chicken stock, remaining 1 teaspoon garlic, salt, and pepper. Add the broccolini and simmer for 5 minutes.
3.   Fluff the couscous with a fork and transfer to a serving platter. Make a long, narrow indentation in the middle. Arrange the broccolini in the indentation and spoon the cooking liquid over the couscous. Serve at once.

Simple Sexy Kitchen Tip: Submerging onions or running cold water over them also reduces the problem, but this can be a bit impractical. If you can remember, follow the National Onion Association's advice and chill the onions for 30 minutes or more to reduce the onion's metabolism and release of the enzymes that produce the offending LF gas. As a last resort, put on a sexy pair of glasses or goggles to block the gas from reaching your eyes!

Aphrodite Says: Onions were served at wedding feasts of both the ancient Greeks and Romans to "seek the door of Venus." In a later era, *The Perfumed Garden* provides a love potion of onions and honey, a simplified version of Galen's recipe that also included pine nuts and almonds. To this day several Indian sects prohibit the eating of onions to prevent wanton sexual desire.

Pepper Steak with Cognac

SEXY FOODS: pepper, spirits, steak, onion (shallots), parsley
2 SERVINGS

Steak
1 tablespoon black peppercorns
2 boneless beef steaks, rib-eye, sirloin, or filet mignon, 3/4 to 1 inch thick, 6
to 8 ounces each
1 tablespoon vegetable oil
1 1/2 teaspoons butter
Salt to taste

Sauce
1 1/2 teaspoons butter plus 1 to 2 tablespoons softened butter
1 1/2 teaspoons minced shallot
1/4 cup beef stock
2 tablespoons Cognac

Garnish
Flat-leaf parsley or watercress

1.   **To prepare the steaks:** Roughly crush the peppercorns.
2.   Trim excess fat from the steaks and dry the meat with paper towels.
Sprinkle half of the peppercorns on one side of each steak and press into
the meat. Repeat on the other side of the steaks. Cover with wax paper and
set aside for at least 30 minutes or up to 1 hour to allow the pepper flavor to
penetrate.
3.   Preheat a warmer drawer or an oven to 180°F.
4.   Add the oil and butter to a small-to-medium, heavy skillet just big
enough to hold both steaks in one layer. Heat on medium-high until the butter
foam begins to subside.
5.   Sauté the steaks on one side for 3 to 4 minutes, keeping the fat hot,
but not burning. Turn the steaks and cook the other side, about the same time
for medium rare, less for rarer meat (see Tip.)
6.   Remove the steaks from the pan, sprinkle with salt, and keep warm in
the oven or warmer drawer.
7.   **To make the sauce:** Pour out the fat but do not clean the skillet. Set
the skillet over medium heat and add the 1 1/2 teaspoons butter and shallots.
Cook slowly for 1 minute, then add the stock. Raise heat to high and boil
down the liquid rapidly, while scraping up cooking bits and juices.

8.   Add the Cognac and boil rapidly for about 1 minute to evaporate the alcohol. Remove the pan from heat and swirl in the softened butter, 1 1/2 teaspoons at a time.

9.   Pour the sauce over the steaks and **garnish** with parsley or watercress. Serve immediately.

Simple Sexy Kitchen Tip: Steak is sexiest when it's tender, juicy, and blushing inside with rosy shades. If you're used to steak cooked through, be adventurous and try it medium rare, just this once. It might inspire a little adventure in the bedroom as well!

Survey Secrets: When participants were asked to create their own sexy menu, steak was among the top main dish choices, particularly among young men, 22-25. Potatoes were a favorite pairing, which just goes to prove that certain mainstay combinations hold definite aphrodisiac appeal.

Aphrodite Says: Peppercorns are spicy berries native to India or Malaysia. Their aphrodisiac reputation as sexual "energy" boosters dates back thousands of years. They are mentioned in both *The Kama Sutra* (2nd century, BCE) and in the 15th century Arabic text, *The Perfumed Garden of Sensual Delight.* Like sweet peppers, their color variations reflect changes with time. At the time of picking, they're green; as they dry in the sun, they transform from red, to yellow, to brown, and finally to black. If the black husk is removed after the drying process, the result is white peppercorns, the very spiciest. Pepper ground from peppercorns was so valued in early European times that it was used as currency. Pepper in all forms stimulates saliva flow, so it's a perfect choice to "whet" your appetite in many ways!

Mussels in Saffron-laced White Wine Broth

SEXY FOODS: mussels, saffron, tomatoes, white wine, onion (chives)
2 TO 3 SERVINGS

2 pounds mussels
8 ounces tomatoes
1/2 teaspoon butter
1 medium clove garlic, chopped
1/4 cup dry white wine
1 1/2 teaspoons half-and-half
1/2 rounded teaspoon saffron threads
1/4 cup clam juice
1 green onion, thinly sliced
2 1/4 teaspoons lemon juice
2 teaspoons thinly sliced chives

1.   Scrub and debeard the mussels. Cover with damp paper towels and refrigerate until needed.
2.   Core the tomatoes then halve crosswise. Gently squeeze out seeds and excess juice and chop the tomatoes. You should have about 3/4 cup. Set aside.
3.   In a large nonreactive pot over medium-low heat, melt the butter, then sauté the garlic until fragrant, about 1 minute. Do not brown.
4.   Add the wine, half-and-half, and saffron, raise the heat to medium, and simmer for 5 minutes.
5.   Add the clam juice, green onion, lemon juice, and reserved tomato, and simmer for 5 minutes more.
6.   Add the mussels and cover the pot. Let steam until the mussels open, about 5 to 7 minutes. About halfway through cooking, hold down the lid with a pot holder and gently shake the pot to rearrange the mussels so that they cook evenly.
7.   Divide the opened mussels between two bowls, discarding any mussels that do not open. Divide the broth between the servings and sprinkle with chives.

Survey Secrets: Seafood, especially oysters, lobster and shrimp, ranked in the top 10 of all three categories—reputation, chosen-from-list, and free choice—but caviar, clams (including mussels) and sushi also made at least one of the three top ten lists! When it comes to sexy eats, seafood gets us rocking and rolling!

Love Skills: Does cleaning up a huge mess after a meal deter you from cooking? Instead, engage your partner in a little love play to turn a daunting task into something you can't wait to do.

Aphrodite Says: While the Greeks valued temperance and moderation, alcohol played a role in overriding that mindset. The Cult of Dionysus favored wine-fueled revelry steeped in mysterious rituals deeply associated with notions of life and death and fertility. Bacchanalian traditions were originally connected to agriculture and theater, and involved liberation of oneself through wine and ecstatic behavior. Though complicated and controversial today, for the ancients, sexuality was an early byproduct of alcohol consumption. The Romans even had a slogan for it: *sine baccho, venus friget,* or "without wine, love grows old."

Spice-infused Rice with Lamb

This is a great accompaniment to the Shish Kebab or as a side to another meal. It can be made ahead, if desired.

SEXY FOODS: rice, cinnamon, nutmeg, onion, tomato, mushroom, almond

2 tablespoons butter
1 1/4 cups long-grain brown rice
1/2 cup chopped onion
2 1/4 cups Lamb Broth (recipe follows), chicken broth, or water
1 (14-ounce) can whole tomatoes, drained, 1/4 cup of juice reserved
1 1/2 teaspoons dark brown sugar
1/2 teaspoon ground cinnamon
Rounded 1/4 teaspoon freshly grated nutmeg
3/4 teaspoon salt
1/4 teaspoon freshly ground black pepper
1/4 California bay leaf or 1/2 Turkish bay leaf
1/2 cup grated Cheddar cheese
1/4 cup sliced white mushrooms, optional
1/4 cup cooked lamb bits from lamb bones if making the Lamb Broth, optional
2 tablespoons slivered almonds, optional

1.   Preheat an oven to 350°F. (Note: If making the Lamb Broth, prepare it at least 8 hours in advance, or the day before.)
2.   Over medium heat, in a large ovenproof pan with a tight-fitting lid, melt the butter and sauté the rice and onion for about 5 minutes.
3.   Add the broth, tomatoes and reserved juice, brown sugar, cinnamon, nutmeg, salt, pepper, and bay leaf. Cover the pan, transfer to the oven, and bake for 45 minutes.
4.   Stir the rice well and then fold in the cheese, mushrooms if using, and lamb bits if using.
5.   Re-cover the pan and bake for 30 to 40 minutes more, or until all liquid is absorbed and rice is tender.
6.   Just before serving, sprinkle with almonds if using.

Lamb Broth

3 TO 4 SERVINGS

1 tablespoon olive oil
Bone and trimmings from a leg of lamb, or 1 1/3 pounds lamb shank
1 1/2 cups chopped onion
6 cups water
1/2 California bay leaf or 1 Turkish bay leaf
8 black peppercorns

1.   In a large Dutch oven or heavy soup pot over medium heat, heat the oil and brown the lamb bone and trimmings or lamb shank for about 5 minutes. Add the onion and brown several minutes more, until the onion is soft and translucent.

2.   Add the water and bring to a vigorous boil. Skim off scum that rises to the top for several minutes, until no more rises.

3.   Add the bay leaf and peppercorns and reduce heat so that broth simmers, uncovered, for about 2 hours.

4.   Cool. Then strain the broth and refrigerate for several hours so that fat rises to the top.

5.   Pick the lamb meat from the bones and reserve separately, refrigerated. Discard connective tissue, gristle, onion, and spices.

6.   Just before using the broth, skim off and discard fat. Extra broth can be frozen for up to 6 months.

Aphrodite Says: The Indian love manual, *The Ananga-Ranga,* includes a wild rice recipe that was to be eaten at night to provide a man with "enormous vigour and the enjoyment of one hundred women." If it can help a guy handle one hundred women, imagine what it might do if he was just "handling" you!

Shish Kebab

You marinate the lamb the day before, but it cooks quickly at the last minute. Serve with a fragrant rice dish, such as the Spice-infused Rice with Lamb basmati rice, or your favorite pilaf. You'll need long metal skewers, at least one for each of you.

SEXY FOODS: oregano, onion, tomato, black pepper, mushroom
6 TO 8 SERVINGS

Lamb and Marinade
1 1/4 pounds boneless leg of lamb
1 large onion, sliced
1 1/2 teaspoons dried Greek oregano
1 1/2 teaspoons salt
1 teaspoon cracked black pepper
1 1/4 cups dry sherry, or more as needed
1/2 cup olive oil, or more as needed

Vegetables (per person)
Two 1 1/2- to 2-inch-diameter onions, peeled, root end trimmed but left intact
Two 2-inch-diameter tomatoes
3 or 4 medium white mushrooms
1/2 bell pepper, cut into 1- to 2-inch squares

1.   **To prepare the lamb:** Cut the lamb into 1 1/2-inch cubes.
2.   In a large nonreactive dish, layer half the onions. Next, layer the lamb, then the remaining onions.
3.   Sprinkle with the oregano, salt, and pepper.
4.   Pour the sherry and oil over to cover. If more marinade is needed, use more sherry and oil in the same proportions.
5.   Cover and refrigerate overnight, occasionally stirring gently.
6.   **To prepare the skewers and cook the kebabs:** Remove the lamb from the marinade and set aside at room temperature for 1 hour before needed. Discard marinade.
7.   If you prefer onions without the raw "edge," microwave the required number of onions on high for 1 minute. Set aside to cool.
8.   Oil a grill grate or broiler pan, and heat grill or broiler to high. (Select plain, not scented, briquettes, if using.) Place grill grate or broiler pan about 6 to 8 inches from heat and heat until hot.
9.   Place the drained lamb and the vegetables in separate lazy-Susan bowls or on a large platter.
10.   Thread the vegetables and meat, alternately, on metal skewers. Un-

less it's a surprise meal for your lover, it's fun to each assemble your own skewer, according to personal preferences.

11.   Cook the kebabs for 3 to 4 minutes on one side; turn the skewers and cook to desired doneness, about 3 to 4 minutes more for medium-rare meat.

Simple Sexy Kitchen Tip: If your boneless leg of lamb weighs significantly more than what's needed here, freeze the remainder for another use or for another wonderful shish kebab in the future.

Aphrodite Says: The tomato is both the "love apple" and a forbidden fruit, in part because of the historical bias against red foods, and in part because it's a member of the nightshade family and was feared poisonous. Thankfully, redness-means-passion has won out over redness-means-death, for the beautiful and delicious tomato is worthy of inclusion in any love feast!

Tomatoes and Olives with Cumin Dressing

This is a wonderful accompaniment to grilled shrimp or lamb kebabs. You might also include it as a side dish for a quick summer dinner or picnic.

SEXY FOODS: tomato, olive, cumin, turmeric, onion, cilantro
4 SERVINGS

1 pound medium, vine-ripened tomatoes
1/2 cup drained, pitted, black olives, such as kalamata
1 medium yellow or white onion, chopped
1 tablespoon chopped fresh cilantro or flat-leaf parsley
2 tablespoons fresh lemon juice
3 tablespoons extra-virgin olive oil
1/2 teaspoon salt
1 teaspoon sugar
1/16 teaspoon ground turmeric
Rounded 1/4 teaspoon ground cumin
Freshly ground black pepper to taste

1.   In a ceramic or other nonreactive shallow serving bowl or an 8-inch-square glass dish, lay out the tomatoes and sprinkle evenly with the olives, onion, and herb.
2.   Put the lemon juice in a small bowl and drizzle in the oil while whisking constantly.
3.   Add the salt, sugar, turmeric, cumin, and black pepper, and mix well. Pour over the tomato mixture. Cover and refrigerate.
4.   Let marinate for 2 hours and serve ice cold.

Simple Sexy Kitchen Tip: Leftover salad will keep, refrigerated, for about two days. Layer it with sliced cold cuts for an effortless sandwich filling or toss with lettuce and arugula for a quick green salad.

Ghee

Ghee holds a special place in the lore and history of both sexuality and food. Especially prevalent in India, it also holds strong value for several Middle Eastern and African cultures. It's featured in the love manual Kama Sutra and in Ayurvedic writings:

"A person who takes ghee and milk,
who is free from fear, complexion and diseases,
who indulges in sex every day, who is youthful,
and who has determination, gets sex vigour with women"

This recipe whispers, "Slow down, take your time." Watch the butter slowly transform into a rich caramel hue. Passing the time fantasizing about your lover while making this wouldn't hurt either!

SEXY FOODS: ghee (caramelized butter)
ABOUT 1 1/2 CUPS

1 pound high-quality, unsalted butter, cut into 1 1/2-inch chunks
You'll also need:
Wooden spoon
Fine-mesh strainer
Fine cheesecloth
Ladle
Heat-resistant glass container with a tight-fitting lid

1.   In a heavy saucepan, melt the butter over medium-low to low heat for about 5 to 8 minutes. Meanwhile, place a heat-resistant glass container on a folded kitchen towel in a sink; line a fine-mesh strainer with 4 layers of cheesecloth and place over the container. Once the butter is melted, stir once a minute until the butter begins to froth and boil.
2.   Adjust heat to a slow boil. Expect foam to rise to top surface of the butter. Every few minutes, for about 30 minutes, stir and scrape bottom of pan with a wooden spoon to disperse milk solids as they settle there.
3.   After about 30 minutes, the surface foam will separate; the milk solids in the butter will begin clumping together. As the milk solids start to cook, the aroma will intensify. You've reached the clarified butter stage.
4.   During the next 5 to 10 minutes, continue stirring and scraping bottom of pan. Also scrape down the foamy residue accumulating on sides of pan. Watch the butter carefully as the milk solids caramelize into a light-to-medium brown and the butter becomes an alluring orange color. Fizzy bubbles will begin to form. The aroma will be more sweet and caramel-like.

5.   As soon as the milk solids are medium brown, remove pan from heat. Working carefully so as not to disturb the milk solids at bottom of pan, immediately ladle the butter oil into the cheesecloth-lined strainer set on the glass container. Don't ladle in any of the milk solids. Allow the ghee to cool, uncovered, before closing the lid.

Simple Sexy Kitchen Tip: If you stopped before the milk solids caramelized, you've made clarified butter, which also tastes great. It should be stored in the refrigerator and will last up to 3 months. If you've succeeded in making ghee, it can be stored at room temperature for up to a year (as if this delicious stuff is going to last that long!).

Love Skills: Making ghee yourself takes a little attention, a light hand and a bit of time. Think of it in terms of extensive, delicious foreplay. The care you take now will pay off in heightened satisfaction later. Slow down and enjoy the transformation!

*****

Spicy Shrimp and Rice

Serve this delicious dish with crusty bread and steamed artichokes with lemon butter.

SEXY FOODS: shrimp, chili, tomatoes, olives, orange, rice
4 SERVINGS

3 tablespoons olive oil
2 medium yellow onions, finely chopped (about 1 1/3 cups)
3 cloves garlic, chopped or crushed
1 medium green or red bell pepper, coarsely chopped
1 (8-ounce) bottle clam juice
3/4 cup fresh orange juice
Two 1/2-by-2-inch strips orange zest
1 cup chopped tomatoes
10 pitted ripe black olives, halved
1 California bay leaf or 2 dried Turkish bay leaves
2 teaspoons hot chili sauce
3 cups cooked brown or white rice
1 pound shrimp, peeled and deveined

1. Preheat an oven to 350°F.

2. In a Dutch oven or other stove-to-oven pot, heat the oil over medium heat for 1 minute.

3. Add the onions and garlic and cook, uncovered, until golden, about 10 minutes. Do not brown the garlic.

4. Add the bell pepper and cook for 5 minutes more.

5. Stir in the clam juice and orange juice and zest. Raise heat to high and cook, uncovered, for 2 minutes.

6. Add the tomatoes, olives, bay leaf, and chili sauce, and bring to a boil. Stir in the cooked rice.

7. Add the shrimp, cover, and bake for 15 minutes, or until the shrimp are pink and just cooked through.

Variation: To serve as a salad, let cool, uncovered, to room temperature. In a small bowl, whisk together 1/3 cup olive oil and 2 1/2 tablespoons lemon juice. When the rice and shrimp have cooled, thoroughly fold in the oil and lemon juice mixture. Serve immediately at room temperature.

Simple Sexy Kitchen Tip: This dish can be made in advance. Omit adding the shrimp and let the casserole cool, uncovered, to room temperature. Cover and refrigerate for up to 3 days. One hour before baking, remove from refrigerator. Then add the shrimp and bake for 25 to 30 minutes.

Aphrodite Says: During his travels in the 18th century, Capt. Cook reported that, on one island, the king's task was to deflower all the maidens on the island, and that the king attributed his virility to a precoital shrimp dish.

Scallops with Garlic and Cilantro

I like to serve the scallops over rice or with toasted French bread for sopping up the flavorful juices.

SEXY FOODS: scallops, garlic, chili sauce, zucchini, cilantro, garlic, tomato
3 TO 4 SERVINGS

1 pound large scallops (about 20)
2 plum tomatoes
2 medium zucchini (about 11 ounces total)
3 tablespoons butter
1 tablespoon olive oil
4 medium cloves garlic, chopped
2 tablespoons hot chili sauce, such as Sriracha or Tapatio brand, or to taste
2 tablespoons fresh lime juice (about 1 or 2 limes)
2/3 cup finely chopped fresh cilantro

1.   Rinse the scallops with cold water and pat dry. Set aside.
2.   Quarter each tomato lengthwise and lightly squeeze to remove seeds and juice. Set quarters aside.
3.   Cut each zucchini in half crosswise, and then quarter each piece lengthwise.
4.   In a large skillet over medium heat, melt the butter. Add and heat the oil, then add the zucchini, cut side down. Cook, turning pieces occasionally, for about 4 to 5 minutes, until browned on all sides and just tender. Remove the zucchini from pan and set aside.
5.   Add the garlic to pan and cook for about 2 minutes, or under golden. Stir in the hot sauce.
6.   Add the reserved scallops and cook, stirring constantly, for 2 to 3 minutes.
7.   Stir in the lime juice and cilantro. Add the reserved tomato and zucchini to pan, and cook for about 2 minutes more, until scallops are fully cooked.

Survey Secrets: In my 21st Aphrodisiac Foods Survey, zucchini was recognized as one of the top five sexiest vegetables.

Aphrodite Says: As you might have guessed by now, zucchini (aka courgette), is a Doctrine of Resemblances food, rivaled only by the cucumber and banana in its approximation of part of the male anatomy. Perhaps that's why no less a source than the UCLA School of Medicine's training program in human sexuality used to encourage the use of zucchini for certain personal gratifications. That's quite an endorsement for this veggie's erotic potential.

Balsamic Squash Purée

SEXY FOODS: squash, shallots, nutmeg
4 SERVINGS

1 butternut squash (about 1 1/2 pounds) or 2 cups roasted butternut squash
pulp
2 tablespoons minced shallots
4 tablespoons butter
3 tablespoons balsamic vinegar
1 teaspoon salt
Freshly grated nutmeg

1.   If starting with a whole squash, preheat an oven to 400ºF. Cut the
squash in half lengthwise; scrape out and discard the seeds. Place the halves
cut side down in a roasting pan, add 1/4 inch of water, and bake for about 30
to 40 minutes, or until soft when pierced with a fork.
2.   Remove from oven and set aside until cool enough to handle. Scrape
out and mash 2 cups of squash pulp; set aside. (Reserve any remaining
squash for another use.)
3.   In a medium saucepan over medium heat, heat 1 tablespoon of the
butter and sauté the shallots for 3 to 5 minutes. Add the vinegar, increase heat
to high, and cook for about 3 to 5 minutes, until the vinegar is reduced to a
syrup.
4.   Stir in the squash pulp and salt, reduce heat to low, and cook until
heated through, about 5 minutes.
5.   Cut the remaining butter into small pieces, add to squash, and beat
with a fork or wooden spoon until fairly smooth. Sprinkle with the nutmeg
and serve immediately.

Balsamic-braised Cipollini Onions with Pomegranate

SEXY FOODS: onion, pomegranate seeds, spirits (wine)
2 TO 4 SERVINGS

1 pound cipollini onions or small boiling onions
1 tablespoon extra-virgin olive oil
Salt to taste
Freshly ground black pepper to taste
3/4 cup low-sodium chicken broth
2 tablespoons dry red wine
2 tablespoons balsamic vinegar
1/2 teaspoon light brown sugar
2 tablespoons crème fraîche or heavy whipping cream
1/4 cup pomegranate seeds (about 1 1/2 ounces)

1.   Bring a large saucepan of water to a full boil over high heat. Add the
onions to blanch for 1 minute. Drain and let cool briefly. Peel and trim the
onions.
2.   In a large skillet over medium-high heat, heat the oil, add the onions,
and sprinkle with salt and pepper. Sauté the onions until brown, about 12
minutes.
3.   Add the broth, wine, vinegar, and brown sugar. Bring to a boil, then
reduce heat, cover, and simmer for 15 minutes.
4.   Increase heat, return to a boil, and cook, stirring often, until onions
are tender and liquid is thickened, about 18 minutes. (If desired, the dish can
be made ahead to this point, cooled, covered, and refrigerated for up to 1 day.
When ready to proceed, warm over medium heat and resume with Step 5.)
5.   Stir in the crème fraîche. Simmer for about 2 minutes, until the sauce
coats onions thickly.
6.   Adjust the seasoning with additional salt and pepper if desired.
Spoon individual servings onto warmed plates or transfer the onions to a
serving bowl. Sprinkle with pomegranate seeds.

Aphrodite Says: As we've seen before, many ancient and pre-modern cultures
viewed a food's physical characteristics as an indication of what it could do
for them. Thus the pomegranate's many, many seeds were an obvious nod to
fertility. They were native to Persia and then spread to Egypt, the Near East,
and Greece. As with the pear and certain other fruits, some suggest it was the
pomegranate, not the apple, that tempted Eve in the Garden of Eden.

Herbed Lamb Meatballs

I like to serve the meatballs over garlic couscous or make a killer meatball sandwich with pita bread using leftovers.

SEXY FOODS: onion, tomato, nutmeg, ginger, cloves, parsley, cilantro

4 MAIN-DISH SERVINGS... OR 2 MAIN-DISH SERVINGS, PLUS
2 KILLER MEATBALL SANDWICHES (WRAPPED IN BIG PITAS) LATER

Sauce

1 pound vine-ripened tomatoes
1 1/2 teaspoons olive oil
1 cup chopped onion
1 clove garlic, chopped
1 teaspoon sugar
1 tablespoon tomato paste
1/2 teaspoon quatre épices (see Tip)
1 teaspoon salt
1/4 teaspoon freshly ground black pepper
1/2 cup unsalted beef stock

Meatballs

1 clove garlic, minced
2 cups minced onion
2/3 cup minced fresh flat-leaf parsley, including stems
2/3 cup minced fresh cilantro
2/3 cup minced fresh dill
1 pound lean ground lamb
1 teaspoon salt
1/4 teaspoon freshly ground black pepper
Fresh dill for garnishing

1.   **To make the sauce:** Wash and dry the tomatoes, then purée them in a blender or food processor. Set aside.
2.   In a large nonreactive saucepan, heat the oil and sauté the onion for about 1 minute. Add the garlic and sauté for 1 minute more.
3.   Stir in the reserved tomato purée, sugar, tomato paste, quatre épices, salt, and pepper.
4.   Stir in the broth and cook for 20 minutes over low heat.

5.   **Meanwhile,** preheat an oven to 450ºF. Lightly oil a rimmed baking sheet and set aside.

6.   **While the sauce is simmering, make the meatballs:** In a large bowl, mix the garlic, onions, parsley, cilantro, and dill.

7.   Break up the lamb and mix in, taking care not to compact the mixture.

8.   Season with the salt and pepper.

9.   With wet hands, form small portions of the meat mixture into 1 1/2-inch diameter meatballs (about 24 total.) Dip your hands in a small bowl of water as needed. As the balls are formed, place them, spaced apart, in a single layer on the baking sheet.

10.   Bake the meatballs for about 12 minutes, or until a crust has formed on the outside.

11.   Add the meatballs to the tomato sauce and simmer gently for 5 minutes.

12.   Serve hot, garnished with dill.

Simple Sexy Kitchen Tip: The four spices included in the quatre épices blend—nutmeg, ginger, cloves, and pepper—all have aphrodisiac reputations. Leave it to the sexy French to use it often in their cooking. You'll find the blend—not to be confused with Chinese five-spice—in the spice section of most supermarkets.

Pork Tenderloin with Fruit Sauces

SEXY FOODS: cherry, apricot, garlic, thyme, ginger
4 SERVINGS

1 1/2 pounds pork tenderloin
1/4 cup dry sherry
1/4 cup low-sodium soy sauce
1 large clove garlic, minced
1 1/2 teaspoons Dijon mustard
1/2 teaspoon ground ginger
1/2 teaspoon dried thyme
Apricot Sauce (recipe follows)
2 teaspoons vegetable oil
Cherry Sauce (recipe follows)

1.   **To prepare the pork:** Place the meat in a lidded, nonreactive dish that will just hold the meat and marinade, or in a zip-style plastic bag.
2.   In a small bowl, whisk together the sherry, soy sauce, garlic, mustard, ginger, and thyme until thoroughly mixed. Set aside 1 to 2 tablespoons of the marinade for basting, and pour the remaining marinade over the pork, making sure it is thoroughly coated. Cover the dish or seal the bag, and refrigerate for 2 to 3 hours, turning the meat about halfway through.

3.   While the meat is marinating, **prepare the Apricot Sauce.**

4.   When ready to cook the meat, preheat an oven to 350ºF. Place a rack in a broiler pan or other shallow pan, and set aside.
5.   Discard the used marinade, and pat the meat dry.
6.   Heat the oil in a sauté pan over medium heat, and sear the meat for about 2 to 3 minutes on each side.
7.   Transfer the meat to the reserved pan and place in oven. After 10 minutes, baste the meat with the reserved marinade and turn the meat. Cook for another 5 minutes, or until a meat thermometer reads 155º to 160ºF.

8.   Meanwhile, **prepare the Cherry Sauce**.

9.   When the meat is done, remove from oven and let rest for 5 minutes.
10.   Slice on the diagonal into 1/4-inch-thick slices. Serve with the fruit sauces.

Apricot Sauce

2 teaspoons oil or butter
3 tablespoons minced green onion (mix of green and white parts)
1 (12-ounce) jar apricot preserves, such as Hero
1/3 cup apricot brandy
1 teaspoon low-sodium soy sauce
1 teaspoon seasoned rice vinegar
1/8 teaspoon ground ginger

1.   Heat the oil in a saucepan over medium heat, and sauté the green onion for 2 to 3 minutes.
2.   Stir in the preserves, brandy, soy sauce, vinegar, and ginger.
3.   Simmer over low heat for 20 to 30 minutes, or until reduced to desired consistency. Keep warm.

Cherry Sauce

1 tablespoon dry sherry
1 1/2 teaspoons low-sodium soy sauce
1/2 cup plus 2 tablespoons currant jelly
2 tablespoons dried tart cherries (see Tip)

1.   Combine all the ingredients in a saucepan.
2.   Bring to a simmer over medium-low heat and cook for 2 minutes. Keep warm.

Simple Sexy Kitchen Tip: Dried tart cherries are available from Trader Joe's and other specialty markets.

Aphrodite Says: In the Middle Ages Europeans thought thyme encouraged lust and sexual potency. Even the famous Benedictine monks got in on the act, and thyme is still an ingredient in their decadent liqueur.

Moroccan Honey Chicken

Serve this enticing dish with couscous, rice, rice pilaf, or potatoes to soak up all the delicious sauce.

SEXY FOODS: honey, cinnamon, ginger, onion, mushroom, tomato
4 SERVINGS

1 (14.5-ounce) can stewed tomatoes, undrained
1 cup coarsely chopped onion (about 1 medium)
2 large cloves garlic, finely chopped
6 tablespoons tomato paste
3/4 teaspoon salt
1/8 teaspoon freshly ground black pepper
1 teaspoon ground ginger
2 teaspoons ground cinnamon
3 tablespoons honey
2 pounds chicken parts
1 tablespoon olive oil, optional
3 cups sliced white mushrooms (about 8 ounces), optional
1 tablespoon toasted sesame seeds for garnishing

1. In a large, heavy nonreactive skillet, combine tomatoes, onion, garlic, tomato paste, 1/4 teaspoon salt, pepper, ginger, 1 1/2 teaspoons cinnamon, and 2 tablespoons honey. Stir until well blended. Cook over medium-low heat until well blended, about 5 to 10 minutes.
2. Add chicken pieces and spoon the sauce over them. Cook, covered, over medium-low heat until chicken is tender, about 40 to 60 minutes.
3. For mushrooms, heat olive oil in a large sauté pan over medium-high heat. Sauté the mushrooms until browned, about 4 to 5 minutes. Set aside.
4. When chicken is done, remove from skillet & cover to keep warm.
5. Return skillet with the sauce to the stove and bring to a boil over medium-high heat. Stir occasionally, until reduced to thick sauce, 5-10 minutes.
6. Stir in the remaining 1/2 teaspoon salt, 1/2 teaspoon cinnamon, and 1 tablespoon honey.
7. Return the chicken to the skillet, add the mushrooms, and heat through. Adjust the seasoning if needed.
8. To serve, spoon some sauce over each portion of chicken, and sprinkle with sesame seeds.

Aphrodite Says: Writings from Mesopotamia, widely regarded as the birthplace of civilization, include references to the role of honey in enhancing sensual pleasure. These writings express the sexual act, from "tasting the honey-plant," and "doing the sweet thing," to "bringing the sweetness," which likely referred to orgasm.

Crab-stuffed Mushrooms

SEXY FOODS: crab, mushroom, garlic, parsley
2 SERVINGS

8 ounces extra-large white or cremini mushrooms (about 12)
1/2 cup Italian-seasoned dry bread crumbs
4 ounces cooked crabmeat, picked over as needed and pulled apart or chopped
1/4 cup (1 ounce) grated pecorino Romano cheese
1 tablespoon finely chopped parsley
1 small clove garlic, pressed or finely chopped
Pinch of salt
1/8 teaspoon freshly ground black pepper, or more to taste
Extra-virgin olive oil, for drizzling

1.   Preheat an oven to 450°F. Lightly coat a rimmed baking sheet with cooking spray, and set aside.
2.   Wipe the mushrooms with a damp cloth to remove the dirt. Or wash them in cold water but do not let them soak; drain well.
3.   Remove the mushroom stems and finely chop enough of them to make 2 tablespoons. Discard the remaining stems or reserve for another use.
4.   In a medium bowl, mix together the chopped stems, bread crumbs, crabmeat, cheese, parsley, garlic, salt, and pepper.
5.   Evenly stuff each mushroom with the crab mixture, then drizzle a bit of the olive oil over each.
6.   Arrange the mushroom caps on the reserved baking sheet. Bake for 8 to 10 minutes or until bubbling hot. Serve immediately.

Simple Sexy Kitchen Tip: You can prepare both the crab mixture and the mushrooms ahead and store, separately, in the refrigerator. Wrap the mushroom caps in paper towels, not plastic wrap. Stuff the mushrooms and let come to room temperature before baking.

Pasta with Roasted Tomatoes, Olives, and Pine Nuts

SEXY FOODS: tomatoes, garlic, chili flakes, oregano, pasta, olives, capers, pine nuts
3 SERVINGS

1 1/4 pounds cherry or grape tomatoes, halved
2 tablespoons plus 2 teaspoons olive oil
1 1/2 teaspoons balsamic vinegar
2 large cloves garlic, minced
1/8 teaspoon crushed red chili flakes
1 1/2 tablespoons chopped fresh oregano
Salt
8 ounces bow-tie (farfalle) pasta
1/4 cup pitted kalamata olives
2 tablespoons capers, drained
2/3 cup (about 3 ounces) crumbled feta or soft, fresh goat's milk cheese
Freshly ground black pepper
2 tablespoons toasted pine nuts for garnishing

1.   Adjust a rack to the center of an oven and preheat to 375°F.
2.   In an 8-inch-square nonreactive baking dish, combine the tomatoes, oil, vinegar, garlic, and chili flakes.
3.   Roast for about 40 to 50 minutes, stirring occasionally, until the tomatoes are juicy and tender.
4.   Remove from oven & gently mix in oregano. (Tomatoes can be roasted up to 2 hours in advance. Let stand at room temperature until ready to proceed.)
5.   In a large pot, bring 2 to 3 quarts of water to a full boil. Stir in 2 to 3 teaspoons of salt and stir in the pasta. Return to a full boil and cook until tender but still firm to the bite (al dente). Drain pasta and return it to the pot.
6.   Add the tomato mixture, olives, and capers, and stir over medium heat for about 2 minutes, or until heated through.
7.   Add the cheese and continue stirring until melted and creamy. Season to taste with salt and pepper. Garnish with the pine nuts.

Simple Sexy Kitchen Tip: If you select a higher-quality feta, it will typically be less salty . . . keeping you sexy and svelte!

Simple Sexy Love Skills Tip: This is as delicious cold as it is warm. Enjoy as a main dish or refrigerate for an "anytime is the right time" moment. Perfect for a picnic!

Survey Secrets: Pasta made the top ten free-choice aphrodisiac foods, and was recognized by over 25% of all survey participants as a sexy food.

Red Lentil Soup with Ghee-infused Pita Croutons

This hearty and smooth soup transports you to the sensual flavors of the Middle East. "Red" lentils, orange in color when purchased, quickly turn a rich mustard yellow when cooked.

SEXY FOODS: lentils, tomato, cumin, parsley, onion, ghee, parsley
2 MAIN-DISH SERVINGS OR 4 AS A SIDE

8 ounces dried red lentils
2 cups water
1 3/4 cups low-sodium beef or vegetable stock
1 small tomato, quartered and seeded
1 small Yukon Gold potato, quartered
1 small carrot, quartered crosswise
1 teaspoon salt
1 1/2 teaspoons olive oil
1 small yellow or white onion, finely chopped
1 1/2 teaspoons home-made Ghee, or purchased ghee
1 whole-wheat pita round, cut into 1-inch squares
1/2 teaspoon ground cumin, or more to taste
1/4 teaspoon white pepper
1 1/2 teaspoons chopped, flat-leaf parsley leaves

1.   Thoroughly pick over and rinse the lentils in a sieve or colander until all grit has been removed.
2.   In a medium pot, combine the lentils, water, and 1 cup of the broth. Add the tomato, potato, carrot, and 1/2 teaspoon salt, and bring to a boil. Reduce heat to low and simmer for 45 minutes, skimming any froth that forms.
3.   Meanwhile, in another pot, heat the olive oil over medium heat, and sauté the onion until golden, about 10 minutes. Set aside.
4.   While lentils continue to simmer, melt the ghee over medium heat in a sauté pan large enough to hold the pita. Add the pita pieces and sauté until crisp, about 4 minutes per side. Drain on paper towels until ready to use.
5.   Remove lentil mixture from heat, stir in remaining 3/4 cup broth, and purée with an immersion blender (or in a conventional blender) until smooth.
6.   Add the lentil purée and cumin to the onions. Simmer for about 10 minutes, or until the soup thickens. Add the white pepper and remaining 1/2 teaspoon salt, or more to taste.
7.   Pour the soup into warmed bowls and sprinkle with the parsley and reserved pita croutons.

Simple Sexy Kitchen Tip: Happily, red lentils take much less time to cook than brown lentils, especially if freshly purchased.

Poblano Chilies Stuffed with Shrimp and Crab

SEXY FOODS: chilies, shrimp, crab, garlic, onion, cilantro, olive oil
2 SERVINGS

4 large, fresh poblano chilies
1 yellow bell pepper
3 to 4 teaspoons canola oil or other oil with a high smoke point (not olive oil)
3 1/2 tablespoons olive oil
1/4 cup minced shallots
1 cup chicken stock
1/2 cup minced red onion
2 cloves garlic, minced
3 ounces shrimp, peeled, deveined, and coarsely chopped
1 scant cup freshly cut or frozen corn kernels
5 to 6 ounces cooked crabmeat, picked over as needed and shredded
1/2 red bell pepper, diced
4 teaspoons minced fresh cilantro
3 tablespoons pepitas (hulled pumpkin seeds), roasted
1/4 teaspoon salt, or more to taste
1/8 teaspoon freshly ground black pepper, or more to taste
Fresh cilantro leaves for garnishing

1.   Adjust a rack about 4 to 6 inches below a broiler, and turn on the broiler.
2.   Rinse the poblano chilies and yellow bell pepper; pat dry.
3.   Put the canola oil in a small bowl and, using a pastry brush, coat the yellow pepper and chilies evenly with oil.
4.   Put the oiled pepper and chilies, spaced apart, on a broiler pan and set under broiler. Watch them very carefully. After they have black patches, use tongs to turn them to another side to roast. Repeat until all sides have black patches.
5.   Turn off broiler and transfer the chilies and pepper to a 9-by-13-inch baking dish or similar dish. Seal the dish with plastic wrap and set aside for about 15 minutes to steam and cool. (This process loosens the skin and makes the chilies easier to peel.)
6.   While the chilies and pepper are cooling, heat 1 1/2 tablespoons of the olive oil in a medium saucepan over medium heat and sauté the shallots until soft. Set aside.
7.   Peel the poblanos without removing their stems. Make a lengthwise opening in each; carefully remove and discard the seeds. Set the chilies aside. Peel, stem, seed, and chop the yellow pepper.

8.   Add the yellow pepper and 1/2 cup of the chicken stock to the shallots. Bring to a boil and then reduce heat to simmer for 10 minutes.

9.   Purée the yellow pepper mixture in a blender. Transfer the purée to a serving bowl that can be kept warm in a warmer or briefly reheated in a microwave when ready to serve.

10.   In a medium skillet over medium heat, heat the remaining 2 tablespoons olive oil and sauté the red onion and garlic until soft, about 3 minutes. Add the remaining 1/2 cup chicken stock, bring to a boil, and stir up any browned bits to deglaze the pan.

11.   Add the shrimp and cook until pink, about 3 minutes.

12.   Rinse the corn with hot water and drain. Add to the skillet. Stir in the crabmeat, red bell pepper, cilantro, and toasted pepitas; heat through. Season with the salt and pepper.

13.   Spoon the seafood filling into the chilies, and arrange 2 on each serving plate. Pour some of the warm yellow pepper sauce over the poblanos and garnish with cilantro. Serve the remaining yellow pepper sauce on the side.

Thai Lettuce Wraps

SEXY FOODS: romaine lettuce, ginger, chilies, mushroom, onion, garlic, basil
2 MAIN-DISH OR 4 APPETIZER SERVINGS

1 head romaine lettuce
1 cup roughly chopped fresh basil
1/2 cup dry-roasted peanuts, roughly chopped
2 tablespoons low-sodium soy sauce
2 tablespoons Asian fish sauce (nam pla) plus more if desired
1 tablespoon oyster sauce
2 tablespoons lime juice
2 tablespoons vegetable oil
3 cloves garlic
1 thumb-sized piece peeled fresh ginger or galangal, grated
1 red Thai or jalapeño chili, seeded and thinly sliced
2 shallots, thinly sliced
1/2 cup cooked, shredded chicken or pork, or cooked baby shrimp
4 or 5 fresh shiitake mushrooms, thinly sliced
1 carrot, grated or cut into thin strips
1/2 cup shredded red or white cabbage
3 green onions, cut in half lengthwise then crosswise into 2-inch pieces
1 egg
2 cups bean sprouts
Thai chili sauce

1.   Wash the lettuce and cut off and discard 2 to 3 inches from the bottom. Spin dry or towel dry the leaves and set aside in a large bowl.
2.   Place the basil and peanuts in separate serving bowls and set aside.
3.   In a small bowl, combine the soy sauce, fish sauce, oyster sauce, and lime juice, and set within reach of the stove.
4.   Heat a wok or large skillet over medium-high heat. When the pan is hot, swirl in the oil. Add the garlic, ginger, chili, and shallots. Stir-fry until fragrant, about 1 minute. (Anytime the pan gets too dry, add a little bit of water.)
5.   Add the meat or shrimp, mushrooms, carrot, cabbage, and green onions. Stir-frying the ingredients in the wok, add the reserved soy sauce mixture, and continue stir-frying for about 1 minute more.
6.   Push the ingredients to the side of the pan and add the egg, stirring vigorously to ensure that the yolk breaks quickly. Push the ingredients into the egg and mix well.
7.   Add the bean sprouts and stir-fry into the mixture for about 1 minute.

8.   Remove from heat and taste carefully for seasoning. Add 1 table-spoon more fish sauce if more salt is desired.

9.   Transfer the filling to a warm bowl and take to the serving area with the bowls of lettuce, basil, and peanuts and the chili sauce.

10.   To prepare each lettuce wrap tableside, place 1 to 2 heaping table-spoons of filling into a whole lettuce leaf. Add a sprinkling of basil and peanuts and a dash of Thai chili sauce if you like to spice things up. Gently wrap the filling in the lettuce, and eat!

Aphrodite Says: As a "heating" agent throughout ancient times it was felt that ginger, among other qualities, contributed to sexual potency and fertility. Both sperm and the womb were considered "hot and wet," so the best aphrodisiacs possessed these dual SEXY FOODS. "Hot" alone might boost potency but not fertility. Ginger's rare classification as both hot and wet made it the most prized of all the spices. Anyone who has heard a lover say that she is "hot and wet" will appreciate the value of this root.

*****

Picnic Bean and Artichoke Heart Salad

This is a great salad for a romantic picnic and will keep for about a week if covered tightly in the refrigerator.

SEXY FOODS: garbanzo bean (chickpea), olive, olive oil, mushroom, artichoke, onion, garlic, tarragon

12 SERVINGS

Salad

1 pound fresh whole green beans

1 (15-ounce) can kidney beans, drained (see Tip)

1 (8-ounce) can garbanzo beans, drained (see Tip)

1 (12-ounce) jar or 2 (6-ounce) jars marinated artichoke hearts, drained

3 to 4 ounces mixed pitted olives, such as kalamata and green, sliced

1 small red onion (about 6 ounces), thinly sliced

4 to 6 ounces Marinated Mushrooms, sliced, or purchase a brand like Reese

4 to 5 teaspoons small capers, drained

1/4 cup chopped fresh flat-leaf parsley

1 tablespoon chopped green onion or chives

Dressing
1/2 cup olive oil
1/4 cup tarragon vinegar or tarragon–wine vinegar
1 teaspoon minced fresh tarragon
1 teaspoon salt
1/4 teaspoon freshly ground black pepper
1 clove garlic, chopped
1 sprig flat-leaf parsley
Pinch of cayenne pepper

1. **To make the salad:**
Bring 2 quarts of water to a vigorous boil in a large pot; add 2 teaspoons of salt. Toss in the green beans all at once and return to a boil. Boil for about 5 minutes, and test a bean; it should retain a crunch. Drain immediately and run cold water over the beans continuously for several minutes to arrest further cooking. Set aside.
2. In a 9-by-13-inch nonreactive dish, combine the drained kidney beans, garbanzo beans, artichoke hearts, olives, red onion, mushrooms, capers, parsley, and green onion.
3. Use paper towels to dry off the green beans, and then cut them into 1 1/2- to 2-inch lengths. Stir into the salad mixture.

4. **To make the dressing:**
Combine all the dressing ingredients in a blender jar and blend well.
5. Pour the dressing over the salad mixture and toss lightly but thoroughly to coat all ingredients.
6. Cover with plastic wrap and refrigerate overnight before serving.

Simple Sexy Kitchen Tip: When purchasing canned beans, avoid low-salt versions. They invariably contain extra sugar to compensate, which negatively affects the taste of this delicious dish.

Aphrodite Says: Can you name the woman crowned "Miss California Artichoke Queen" in 1947 at the Artichoke Festival in Castroville, California? It was one Norma Jean Baker, whose crown provided a decided boost to her budding career as the sex goddess icon, Marilyn Monroe.

Beet Carpaccio

SEXY FOODS: beets, onions, garlic, olive oil, spirits (wine)
2 SERVINGS

2 large or 4 medium beets (1 pound with greens)
1 clove garlic, unpeeled
1 medium onion (5 ounces), quartered lengthwise and thinly sliced crosswise
1 tablespoon unsalted butter
1/4 teaspoon sugar
1/4 teaspoon salt plus more as needed
1 teaspoon balsamic vinegar
2 1/2 tablespoons dry white wine
Freshly ground black pepper
4 teaspoons extra-virgin olive oil
2 1/2-ounce chunk Parmigiano-Reggiano

1.   Adjust oven rack to the middle position, and preheat oven to 450°F.
2.   Trim beets, leaving 1 inch of stem attached. Reserve any leaves for
another use. Wrap beets & garlic together in double layer of foil; seal tightly.
3.   Put the packet on a baking pan and roast beets until tender, about 60
to 75 minutes. Remove from oven and set aside to cool slightly.
4.   Meanwhile, in heavy nonreactive skillet over medium-low heat, cook
onion in butter, covered, stirring occasionally until soft, about 15 minutes.
5.   Add the sugar, 1/4 teaspoon salt, and vinegar. Cook uncovered,
stirring occasionally, until onions are tender and caramelized to deep brown,
about 15 minutes more.
6.   Add the wine and boil, stirring occasionally, until liquid is reduced to
about 2 teaspoons, about 3 minutes.
7.   Transfer onions to food processor, reserving the skillet. Pulse onions
to a coarse purée then return to skillet. Season with salt and pepper to taste.
8.   When you are ready to serve, reheat the onion marmalade in the skillet, covered, over low heat. Keep warm.
9.   Unwrap beets; remove and discard skins, stems, and root ends; cut
beets crosswise into 1/8-inch-thick slices. (For a make-ahead idea, see Tip.)
10.   Divide warm onions between 2 dinner plates, spreading in a thin
layer over the bottom of each plate. Arrange beet slices in a single layer over
onions, overlapping slices only enough to cover onions. Drizzle 2 teaspoons
oil over each serving and season with pepper. Using a vegetable peeler, shave
curls of Parmigiano-Reggiano over the beets. Serve immediately.

Simple Sexy Kitchen Tip: Beets can be roasted and peeled 1 day ahead and
chilled in sealed plastic bag. To reheat, slice beets, then stack slices in 2 piles,
wrap in foil, and reheat in 400°F oven until warm, about 10 minutes.

Part IV
Late Night Rendezvous
(desserts, drinks, and more)

Introduction

For some of us, the evening and over-night hours can be the most love-compatible periods in otherwise busy days. For one thing, we all go to bed at some point, and it may be the only opportunity we have to let go of the stresses of the day and truly connect with our lover.

For others, we may be so tired at the end of the day that stirring up energy for passion hasn't been easy. That's where simple and sexy often converge, at the place where good intentions meet the realities of modern life. If you're looking to spice up your love life but aren't sure where to start, this section might be just what you're looking for.

Whether it's a luscious dessert following a romantic meal, a tasty little sweet shared between sips of champagne or liqueur before a crackling fire, or a midnight snack shared in bed after a bit of lovemaking, the recipes in this section lend themselves to night moves.

No mention of aphrodisiac desserts and sweets would be complete—or even possible—without chocolate. While especially important for women, chocolate in all its splendid variations ranks high for men, too, especially when it comes to men wanting to please and tempt their partners with something both special and sexy!

The aphrodisiac qualities of chocolate are many and not limited to physical responses. As I've already mentioned, the aphrodisiac effect can stem from many causes, not the least of which is how you feel about a food, or how it makes you feel emotionally. Many of us harbor titillating memories of particularly powerful love scenes from our past, and if there was food associated with the memory, the presence or even the thought of that food can arouse that loving feeling as if it were yesterday. Chocolate is one of those foods that triggers both physical and emotional responses wherever we encounter it. It has become so ubiquitous in our repertoire of love-related foods that the only holiday devoted to lovers—Valentine's Day—is now built around the giving and enjoyment of chocolate.

One more thing about chocolate (for it's not the only ingredient that makes these recipes sexy): It is a remarkably flexible and convenient food. Served cold or hot, on its own or as a companion to or ingredient in other foods, the uses of chocolate and its variants are nearly limitless. In fact, while I don't recommend it, if you could choose only one aphrodisiac food to enhance your love life, you'd probably choose good old chocolate.

Desserts and midnight snacks also lend themselves to creativity, both in the kitchen and wherever you make love. For example, if you've wondered about using your lover's body as a spoon or a plate, dessert items provide myriad sexy options. The sweetness, texture, visual appeal, and even temperature of desserts convert easily to edible clothing. So lay in some basic ingredients for simple, sexy desserts and snacks, let your imagination run, and you'll never find yourself without a sweet little something you can add to the moment to make a nighttime rendezvous memorable.

Love Skills: Timing is often critical in determining whether or not we have sex. Wherever possible or appropriate, consider making part or all of your sexy food ahead of time to minimize interruptions of the flow of an evening and to maximize the spontaneity factor.

Aphrodite Says: Aztec lore suggests that Montezuma drank 50 cups of cocoa before his rendezvous with a harem of 600 women. So who says only women find chocolate sexy!

Survey Secrets: Chocolate in all its wonderful variety was the overall winner in the favorite aphrodisiac food category of my survey. The best of the best? Chocolate covered strawberries and chocolate sauce or syrup.

Love Skills: A simple, foil wrapped chocolate on the pillow transforms a bedroom into an exotic getaway for two. When in doubt, chocolate is simple, sexy food at its best. It exudes relaxation and getting away from it all. Try surprising your partner with a chocolate treat on her pillow, followed by a massage. Trust me, she'll appreciate the gesture!

Chocolate-covered Strawberries

This dessert is ridiculously simple & elegant, leaving room for your creative energies and imaginations to run freely about where, when, and how to serve the berries! Anytime, anywhere to pique erotic inclinations is a good bet!

SEXY FOODS: chocolate, strawberries
2 SERVINGS

10 to 12 large, fresh strawberries with stems, at room temperature
8 ounces semi-sweet chocolate
2 tablespoons vegetable shortening
1/2 teaspoon orange extract, or another extract, like coffee, chocolate, or rum

1.   Carefully wash and thoroughly dry room temperature strawberries. Ideally, they should not be purchased more than a day ahead.
2.   Line baking sheet or flat surface with waxed paper or aluminum foil.
3.   Add water to bottom of double boiler, making sure water level does not touch upper container, & bring to a simmer. Combine chocolate and shortening in upper container & stir until chocolate is melted and smooth. Remove from heat, keeping chocolate over the hot water, and stir in extract.
4.   One by one, hold each strawberry by the stem and dip into the chocolate, coating about 3/4 of the berry. Let any excess chocolate drip back into the container. Place each dipped berry on the reserved baking sheet.
5.   After all berries are dipped, place in the refrigerator for 15 to 20 minutes to harden. (Do not leave them in the refrigerator for more than 1 hour.)
6.   Remove from the refrigerator and gently loosen berries from waxed paper with a spatula. They can remain at room temperature for about an hour.

Variation: Use this same procedure to dip other dry-surfaced fruit: diagonally sliced bananas, mandarin oranges with membrane on, cherries, or dried fruit.

Simple Sexy Kitchen Tip: For a truly delicious and sensual flavor experience, inject the strawberries with Grand Marnier or other liqueur after the chocolate has hardened. Use a hypodermic needle and syringe (available at kitchen supply stores) for injecting them.

Love Skills: You and your lover will surely want to feed each other at least one strawberry, if not several. For added aphrodisiac effect, eat them slowly, taking small bites. The juices are more likely to drizzle down your lips and chin, so why not use the opportunity for a bit of sensual licking?

Survey Secrets: Of all the personal favorite aphrodisiac foods, chocolate and strawberries hit the top in my 21st Century Aphrodisiac Foods Survey list, in a dead heat! A full 73% of the respondents selected these two!

Pumpkin Chiffon Pie with Gingersnap Pecan Crust

Anecdotally speaking, pie turns men on. Cinnamon, ginger and cloves all have sexy reputations, as will you when you serve your lover this delicious treat.

SEXY FOODS: pumpkin, pumpkin pie spice, pecan, whipped cream
8 SERVINGS

Crust

14 (2-inch-diameter) gingersnap cookies (about 4 ounces)
1 cup pecans (about 4 ounces)
1/4 cup granulated sugar
4 tablespoons (1/2 stick) unsalted butter, melted and cooled

Filling

2 envelopes unflavored gelatin (4 teaspoons total)
1 1/4 cups fat-free evaporated milk, or 1 cup evaporated milk plus 1/4 cup rum
1 can (16 ounces) plain pumpkin (not spiced pumpkin-pie filling)
1/2 cup firmly packed light brown sugar
1 teaspoon ground cinnamon
1/4 teaspoon ground ginger
1/8 teaspoon ground cloves
1 teaspoon grated lemon zest
3 large egg whites or equivalent meringue powder (see Tip)
2/3 cup granulated sugar

1.   To make the crust: Adjust a rack to the middle and preheat an oven to 350°F. Lightly grease a 9-inch glass pie pan and set aside.
2.   In a food processor, combine the cookies, pecans, and sugar, and process together until finely ground. Add the butter and blend until mixture is well combined.
3.   Press the crust mixture into the bottom and up the sides of the reserved pie pan.
4.   Bake for 15 minutes, or until edge of crust is crisp and golden. Cool on a wire rack.
5.   Meanwhile, prepare the filling: In a medium saucepan, sprinkle the gelatin over the milk; let stand for 1 minute. Cook over low heat, whisking constantly, until the gelatin dissolves completely, about 5 minutes. Remove from heat.
6.   In a large bowl, combine the pumpkin, brown sugar, cinnamon, ginger, cloves, and lemon zest. Stir in the gelatin mixture. Refrigerate the mixture for 30 minutes, stirring occasionally.

7.   Using an electric mixer in a deep, clean, dry mixing bowl, whip the egg whites and granulated sugar on medium speed until foamy. Raise speed to high and continue beating until stiff peaks form. Beat egg whites to stiff peaks but do not overbeat. If using meringue powder, follow the manufacturer's instructions.

8.   Fold the meringue mixture into the pumpkin mixture. If necessary, refrigerate until the mixture mounds slightly when dropped from a spoon. Spoon the filling into the baked crust. Cover and refrigerate for at least 4 hours, or until set.

Survey Secrets: Whipped cream. Ranked 3rd in both free-choice personal favorites and most recognized aphrodisiac food (tied with oysters), this sweet foam is also the #1 ranked dairy aphrodisiac, followed closely by ice cream. It ranked high in reputation with women, young people, and those with a high school education.

Love Skills: Sometimes overindulging in food can make you sleepy, which might take your focus away from sexy pursuits. Though sweet and satisfying, this dessert is light and airy, and won't sidetrack your amorous intentions by putting you to sleep!

Simple Sexy Kitchen Tip: If you're not gifted at separating eggs or don't like having spare egg yolks lying around, use pasteurized egg whites, readily available at your local market. What's more, they assure you of egg safety. Simply beat them with the sugar in an electric mixer, no heat needed.

Aphrodisiac Chocolate Fondue Sauce for Sensual Fruits

The fruits suggested are especially delectable served in this way, but you can add or substitute any other fruits and/or pieces of waffle cookies or pound cake that suit your taste. Use your imagination to cut your selections into sensually appealing shapes.

SEXY FOODS: whipped cream, chocolate, liqueur, a variety of fruits with aphrodisiac reputations—kiwi, figs, bananas, strawberries, oranges
2 SERVINGS

8 whole organic strawberries, with stems, wiped with damp paper towel and patted dry
2 kiwis, peeled and cut into thick rounds
1 large banana, peeled and cut on the bias into 8 pieces
1 orange, peeled and sectioned, with pith removed
8 dried Calimyrna figs
1/3 cup whipping cream
1 1/2 teaspoons grated orange zest
8 ounces semisweet or bittersweet chocolate, finely chopped
3 tablespoons Grand Marnier, Cointreau, or other orange-flavored liqueur

1.   Arrange the fruit attractively on a large plate or place each type of fruit in a separate dish of a lazy Susan.
2.   In a heavy medium saucepan, combine the cream and orange zest and bring to a simmer over medium heat.
3.   Add chocolate & 1 tablespoon of Grand Marnier. Whisk until smooth. Remove sauce from heat & whisk in remaining Grand Marnier.
4.   Transfer sauce to fondue pot that is heated by candle or canned-heat burner. Be sure to keep the heat low; too much heat will burn the chocolate.
5.   Use fingers or long fondue forks to dip pieces of fruit into the warm chocolate sauce.

Simple Sexy Kitchen Tip: Strawberries are at their delicious best when in season. When they're organic, you can gently clean them with a damp paper towel, dispensing with the need to thoroughly rinse them to remove pesticides, and water-logging them in the process.

Love Skills: You're very likely to have plenty of leftover sauce . . . surely you can figure out something creative to do with it!

Survey Secrets: Chocolate. Interestingly, younger people (age 18-25) were significantly more likely to select chocolate (73%) from a list of aphrodisiacs than any other age group. Less surprisingly, 73% of females chose chocolate as sexy food, far more than the males.

Strawberries and Figs

SEXY FOODS: figs, strawberries, whipped cream, mint
2 SERVINGS

1 (12-ounce) package unsweetened frozen strawberries, thawed
1/2 cup superfine sugar
1/2 cup whipping cream, optional
1 tablespoon confectioners' sugar, if making whipped cream
6 fresh Calimyrna figs or, if not in season, substitute other figs, washed, dried, and halved lengthwise
2 sprigs fresh mint for garnishing
2 tablespoons finely minced fresh mint

1.   In a food processor, purée the strawberries with the sugar.
2.   Whip the cream, if using; when it is partially whipped, gradually add the confectioners' sugar.
3.   On each individual dessert plate, place 3 fig halves, cut side up.
4.   Swirl some of the strawberry purée decoratively over the figs. (Leave the use of the remaining purée to your imagination!)
5.   If desired, add a dollop of whipped cream to each serving. Place a sprig of mint on top.
6.   Serve with a small bowl of minced mint as additional garnish.

Simple Sexy Kitchen Tip: Using defrosted frozen strawberries guarantees the sumptuous color and sweetness of the sauce.

Walnut Torte with Whipped Cream

SEXY FOODS: walnuts, whipped cream (a survey favorite), vanilla
6 TO 8 SERVINGS

20 Keebler Club crackers
1 teaspoon baking powder
3/4 cup (3 ounces) chopped nuts, such as walnuts
3 egg whites, at room temperature
1/8 teaspoon salt
1 teaspoon vanilla extract
1 cup granulated sugar
1/2 cup whipping cream
1 tablespoon confectioners' sugar

1.   Preheat an oven to 350°F.
2.   Pulse crackers in a food processor (not a blender) to make crumbs or
crush them in a plastic bag; you should have about 3/4 cup of crumbs. In a
small bowl, mix the crumbs, baking powder, and walnuts. Set aside.
3.   Using electric mixer in a deep, clean, dry mixing bowl, whip egg
whites, vanilla, & salt on medium speed until foamy. Raise speed to high and
continue beating until firm peaks form. Add granulated sugar in 3 parts, beating thoroughly after each. Beat egg whites to stiff peaks but do not overbeat.
4.   Gently fold the crumb mixture into the egg whites. Spread evenly in
a 9-inch ungreased pie pan.
5.   Bake 20 to 25 minutes, until light golden brown. Cool completely.
6.   In small deep bowl, whip cream & confectioners' sugar until stiff.
Spread the cream over the cooled torte, cover with nonstick aluminum foil,
and refrigerate for at least 8 hours or up to overnight.
7.   To serve, cut the torte into wedges.

Survey Secrets: It seems women may have a sweet tooth when it comes to
sexy food. Females are significantly more likely than men to recognize or select chocolate, vanilla, strawberries, cherries & whipped cream as an aphrodisiac. Hint for guys: If you want to trip your woman's trigger, think dessert!

Love Skills: Love play takes on a sweet & sensual tone when whipped cream
is handy. Highly popular today as a sexy food, nothing rivals whipped cream
for topping your lover's body as a prelude to enjoying your just desserts!

Aphrodite Says: Both Dionysian myth and the more blatant Roman reference
to sexual prowess help to explain the Roman use of walnuts during fertility
rites, including the practice of throwing them, not rice, at wedding ceremonies. Even King Solomon, in his highly erotic *Song of Solomon*, declares his
pleasure in visiting and gazing at his walnut grove!

75 Cherries Jubilee Crêpes

SEXY FOODS: cherries (a survey favorite), liqueur, vanilla, ice cream (a survey favorite)
4 SERVINGS

1 recipe Dessert Crêpes
1 (24.7-ounce) jar dark Morello cherries in light syrup, such as Trader Joe's, drained, 1/2 cup syrup reserved separately
3 tablespoons unsalted butter
3 tablespoons sugar
1/4 cup ruby Port
1 teaspoon cornstarch
1 tablespoon fresh lemon juice
3 tablespoons brandy or Cognac
Vanilla frozen yogurt or ice cream

1.   Make the crêpes and keep them warm in a 200°F oven while you prepare the cherries. Or, if crêpes have been made ahead, reheat them, wrapped in aluminum foil, on a baking sheet in a preheated 325°F oven for 5 to 10 minutes, or until heated through.

2.   In a large skillet over medium heat, melt the butter until it foams. Sprinkle in the sugar and cook for 1 to 2 minutes.

3.   Add the wine and reserved syrup and cook until reduced by about half, to the consistency of a thick syrup.

4.   In a small bowl, mix the cornstarch with a little of the hot sauce until smooth. Then, stirring the sauce constantly, mix in the cornstarch mixture and bring the sauce to a boil to thicken.

5.   Add the reserved cherries, heat through, and stir in the lemon juice.

6.   Fold the crêpes into triangles and add them to the skillet, coating them in the sauce. Push the crêpes to one side of the pan.

7.   In a small pan, carefully heat the brandy, then ignite with a match, and spoon the flaming brandy over the sauce.

8.   When the flames subside, serve 2 crêpes and a spoonful or two of sauce on each plate.

9.   Top with a dollop of frozen yogurt or ice cream.

Survey Secrets: Cherries were chosen #3 from a list of aphrodisiac foods, with women and younger people especially finding them to sweeten their lust.

Date and Oat Squares

SEXY FOODS: dates, oats, vanilla
16 (2-INCH) SQUARES

2 1/4 cups pitted dates, chilled
2/3 cup water
3/4 teaspoon vanilla extract
8 tablespoons (1 stick) unsalted butter
1/2 cup packed light brown sugar
1 1/2 tablespoons golden syrup, or substitute light corn syrup
3/4 teaspoon dark molasses
2 cups rolled oats
1 cup whole-wheat flour
1 1/2 tablespoons raw wheat germ, optional
1/4 heaping teaspoon
Rounded 1/4 teaspoon baking soda
Pinch of salt

1. Adjust a rack to the middle of an oven and preheat to 350°F. Spray an 8-inch-square glass baking dish with cooking spray and line with parchment paper. Set aside.
2. Slice the dates lengthwise and roughly chop.
3. In a saucepan over low heat, warm the dates and water, stirring occasionally, until the dates have softened and absorbed all of the water. Stir in the vanilla and set aside.
4. In another small saucepan, combine the butter, brown sugar, golden syrup, and molasses, and stir over low heat until the butter has melted.
5. In a medium bowl, mix together the oats, flour, wheat germ if using, baking soda, and salt.
6. Pour the butter mixture into the flour mixture and blend thoroughly until crumbly.
7. Spread half of the mixture in the baking pan and press into an even layer. Spread the reserved dates evenly over the oat layer. Sprinkle the remaining oat mixture over the dates.
8. Bake for about 30 minutes, or until the top is golden. Remove from the oven and place on a rack to cool.
9. Cut into 2-inch squares.

Aphrodite Says: The 2nd century physician Galen included date piths in the love potion he recommended to "excite the desire of women." The Shields Date Farm near Palm Springs, CA keeps alive the centuries-old "date-mating" process, and even promotes it in the form of a vegetative super-soft porn film seen by thousands: "The Romance and Sex life of a Date."

Fresh Fruit with Honey–Lemon Sauce

Feel free to vary the suggested fruits to reflect both what's at its juicy peak of season and what holds the most personal sex appeal. Serve the fruit on bamboo skewers so that you can readily pluck off pieces, one at a time, to serve your lover.

SEXY FOODS: honey, watermelon, orange, melon, kiwifruit, red grapes (a survey favorite), pepper
2 TO 3 SERVINGS

Sauce
1 (3-ounce) package cream cheese
2 tablespoons honey
3 tablespoons fresh lemon juice
1/2 teaspoon grated lemon zest (preferably from organic lemon)
1/4 cup vegetable oil
1/8 teaspoon white pepper
Salt to taste, optional

Fruit
1/2 cup fresh cantaloupe chunks
1/2 cup fresh pineapple chunks
1/2 cup watermelon chunks
1/2 cup honeydew melon chunks
1 kiwifruit, peeled, halved crosswise, then each half quartered
1/2 cup fresh orange segments
1/2 cup red grapes

1.   To make the sauce: Whirl the cream cheese in a blender until smooth, then blend in the honey, lemon juice and zest.
2.   With blender on low speed, gradually add oil in a slow steady stream.
3.   Add the white pepper and salt if using, and blend in.
4.   Chill the sauce until ready to serve.
5.   While the sauce is chilling, prepare the fruit: If starting with whole fruit, wash and dry before cutting as indicated.
6.   Thread the fruit, alternating types, on bamboo skewers. Or, arrange fruit in rows on a serving platter. Drizzle the sauce over individual servings.

Simple Sexy Kitchen Tip: If you're pressed for time, head to the salad bar or produce section of your local market to pick up many of the fruits, already cut. Refrigerate leftover fruit for the next day.

Love Skills: This is another sauce to drizzle onto your lover's body. But given the lemon juice and pepper included, you might want to ensure you use it for "external application only."

Tropical Coconut Flan

This light, satisfying dessert will keep you inspired for the rest of the night.

SEXY FOODS: coconut, vanilla
4 SERVINGS

Caramel
6 tablespoons sugar
1/4 cup water

Custard
3/4 cup nonfat milk
3/4 cup coconut milk
2 1/2 tablespoons sugar
2 eggs
1/2 teaspoon vanilla extract
2 tablespoons unsweetened grated dried coconut

1.   Preheat 325°F. Set four 1/2-cup ramekins within reach of stove.
2.   **Caramel**: Add the sugar and water to a heavy, preferably easy-pour, saucepan. Stir and heat the mixture over medium-high heat until the sugar dissolves. Cook, without stirring, until the mixture turns a rich caramel color, about 8 to 12 minutes. Watch carefully to avoid burning.
3.   Remove from heat and immediately pour the caramel into the ramekins, tilting them to coat bottoms evenly. Set aside.
4.   **Custard**: In a small heavy saucepan, mix the milk, coconut milk, and sugar and heat over medium heat just until hot. Remove from heat.
5.   In medium bowl, beat eggs. Slowly stir in hot milk mixture and then vanilla. Pour mixture through fine-mesh sieve into another bowl.
6.   Gently fold in the dried coconut.
7.   Place the caramel-lined ramekins, not touching, in a 9-by-13-inch glass baking dish. Pour hot water into the baking dish to reach halfway up the sides of the cups. Ladle the egg mixture into the cups, dividing evenly.
8.   Bake until the custards are set and a knife inserted into the middle of custard comes out clean, 30 to 35 minutes. Remove the custards from the water bath and let cool. Cover and refrigerate to chill well before serving.
9.   To serve, run knife around edge & unmold onto individual plates.

Simple Sexy Kitchen Tip: Stir coconut milk thoroughly before measuring.

Aphrodite Says: The great Moroccan 14th century geographer/traveler, Ibn Battuta, who traveled over 75,000 miles just 60 years after Marco Polo, sang the praises of coconuts, bananas and mollusks after finding them in abundance in Dhofar, Oman. Referring to the coconut, he wrote: "As for its aphrodisiac quality, its action in this respect is wonderful."

214

Poached Pears with Raspberry Brandy Sauce

This is a great make-ahead dessert for a special romantic occasion.

SEXY FOODS: raspberry, pear, mint, spirits (liqueur)
4 SERVINGS

4 firm ripe pears, such as Anjou
2 tablespoons fresh lemon juice
3 cups water
1/2 cup sugar
15 ounces frozen raspberries in syrup, thawed and drained, juice reserved
separately
6 tablespoons seedless raspberry jam
1 tablespoon framboise (raspberry brandy), Cognac or kirsch (cherry brandy)
Mint springs for garnishing

1.   Choose a bowl just large enough to hold the pears. Fill with enough
water to cover pears. Remove pears. Add 1 tablespoon lemon juice to the
water and set aside.
2.   Select a saucepan just large enough to hold the pears. (If the pan is
too large, the pears will not be covered by the poaching liquid.) Set the pan
aside.
3.   Peel the pears, leaving the stem intact. With a melon baller, remove
the seeds, starting at the bottom of the pear and scooping out a ball of the
core and seeds. Continue scooping only until all seeds have been removed;
leave the rest of the pear intact. Cut a thin horizontal slice from the bottom
of each pear so that it will stand upright. As each pear is done, place it in the
bowl of lemon water to prevent discoloration.
4.   In the saucepan, combine the measured 3 cups of water, sugar,
remaining 1 tablespoon lemon juice, and reserved syrup from the berries.
Bring the liquid to a boil. Immediately reduce heat and simmer until the
sugar dissolves, about 5 minutes. (If desired, you can stop at this point and
store the poaching liquid in the refrigerator until ready to proceed.)
5.   With the poaching liquid at a simmer, drain the pears, discarding the
lemon water. Gently add the pears to the saucepan, cover the pan, and
simmer slowly, turning the pears occasionally, until they are tender when
pierced with a knife. This may take as little as 5 minutes or as much as 30
minutes, depending on the size, type, and ripeness of the pears.
6.   Refrigerate the pears in the poaching liquid for several hours or
overnight. Turn them occasionally.
7.   Meanwhile, prepare the sauce. In a medium saucepan, bring the
raspberry jam and reserved raspberries to the boiling point. Remove the pan
from heat and slightly cool.

8.   Press the mixture through a fine-mesh sieve or medium disk of a food mill. Strain a second time so that all seeds are out.

9.   Stir in the brandy and refrigerate until ready to use.

10.   To serve, drizzle a tablespoon of the sauce onto each dessert plate. With a slotted spoon, remove the pears from the syrup and blot pears with paper towels. (If desired, you can save the poaching liquid, refrigerated, and re-use it later to poach more pears or peaches.)

11.   Bathe the pears in the remaining sauce and place one on each plate. Garnish each pear with a sprig of mint at the top. Serve the extra sauce on the side.

Simple Sexy Love Skills Tip: If you think you may want to use the sauce for sex play, double that part of the recipe!

Aphrodite Says: Raspberry tea made from raspberry plant leaves has long been recommended to help morning sickness. In the 17th century, *Culpeper's Complete Herbal* also recommended raspberry tea for "getting the womb back in place" as part of postpartum recovery. In modern terms, it will get you back in the sack quickly after childbirth!

Chocolate Mousse with Brandied Whipped Cream

SEXY FOODS: chocolate (chocolate mousse selected as a survey favorite), whipped cream, (a survey favorite), liqueur
4 SERVINGS

6 ounces bittersweet chocolate, such as Ghiradelli's 60% cacao, chopped
3 tablespoons unsalted butter
2 tablespoons Kahlua coffee liqueur, or substitute coffee
1 teaspoon vanilla extract
3 eggs, separated (let whites come to room temperature)
3 tablespoons water
7 tablespoons sugar
1/4 teaspoon cream of tartar
Brandied Whipped Cream (recipe follows)
Candied pecans, espresso beans, and shaved chocolate for garnishing

1.　　In the lower section of a double boiler, heat 1 inch of water until bubbles begin to form on the bottom. In the top section, combine the chocolate, butter, Kahlua, and vanilla, and place over the warm water. Adjust heat to maintain a simmer; do not let the water boil. Stir the mixture continuously until just melted, about 2 to 3 minutes. Remove and set aside the top section with the chocolate mixture.

2.　　In a heat-proof bowl that fits over the lower section of the double boiler without touching the water, combine egg yolks, 3 tablespoons water, and 3 tablespoons of the sugar, and whisk thoroughly. Set over the simmering water and continue whisking constantly, until mixture becomes voluminous and thick, about 3 to 5 minutes. Remove from heat and whisk the egg mixture thoroughly into the melted chocolate. (Take care to prevent any water droplets from falling into chocolate.) Set aside to cool to room temperature.

3.　　Using an electric mixer in a clean, dry mixing bowl, beat the egg whites on medium speed until foamy. Add the cream of tartar and beat until soft peaks form. Then gradually beat in the remaining 4 tablespoons sugar. Increase mixer speed to high and beat egg whites until stiff peaks form.

4.　　Using a rubber spatula, lighten the cooled chocolate mixture by stirring in one fourth of the egg whites. Then gently and thoroughly fold in the remaining egg whites.

5.　　With a 1/2-cup measure, divide the mousse among serving dishes. Cover with plastic wrap, without touching top surface of mousse, and refrigerate for at least 4 hours, or up to 24 hours.

6.　　When ready to serve, make the brandied whipped cream. Top the mousse with the cream and garnish with candied pecans, espresso beans, and shaved chocolate.

Brandied Whipped Cream

ABOUT 1 HEAPING CUP

1/2 cup whipping cream
2 tablespoons brandy
1 tablespoon confectioners' sugar

1.   Using an electric mixer in a very cold bowl, whip the cream at high speed until it is partially thickened.
2.   Add the brandy and continue beating, then gradually add the sugar and beat cream to desired consistency.

*****

French Dessert Crêpes

SEXY FOODS: apricot, strawberry, raspberry, blueberry, liqueur, whipped cream, ice cream, nuts
4 SERVINGS

Dessert Crêpes
1 large egg
1/2 cup milk
2 tablespoons plus 2 teaspoons water
1/2 cup (2 1/2 ounces) all-purpose flour
1 tablespoon sugar
1/2 teaspoon vanilla extract
1 1/2 teaspoons rum, brandy, Cointreau, amaretto, or other liqueur, optional
1 tablespoon butter, melted, plus about 2 teaspoons more for cooking the crêpes

Fillings
Apricot or strawberry preserves
Confectioners' sugar
Fresh lemon juice
Cointreau, Grand Marnier, rum, or brandy
Fresh berries, such as strawberries, raspberries, blueberries, or a mixture

Toppings
Whipped cream
Vanilla ice cream or frozen yogurt

Grated bittersweet chocolate

Candied walnuts or pecans, chopped hazelnuts or almonds

1.   **To mix the crêpe batter in a blender or food processor:** Add the egg, milk, water, flour, sugar, vanilla, spirits, and the 1 tablespoon melted butter, and blend for 5 seconds. Stop the machine and stir down the sides. Blend again for 5 seconds, or until batter is smooth.

To mix the batter by hand: Sift the flour into a medium bowl and stir in the sugar. In a separate bowl, whisk the egg well, and then stir in the milk, water, vanilla, and spirits. Thoroughly whisk the egg mixture into the flour mixture until smooth, and then stir in the 1 tablespoon melted butter.

2.   Cover and refrigerate the batter for at least 2 hours, or up to 24 hours.

3.   Gently stir the batter before using. Set a 6- to 7-inch nonstick crêpe pan over medium-high heat and heat until hot.

4.   Brush the pan lightly with butter, put 2 to 3 tablespoons of batter into the pan, and swirl to coat bottom of pan with batter.

5.   Cook until almost dry on top and lightly browned on the edges, about 1 minute. Loosen the edges with a spatula, flip the crêpe over, and cook for 10 to 15 seconds more, or until very lightly browned on second side.

6.   Transfer the crêpe to a warm plate and cover with aluminum foil. Or, if not using immediately, let the crêpe cool on a clean, flat-weave kitchen towel.

7.   Repeat with the remaining batter, reheating the pan and coating it with butter as needed.

8.   **If serving immediately,** stack the crêpes, with foil between, and cover with foil. Keep warm in a preheated 200°F oven or warming drawer. If using within 24 hours, first cool the crêpes, then stack with foil or waxed paper between each; wrap the stack in foil and refrigerate.

9.   **To freeze,** leave the dividers between the crêpes and wrap them, in quantities intended for each use, tightly in plastic wrap. Put into a zip-style plastic bags and freeze for up to 1 month.

10.   Reheat the crêpes, wrapped in foil, on a baking sheet in a preheated 325°F oven for 5 to 10 minutes, or until heated through.

11.   To serve the crêpes, set out the fillings and toppings and create your own crêpes.

Survey Secrets: Strawberries. Perhaps because the media has paid them so much attention, or perhaps just because they're red, sweet and juicy, and bite-sized, strawberries were not only the top choice overall, but were especially recognized and preferred by younger people (73% have heard of their reputation; 85% selected-from-list) and by women (66% knew of their reputation; 76% selected-from-list). But given the connection between women and chocolate, and strawberries and chocolate, this may not come as such a surprise!

Indonesian Banana Fritters

SEXY FOODS: banana, cinnamon
2 SERVINGS

1/2 cup (2 1/2 ounces), all-purpose flour, or as needed
1/4 cup (1 ounce) rice flour
1 teaspoon baking powder
1/4 teaspoon salt
1/2 cup water, or as needed
Peanut oil or other high-smoke-point vegetable oil for deep-frying
4 small firm bananas, peeled
4 (6-inch) bamboo skewers
Confectioners' sugar or ground cinnamon for dusting
1 lime, cut into wedges

1.   Line a baking sheet or rack with paper towels. Set aside near stove.
2.   In a bowl, combine both flours, baking powder, and salt. Whisk to mix well. Whisk in 1 cup of water to make a smooth, thick batter the consistency of pancake batter; add a little more all-purpose flour or water if needed.
3.   In a wok or deep frying pan, add oil to a depth of 2 inches and heat to 365°F on a deep-fry thermometer.
4.   Meanwhile, thread each banana onto a bamboo skewer, running it all the way through the fruit from one end to the other.
5.   Dip a banana into the batter, coating evenly and letting excess batter drain back into bowl. Carefully lower the banana into the hot oil. Repeat, adding more bananas, but do not crowd the pan or let the oil temperature drop too much. Fry the bananas for about 3 minutes, or until they are nicely golden and crispy. As the bananas are done, transfer them with a slotted spoon to the reserved paper-lined baking sheet to drain. Batter and fry the remaining bananas.
6.   Serve hot, leaving skewers in place. Dust fritters with confectioners' sugar or cinnamon, and pass the lime wedges for squeezing over the fruit.

Survey Secrets: The spices vanilla and cinnamon both made the top ten sexy food by reputation list, but neither one cracked the top ten for choice from a list or free choice. Given the recent studies on the effect of smelling vanilla and cinnamon on male sexual response, this result may change as quickly as an after-dessert quickie!

Aphrodite Says: Here's a fascinating fact: If you're allergic to bananas, you probably steer clear of latex condoms as well, since an allergy to both, known as the "latex-fruit syndrome," is a common condition!

Banana Crêpes Flambées

SEXY FOODS: bananas, cinnamon, coconut, spirits (rum)
2 SERVINGS

4 crêpes from Dessert Crêpes recipe
1 cup chopped banana (about 2 small)
1 1/2 teaspoons fresh lemon juice
1/2 teaspoon ground cinnamon
1/4 cup shredded coconut, toasted
2 tablespoons butter
1/4 cup plus 2 tablespoons low-fat (2%) evaporated milk
1/4 cup plus 2 tablespoons marshmallow cream
Pinch of salt
1/4 cup rum

1.   Lay out the crêpes, browned sides down, on a clean work surface.
2.   Toss the banana with lemon juice to coat, and then sprinkle in the cinnamon and 2 tablespoons coconut. Mix gently but thoroughly.
3.   Spoon 1/4 cup of the banana mixture along the center of the unbrowned side of each crêpe. Fold up two opposite edges of each crêpe to overlap atop the filling. Set aside.
4.   In a saucepan, over medium heat, cook the butter until brown. Remove from heat.
5.   Whisk in the evaporated milk. The mixture will bubble up.
6.   Return to low heat. Add the marshmallow cream and whisk until smooth. Whisk in the salt.
7.   Pour half the sauce into a skillet or chafing dish, carefully add the crêpes, and then cover with the remaining sauce. Sprinkle with the remaining 2 tablespoons coconut.
8.   Heat gently until crêpes are heated through.
9.   In a small saucepan, warm the rum until just hot, and then ignite. Pour the flaming rum over the crêpes.
10.   Serve immediately.

Simple Sexy Kitchen Tip: Adding 1/2 teaspoon of ground cinnamon to the Dessert Crêpes recipe creates a "spicy" crêpe that pumps up the mouth-watering, sensuous aroma of this wonderful dessert!

Aphrodite Says: If the Doctrine of Resemblances needed a poster child, it would surely be the banana. Long, thick, and slightly curved, you have to "undress" it to eat it. Whew! It almost makes me blush to write about it!

Forget-Me-Not Cookies

SEXY FOODS: pecans (or nuts), chocolate (a survey favorite), vanilla
ABOUT 2 DOZEN COOKIES

2 egg whites, at room temperature
2/3 cup superfine or granulated sugar
1 cup (6 ounces) semi-sweet chocolate chips
1 cup (4 ounces) chopped pecans or walnuts, or 1/2 cup of each
1 teaspoon vanilla or peppermint extract

1.   Preheat an oven to 350°F. Cover 1 very large or 2 smaller baking
sheets with silicon liners or line with aluminum foil and spray with cooking
spray. Set aside.
2.   Using an electric mixer in a medium, deep, clean, dry mixing bowl,
whip the egg whites on medium speed until foamy. Raise speed to high and
continue beating until stiff peaks form. Gradually add the sugar, beating thoroughly after each addition. Do not overbeat the egg whites.
3.   Fold in the chocolate chips, nuts, and extract.
4.   Drop by scant tablespoonfuls onto reserved baking sheet(s).
5.   Place in oven and immediately turn oven off. "Forget them" overnight or for at least 7 hours. Do not open oven until cookies are ready to be
removed.

Sparkling Cocktails—a French twist, an Italian twist

Kir Royale

SEXY FOODS: Champagne, the survey's top beverage!
2 SERVINGS

12 ounces chilled Champagne
1 to 2 ounces crème de cassis, preferably from Dijon, France

1.   Fill 2 Champagne flutes with Champagne.
2.   Slowly pour in the desired amount of cassis.
3.   Gently swirl.

Survey Secrets: Champagne. Ranked 2nd overall and 1st in beverages with a sexy reputation, bubbly is most recognized as an aphrodisiac by women (67%), younger people (66%), and those with some college education (65%).

Simple Sexy Kitchen Tip: Since you're adding a strong flavor, there's no need for top-quality Champagne. Opt instead for high-quality cassis! If you're splurging, make both upscale.

*****

Bellini

In 1943, Giuseppe Cipriani, then owner of Harry's Bar in Venice, Italy, created this sparkling drink to honor the Italian Renaissance painter, Giovanni Bellini. Although he used white peaches, use whatever color peach suits your fancy. The hint of raspberry adds a warm glow, perhaps matching the glow of your lover's cheeks after a few sips of this decadent drink.

SEXY FOODS: peach, spirits
4 TO 6 SERVINGS

2/3 cup peach purée
1 teaspoon raspberry purée
1 (750-ml) bottle Prosecco or other Italian sparkling wine, chilled

1.   Place 1 1/2 tablespoons peach purée in the bottom of each Champagne flute and add 2 to 3 drops raspberry purée.
2.   Pour 5 - 6 ounces sparkling wine into each glass. Serve immediately.

Simple Sexy Kitchen Tip: To make peach purée, process peeled ripe peaches in blender or food processor, or purchase purée from a liquor supply store. To make raspberry purée, press fresh or thawed frozen berries through a sieve.

Chelada

SEXY FOODS: beer, a survey favorite.
2 SERVINGS

2 ounces fresh lime juice
2 (12-ounce) bottles or cans Mexican beer, thoroughly chilled
2 lime twists for garnishing

1.　　Have the beer glasses very cold.
2.　　Pour 1 ounce lime juice into each glass, and then add beer.
3.　　Garnish with a lime twist.
4.　　Serve any remaining beer on the side.

Variation: A chelada can also be served over ice in a salt-rimmed glass. Add tomato juice and hot pepper sauce for a michelada.

Survey Secrets: Beer was among the sexy favorite beverages, with males and younger people tending to rank it as having an aphrodisiac reputation.

*****

Dirty Martini

SEXY FOODS: spirits, olive, a dirty name
2 SERVINGS

4 ounces gin
1 ounce dry vermouth
1/2 ounce olive brine from green olives
2 green olives for garnishing

1.　　In a cocktail shaker, combine the gin, vermouth, and brine.
2.　　Fill with ice cubes and stir with a stirring rod or bar spoon.
3.　　Strain into chilled cocktail glasses.
4.　　Garnish and serve immediately.

Simple Sexy Kitchen Tip: Keep this drink classic and sexy by using high-quality ingredients.

Watermelon Martini

SEXY FOODS: spirits, watermelon
2 SERVINGS

1 to 1 1/2 cups peeled chunks ripe watermelon
3 ounces vodka
3/4 ounce fresh lime juice
1 teaspoon Simple Syrup
2 small wedges watermelon for garnishing

1. Press the watermelon through a fine sieve to obtain 3 ounces of juice.
2. In a cocktail shaker, combine the watermelon juice, vodka, lime juice, and simple syrup.
3. Fill with ice cubes and shake hard for 10 seconds.
4. Double strain into chilled cocktail glasses.
5. Garnish each serving with a small wedge of watermelon.

Simple Sexy Kitchen Tip: To double strain a cocktail, hold a small fine-mesh sieve over the serving glass with one hand and, with your other hand, pour the drink so that it passes first through your shaker's attached strainer or a Hawthorn strainer and then through the sieve.

*****

Apricot Cosmopolitan

SEXY FOODS: apricot, orange
2 SERVINGS

2 ounces vodka
1 ounce apricot brandy
1 ounce cranberry juice
1 ounce fresh lime juice
2 teaspoons apricot preserves
2 orange twists or lime wheels for garnishing

1. In a cocktail shaker, combine the vodka, brandy, both juices, and preserves.
2. Fill with ice cubes and shake hard for 10 seconds.
3. Strain into chilled cocktail glasses.
4. Garnish each with an orange twist or lime wheel.

Flirty Fig and Honey

SEXY FOODS: spirits (tequila, a survey favorite), fig, honey
2 SERVINGS

4 ounces reposado tequila
1 1/2 ounces Fig Syrup (recipe follows)
1 ounce fresh lime juice
2 wedges fig for garnishing

1.   In a cocktail shaker, combine the tequila, syrup, and lime juice.
2.   Fill with ice cubes and shake hard for 10 seconds.
3.   Strain into chilled cocktail glasses and garnish each glass with a wedge of fig.

*****

Fig Syrup

The recipe can be doubled or tripled.

ABOUT 1 1/2 OUNCES

4 ripe fresh figs, stemmed and halved
1 1/2 ounces water
4 teaspoons mild honey

1.   In a small saucepan, crush the figs with a potato masher or bar muddler. Add the water and honey and bring just to a boil. Immediately reduce heat, cover loosely, and simmer for 3 minutes.
2.   Remove from heat and let steep, covered, until cooled to room temperature.
3.   Strain through a fine sieve to remove all seeds.
4.   Refrigerate until thoroughly chilled, or up to 5 days.

Blueberry Mojito

This drink is built in the serving glass, so it's easy to prepare two side by side.

SEXY FOODS: blueberries, spirits, mint
1 SERVING

4 sprigs mint
3 tablespoons fresh or frozen blueberries
1 ounce Simple Syrup (recipe follows)
1 lime, halved
1 1/2 ounces light rum
3 ounces soda water
1 small sprig mint, for garnishing

1.   In a pint glass, muddle 4 sprigs mint and 2 tablespoons of the berries in the simple syrup until the berries have released their juice and the mixture is fragrant.
2.   Squeeze the lime halves into the glass then drop in.
3.   Fill the glass with ice.
4.   Add the rum, soda water, and remaining 1 tablespoon berries, and stir with a stirring rod or bar spoon.
5.   Garnish with mint.

*****

Simple Syrup

This recipe can be multiplied for larger quantities.

ABOUT 3/4 CUP

2/3 cup sugar
1/3 cup water

1.   In a small saucepan, heat the sugar and water over medium heat, stirring until the sugar dissolves. Raise the heat, bring just to a boil, then cool to room temperature.
2.   Transfer to a clean glass container and store refrigerated for up to 6 months.

Cucumber Cooler

SEXY FOODS: cucumber, apple, mint, spirits
2 SERVINGS

1 small cucumber, quartered lengthwise
1 large sprig mint
3 ounces Hendrick's gin
1 1/2 ounces apple juice
1 1/2 ounces cranberry juice
Crushed ice for serving

1.   Cut 2 of the cucumber spears into medium dice and drop into a cocktail shaker. Set aside the remaining spears for garnish.
2.   Add the mint sprig to the shaker and muddle the cucumber and mint together to release their flavors.
3.   Add the gin and both juices, fill the shaker with ice cubes, and shake hard for 10 seconds.
4.   Fill highball glasses with crushed ice and strain the drinks into the glasses.
5.   Insert a cucumber spear in each serving for garnish.

*****

Great Balls of Melon

SEXY FOODS: melon, pineapple, spirits
2 SERVINGS

2 1/2 ounces vodka
1 ounce melon liqueur
6 ounces chilled pineapple juice
Watermelon, honeydew, and cantaloupe melon balls on cocktail picks for garnishing

1.   In a cocktail shaker, combine the vodka, liqueur, and 3 ounces pineapple juice.
2.   Fill with ice cubes and shake hard for 10 seconds.
3.   Fill highball glasses with ice and strain the drinks into the glasses.
4.   Top up each drink with 1 1/2 ounces of the remaining pineapple juice and stir with a bar spoon.
5.   Garnish each serving with melon balls on a cocktail pick.

Screaming Orgasm

You can easily create two simultaneously as the drink is made right in the serving glass.

SEXY FOODS: spirits, a sexy name!
1 SERVING

1/2 ounce vodka
1 1/2 ounces Baileys Irish cream
1/2 ounce Kahlua coffee liqueur
1/2 ounce Cointreau or triple sec

1.   Pour the vodka, Baileys, Kahlua, and Cointreau into a cocktail glass over crushed ice.
2.   Stir gently.

Simple Sexy Kitchen Tip: Use a high-quality vodka to ensure smooth mixing with the Baileys. To test in advance, mix a little of each before making the cocktail.

*****

Between the Sheets

SEXY FOODS: spirits, lemon, an inspiring title
2 SERVINGS

1 1/2 ounces Cognac
1 1/2 ounces Cointreau or triple sec
1 1/2 ounces light rum
2 ounces fresh lemon juice
2 lemon twists for garnishing

1.   In a cocktail shaker, combine the Cognac, Cointreau, rum, and lemon juice.
2.   Fill with ice cubes and shake hard for 10 seconds.
3.   Strain into large, chilled cocktail glasses.
4.   Garnish each drink with a lemon twist.

Cherry Lover's Aviation

SEXY FOODS: spirits, cherries
2 SERVINGS

8 sweet cherries
3 ounces gin
1 1/2 ounces maraschino liqueur
1 ounce fresh lemon juice
2 dark sweet cherries, with stem, for garnishing

1.   Muddle 8 cherries in a cocktail shaker to release their juice.
2.   Add the gin, liqueur, and lemon juice.
3.   Fill with ice cubes and shake hard for 10 seconds.
4.   Double strain into chilled cocktail glasses.
5.   Garnish each serving with a cherry.

Simple Sexy Kitchen Tip: There's no need to pit the cherries since you strain this drink. Cherry aficionados even believe the pit adds flavor. Maraschino liqueur is a clear, rather dry liqueur made from whole Marasca cherries, including their crushed pits, which impart a subtle hint of almond. Don't confuse it with other cherry liqueurs or juice from maraschino cherries.

*****

Easy Breeze
This tall drink is light and refreshing. If you like a drier cocktail, try making it with unsweetened 100% cranberry juice.

SEXY FOODS: pineapple, spirits
1 SERVING

1 1/2 ounces coconut rum
2 ounces cranberry juice
2 ounces pineapple juice
1 wedge fresh pineapple for garnishing

1.   In a cocktail shaker, combine the rum and both juices.
2.   Fill with ice cubes and shake hard for 10 seconds.
3.   Fill a highball glass with ice and strain the drink into the glass.
4.   Garnish with a wedge of fresh pineapple.

Simple Sexy Kitchen Tip: Unless you have a very large cocktail shaker, it's best to make this drink one at a time. Otherwise, the cocktail shaker will be too filled to the brim.

Long Sloe Comfortable Screw

SEXY FOODS: sexy title, spirits, orange
1 SERVING

3/4 ounce vodka
3/4 ounce Southern Comfort
3/4 ounce sloe gin
3 ounces fresh orange juice
1 orange slice for garnishing

1.   In a cocktail shaker, combine vodka, Southern Comfort & sloe gin.
2.   Fill with ice cubes and shake hard for 10 seconds.
3.   Fill a highball glass with ice and strain the drink into the glass.
4.   Garnish with an orange slice.

*****

Sexy Chai

This recipe uses coconut milk, but you can make it with almond milk, hemp milk, rice milk, cow's milk, etc. And you can use any black tea, or try an herbal tea, such as African red bush.

SEXY FOODS: cinnamon, pepper, nutmeg, star anise, cloves, vanilla, ginger
4 SERVINGS

1 1/2 cups water
1/4 teaspoon black peppercorns
1/8 teaspoon pink peppercorns
1/8 teaspoon cayenne pepper
1/8 teaspoon freshly grated nutmeg
1/2 California bay leaf or 1 dried Turkish bay leaf
2 star anise pods
1/4 vanilla bean, split lengthwise
4 green cardamom pods, cracked
4 cinnamon sticks, broken into several pieces
3 cloves
1 1/2 cups coconut milk
3/4-inch piece unpeeled fresh ginger, thinly sliced
3 tablespoons packed dark brown sugar, or to taste
1 1/2 tablespoons Darjeeling tea

1.   In a medium stainless steel saucepan, combine the water and all the spices and bring to a boil.

2.   Reduce heat, cover, and simmer for 5 minutes. Remove from heat and steep, covered, for 10 minutes.

3.   Stir in the coconut milk and brown sugar and bring to a high simmer, just below a boil. Watch carefully; do not let the mixture boil.

4.   Immediately add the tea, remove from heat, and steep, covered, for 5 minutes.

5.   Strain the chai through a fine-mesh sieve and serve immediately. Or strain, cool to room temperature, and refrigerate for up to 3 days. Reheat for serving, or serve over ice.

Aphrodite Says: Cinnamon is one of the scents found to trigger an erection response in men. That's the immediate effect! As for its long-term aphrodisiac potential, a long-term study recently showed that cinnamon significantly lowered blood sugar, triglycerides, LDL (bad cholesterol), and total cholesterol. In this 40-day study, 60 subjects were given one gram a day of cinnamon—roughly one-quarter of a teaspoon. Researchers are excited about this small study because the beneficial effects of cinnamon lasted nearly 3 weeks after people stopped taking it.

Survey Secrets: Cinnamon ranked second in preferred sexy spices, and the sixth-most recognized aphrodisiac overall. Surprisingly, given cinnamon's proven effect on the male member, more women recognized it as an aphrodisiac than men!

Sangria

SEXY FOODS: red wine, orange, peach, strawberries
4 TO 8 SERVINGS

1 (750-ml) bottle dry red wine
1/4 cup brandy
1 1/3 cups orange juice
1 fresh peach, halved, pitted, and sliced, or 2/3 cup frozen peach slices
1 small orange, halved, seeded, and sliced
1/2 lemon, seeded and sliced
1 lime, halved, seeded, and sliced
1/2 cup sliced strawberries
Soda water, chilled

1.   Combine the wine, brandy, orange juice, and all the fruit in a large, nonreactive container.
2.   Let stand, refrigerated, for at least 3 hours or up to overnight.
3.   Transfer to a large glass pitcher, and serve the soda water on the side.
4.   Provide large goblets so each of you can pour your own drink., including some fruit and soda water as desired.

Survey Secrets: Red Wine. My data show that people who have sex 5 to 7 times per week were significantly more likely (59%) to recognize wine as an aphrodisiac than those have more or less sex! It may or may not be coincidental that people age 35 and younger were significantly more likely (57%) to have heard of its sexy reputation.

Aphrodite Says: From their sexy scent to their sweet, succulent flesh to their breast-soft outer skin, peaches have been shaking their sexy selves at us for a long time. A well-known 20th century reference to the sexy fruit comes from The Steve Miller Band, under the guise of the Doctrine of Resemblances, "I really like your peaches, let me shake your tree." So break out the peaches, ladies, because the guys just can't leave them alone!

Mango Lassi

SEXY FOODS: mango, banana
2 SERVINGS

12 ounces plain low-fat yogurt
1 ripe mango, peeled and cut into cubes (about 2 cups)
1/2 ripe banana, peeled and cut into chunks
1 to 2 tablespoons sugar, or to taste
10 ice cubes

1.   Combine yogurt, mango, banana, and sugar in blender, and purée.
2.   Add the ice and continue to blend until the ice is almost completely pulverized and the mixture is frothy.
3.   Pour into chilled glasses and serve immediately.

Aphrodite Says: The mango is mentioned in *The Kama Sutra* at least 6 times, including a recommendation to drink the tropical juice before sexual play. There's also a rather homoerotic reference to "sucking the mango fruit," but such pleasures need not be limited to men!

*****

Hotsy Totsy Toddy

SEXY FOODS: spirits, honey
2 SERVINGS

4 ounces Scotch
2 ounces mild honey
1 ounce fresh lemon juice
2 ounces water
2 pieces honeycomb or lemon twist for garnishing

1.   In small saucepan, combine Scotch, honey, lemon juice, and water, and heat gently, stirring to dissolve honey. Heat only to a low simmer.
2.   Pour into small mugs or other heatproof glasses.
3.   Garnish each serving with a small piece of honeycomb.

Aphrodite—and I—Both Say: Alcohol can enhance our sensual experiences, but many a romantic opportunity has been lost to overconsumption of alcohol, not to mention lives lost or damaged from its abuse. As with all the suggestions in this book, a healthy approach to our bodies and minds is the basis for a lifelong enjoyment of that miracle combination of food, drink, and sex. So sip and savor, keep it simple, and let nature take her sexy course!

Selected References

A taste of the references consulted for this book

Albala, K. (2002). *Eating right in the renaissance*. Berkeley, CA: University of California Press.

Amen, D. (2007). *Sex on the brain*. New York: Three Rivers Press.

Anderson, E. (2005). *Everyone eats: Understanding food and culture*. New York: New York University Press.

Benton, D., & Donohoe, R. (1999). The effects of nutrients on mood. *Public Health Nutrition, 2*(3a), 403-409.

Bergh, B. (1992). The avocado and human nutrition. II: Avocados and your heart *Proceedings of Second World Avocado Congress,* 37-47.

Black, R. (Ed.) (2005). *The Gaelic otherworld: John Gregorson Campbell's superstitions of the highlands and islands of Scotland and witchcraft and second sight in the highlands and islands*. Edinburgh: Birlinn.

Boyer, J. & Liu, R.H. (2004, May). Apple phytochemicals and their health benefits. *Nutrition Journal: Department of Food Science and Institute of Comparative and Environmental Toxicology, 3*(5). Doi: 10.1186/1475-2891-3-5.

Brehler, R., Theissen, U., Mohr, C., & Lugar, T. (1997). "Latex-fruit syndrome": Frequency of cross-reacting IgE antibodies. *Allergy, 52*(4), 404-10.
Burton, R. (trans). (1962). *The kama sutra of Vatsyayana: The classic Hindu treatise on love and social conduct*. New York: E. P. Dutton.

Burton, R. (trans). (2010). *The perfumed garden of the Shaykh Nefzawi.* Whitefish, MT: Kessinger Publishing Rare Book Reprints.

Cade, J. E., Burley V. J., Greenwood D.C. (2007, January). Dietary fibre and risk of breast cancer in the UK women's cohort study. *International Journal of Epidemiolology, 36*(2), 431-438. PMID:17251246

Celestin, J., & Heiner, D. (1993, June). Allergy and immunology: Food-induced anaphylaxis. *Western Journal of Medicine 158*(6), 610-611.

Chavarro, J., Rich-Edwards, J., Rosner, B., & Willett, W. (2007, January). Dietary fatty acid intakes and the risk of ovulatory infertility. *American Journal of Clinical Nutrition, 85*(1), 231-237.

Christen, W., Liu, S., Schaumberg, D., & Buring, J. (2005, June). Fruit and vegetable intake and the risk of cataract in women. *American Journal of Clinical Nutrition. 81*(6), 1417-22.
Cressy, D. (1999). *Birth, marriage, and death: Ritual, religion, and the life-cycle in Tudor and Stuart England*. Oxford: Oxford University Press.

Crooks, R., & Baur, K. (2011). *Our sexuality.* (11th Ed.). Belmontt CA: Wadsworth.

De Villers, L. (2016). *Love skills: A fun, upbeat guide to sex-cessful relationships.* (6th ed.) Marina del Rey, CA: Aphrodite Media.

Donovan, J. (1989). *After the fall: The Demeter-Persephone myth in Wharton, Cather, and Glasgow.* University Park, PA: Pennsylvania State University Press.

Dos Passos, J. (1958). *Alfred Lord Tennyson.* New York: Sagamore Press.

Erkkila A.T., Herrington D.M., Mozaffarian D., & Lichtenstein A.H. (2005, July). Cereal fiber and whole-grain intake are associated with reduced progression of coronary-artery atherosclerosis in postmenopausal women with coronary artery disease. *American Heart Journal, 150* (1), 94-101. PMID:16084154.

Edwards, A., Vineyard, R., Wiley, E., Brown, E., Collins, J., Perkins-Veasiz, Baker, R., & Cievidence, B. (2003, April). Consumption of watermelon juice increases plasma concentrations of lycopene and b-carotene in humans. *The Journal of Nutrition, 133*(4), 1043-1050. Doi 0022-3166/03.

Frazer, G. & Fraser, R. (Ed). (1994). *The golden bough: A study in magic and religion.* Oxford, England: Oxford University Press.

Fried, R., & Edlen-Nezin, L. (2006). *Great food, great sex: The three food factors for sexual fitness.* New York: Ballantine.

Gray, J, & Griffin, B. (2009). Eggs and dietary cholesterol—dispelling the myth. *British Nutrition Foundation Nutrition Bulletin, 34,* 66-70.

Hegeneder, F. (2005). *The meaning of trees: Botany, history, healing, lore.* San Francisco: Chronicle books.

Hirsch, A. (2001). *What flavor is your personality?* Naperville, IL: Sourcebook, Inc.

Iriti, M., Rossoni. M., & Faoro, F. (2006, June). Melatonin content in grape: myth or panacea. *Journal of the Science of Food and Agriculture 86*(10),1432-1438.

Kumara, M., Sambaiaha, K., & Lokesh, B. R. (2000, February). Hypocholesterolemic effect of anhydrous milk fat ghee is mediated by increasing the secretion of biliary lipids. *The Journal of Nutritional Biochemistry: 11*(2), 69–75. Doi:10.1016/S0955-2863(99)00072-8.

Manniche, L. (2006). *An ancient Egyptian herbal.* (Rev ed). London: British Museum Press.

Mirza, R., Roisson, J., Fisher, G., D'Aniello, A., Spinelli, P., & Ferrandino, G. (2005, March). *Do marine mollusks possess aphrodisiacal properties?* Paper presented at the 229th national meeting of the American Chemical Society, San Diego, CA.

Paykova, V. (2003). Behind the vegetable: Asparagus. *The Russia Journal.* Archives 1999-2005, 6-11.

Palmatier, R. (2000). *Food: A dictionary of literal and nonliteral terms.* Westport, CT: Greenwood Press.

Prance, G., & Nesbitt, M. (Eds). (2005.) *Cultural history of plants.* New York: Routledge.

Roan, S. (2010, March 16). Study links heart health, vitamin D. *Los Angeles Times,* p. A10.

Rhode, J. M., Huarng J., Fogoros, S., Tan, L., Zick, S., Liu, J. R. (2006, April). *Ginger induces apoptosis and autophagocytosis in ovarian cancer cells.* Abstract #4510, at the 97th American Association for Cancer Research Annual Meeting, Washington, DC.

Santa Ana, R. (2008, June 30). Watermelon may have Viagra-effect: Secrets of phytonutrients are being unraveled. *Agriicultural Life News.* Phytoagnews.tamu.edu/showstory.php?id=554, retrieved 3-18-10.

Sohn, E. (2009, Feb 23). The power of potassium: In the right ratio with sodium, it seems to cut heart-disease risks of a salt-heavy diet. *Los Angeles Times*, p. H1.

Suzuki R., Rylander-Rudqvist, T., Ye, W., Adlercreutz, H., & Wolk, A. et al. (2008, January.) Dietary fiber intake and risk of postmenopausal breast cancer defined by estrogen and progesterone receptor status—a prospective cohort study among Swedish women. *International Journal of Cancer. 122*(2), 403-12. PMID:17764112.

Taverner, P. (1985). *Aphrodisiacs: The science and the myth.* Philadelphia: University of Pennsylvania Press.

Thomson, C., Chisholm, S., McLachlan, S., & Campbell, J. (2008). Brazil nuts: An effective way to improve selenium status. *American Journal of Clinical Nutrition, 87*, 379-384.

Uhley V., Seymour, E., Wunder, J., Kaufman, P., Kirakosyan, A., Al-Rawi, S., & Warber. S. (2009). Pharmacokinetic study of the absorption and metabolism of Montmorency tart cherry anthocyanins in human subjects. *Journal of the Federation of American Societies for Experimental Biology, 23 (Meeting Abstract Supplement)*, 565.4.

Van Dam, R.M., Hu, F.B., Rosenberg, L., Krishnan, S., & Palmer, J.R. (2006, October). Dietary calcium and magnesium, major food sources, and risk of type 2 diabetes in U.S. black women. *Diabetes Care. 29*(10), 2238-43. PMID:17003299.

Ward, E. (2007, February). Not in the mood? Healthful diet and exercise may turn up the heat. *Environmental Nutrition 30* (2), 1, 4.

Zern, T.L., Wood, R.J., Greene , C., West, K. L., Liu, Y., Aggarwal, D., Shachter, N.S., & Fernandez, M.L. (2005, August). Grape polyphenols exert a cardioprotective effect in pre- and postmenopausal women by lowering plasma lipids and reducing oxidative stress. *Journal of Nutrition, 135*(8), 1911-7. PMID:16046716.

Ziff, Stefano. (2010). *Love and the erotic in art.* Los Angeles: J Paul Getty Museum.

About the Author

Linda De Villers, PhD, is a Licensed Psychologist and Diplomate and Supervisor in Sex Therapy with the American Association of Sex Educators, Counselors and Therapists (AASECT).

For over three decades, Dr. De Villers has maintained a private practice and has taught psychology, health psychology and human sexuality courses at major universities and colleges. She is currently an adjunct professor in the psychology departments of Pepperdine University Graduate School, Santa Monica College, and Chaffey College.

She has presented her published research around the world, and is widely quoted and referenced in numerous regional, national and international media. A brief list of her appearances includes *New York Times, USA Today, Washington Post, Los Angeles Times, Cosmo, Glamour, McCalls, Mademoiselle, Better Homes and Gardens, Fitness* and *Men's Health* in print; Discovery Health, Montel Williams, Berman & Berman, Midmorning Los Angeles and Jenny Jones Show on television; and numerous regional and national radio shows. For one year she had a monthly column in *Health* magazine; prior to that she was a weekly Q&A Columnist for Playboy.com.

Dr. De Villers grew up in a medical household in which healthy, sumptuous eating ruled the day. Her marriage to a Frenchman introduced her to the world of French cuisine and Julia Child. From that moment on, she was hooked on cooking, especially in the context of seduction—and is to this day fluent in French!

Following her marriage, Dr. De Villers began exploring world cuisines, starting in the rich cultural diversity of her native Southern California. Over the years she has ventured far and wide, to every continent of the world save Antarctica, savoring regional delights.

She is one of few professionals worldwide to combine a clinical knowledge of sexuality and physical and mental health with a foodies' enthusiasm for fine cuisine. Her playful approach to life and love and food was a major factor in seducing her partner of sixteen years. An avid tennis player, skier, lover of the outdoors, film and art, Linda De Villers makes her home in the Los Angeles area of California.

Sexy Recipes for Lovers (originally published as *Simple Sexy Food*) is her second book and follows on the success of her first book, *Love Skills*, still in print nearly twenty years after publication.